My SOUL IS MY OWN

$\mathscr{M}$Y SOUL
IS MY OWN

Oral Narratives
of African American
Women in
the Professions

Gwendolyn Etter-Lewis

ROUTLEDGE • New York • London

Published in 1993 by

Routledge
29 West 35th Street
New York, NY 10001-2299

Published in Great Britain by

Routledge
11 New Fetter Lane
London EC4P 4EE

Library of Congress Cataloging-in-Publication Data

Etter-Lewis, Gwendolyn.
    My soul is my own : oral narratives of African American women in
the professions / Gwendolyn Etter-Lewis.
        p.   cm.
    Includes bibliographical references and index.
    ISBN 0-415-90559-1 (hard) : $49.95.—ISBN 0-415-90560-5 (pbk.) :
$14.95
    1. Afro-American women executives—Interviews. I. Title
HD6054.4.U6E88   1993
331.4′81658′008996073—dc20   92-39044
                                                                       CIP

British Library Cataloging-in-Publication Data also available.

For
my mother, Georgia
and
For
Ari, my son

CONTENTS

Contents

ACKNOWLEDGMENTS

Many people made this book possible. I will never be able to name or thank them all, but I am deeply appreciative of the assistance and support that I have received during the course of writing this book. I am especially grateful to all of the women who consented to be interviewed, and graciously shared their lives and wisdom.

Grants from the Ford Foundation Postdoctoral Research Fellowships, the National Academy of Education Spencer Foundation Postdoctoral Research Fellowships, and the Western Michigan University Faculty Research and Creative Activities Fund made it possible for me to take time off from teaching to collect data and write the book.

My thanks to transcribers Wendy Miller, Martha Thompson, Mike Baker, Wendy Flanigan, Arlene Morris, and especially to Cyndi Andrus who also took wonderful care of my son. My manuscript was strengthened in its various forms by thoughtful comments and critiques from Gerre Riley, Valena Randolph, Michael Gilbert, Barbara Havira, and Jana Pyle. I am grateful to Michael Hickey for technical computer assistance. Special appreciation goes to Geneva Smitherman who constantly has been a source of support, and to Nancy Miller, Donald Thompson, Sherna Gluck, Daphne Patai, Janet Langlois, Richard Thomas, Beatrice Kachuck, and the late Magdalene Carney for their wisdom and encouragement. Shelly Carpenter and Christine McDowell assisted me with grant-related paper work "beyond the call of duty." Clark Iverson, Suzanne Kent, and Lesley Brill provided exceptional assistance during my postdoctoral research at Wayne State University.

Outside of the university close friends provided moral support lovingly and without being asked. Gail Locke and Hattie Wood have been there for me since we were in first grade. Emily Pane, Donald Garcia, Irene Atkinson and Diane Taherzadeh were staunch supporters and unwavering confidants, Dora Robinson's faith and friendship is a steadying force in my life, and she always has been a marvelous second mother to my son.

I thank my editor, Jayne Fargnoli for enthusiastic and patient support. I am indebted to Roger Dahl and Robert Stockman at the National Baha'i Center and to the staff at the Moorland-Spingarn Research Center at Howard University for providing me with important leads and archival information.

Last, but most important, I am sincerely grateful to my family, particularly my mother, Georgia Etter-Huggins who demonstrated the meaning of strength and who taught me that through God all things are possible; to my stepfather Ray Huggins for his care and generosity; to my brother Terry for his quiet advocacy; and to my son, Ari for being himself and for helping me through difficulties by sharing his delightful sense of humor and wisdom beyond his years. They put up with me and loved me anyway.

Finally, I appreciate the enthusiasm and interest expressed by those who listened to my ideas and liked them without ever reading a single word of the book.

INTRODUCTION

Preparation for this book began many years ago when I sat on my great grandmother's front porch listening to her assess the strengths and weaknesses of the small southern African American community that was our home. Nannie seemed to know something about everything and everyone, and she expressed a unique vision of the past like no other adult I knew. Occasionally she would tell a story about my grandfather, her youngest son, or about a distant relative who, in my child's eyes, seemed larger than life. Nannie was well into her 70's in those days when we sat on the porch surveying the neighborhood or playing dominos or cards. The time spent with her seemed special to me even then. Later, when I discovered a photograph of Nannie as a young woman, I cried because she was so beautiful, and I had only known her as a wise old woman, crippled with arthritis. It never occurred to me that she had been young and vibrant, that she had experienced a rich and full life before any of the great grands were born. So these indelible experiences/memories became a part of my self, my personal identity, and grew into an insatiable curiosity about the past lives of African American women who were the grandmothers and great grandmothers of later generations.

ORAL NARRATIVE AS
RESEARCH METHODOLOGY

Oral narrative, sometimes referred to as oral history, is a dynamic, interactive methodology that preserves an individual's own words and perspectives in a particularly authentic way. Both casual readers and serious researchers can comprehend its meaning and form. Oral narrative is both a process and product that mediates the boundaries between history, language, and literature. It is a collaborative transaction that reconstructs a life once lived; and it is a text that makes relevant to the present metaphors of a narrator's past. Unlike other modes of inquiry that only may provide glimpses of disconnected parts of a person's life, oral narrative offers an intimate perspective of a narrator's interpretation and understanding of her/his own life unabridged. In other words, the spontaneity of oral narration reveals a virtually unedited and sometimes unprocessed view of personal meaning and judgment that is not altered by the usual limitations of written language.

My long-term study of African American women in the professions began in 1985 and has culminated in interviews with over 80 women from across the country.[1] With the assistance of religious and professional organizations, and "networking" women were selected on the basis of profession, education, and geography. They ranged in age from 61 to 101 and were college educated in the decades between 1920 and 1940. Each woman was interviewed for a minimum of 3 hours with some granting up to 6 hours of interview time. All of the audio tapes were transcribed by several different research assistants and checked for accuracy. Due to space limitations, nine of the most interesting narratives were selected for this book.

The nine narrative texts included in Part I are edited minimally. However, "raw" or unedited narratives were used for the actual analysis. Although editing results in a "neat" version of the data and increases readability, it also can obscure the distinct style and subtle linguistic features of a narrator's speech. Thus, there is a need for both edited and unedited narratives depending on the purpose and intended outcome of a research project.

The primary purpose of my study is descriptive, but the data analysis is both qualitative and quantitative. Selected aspects of content *and* form will be examined and discussed. What a narrator says as well as the way she says it is important.

WHAT'S IN A NAME?

The term "oral narrative," "oral history," and "personal narrative" often are inadequate labels for a process and product that surpasses history and conventional narration. Oral history, for example, is not exclusively history, but also sociology, political science, literature, linguistics, anthropology, and a host of other fields. An individual's account of her/his own life is not just personal, but also social, historical, political, and so on. As a result, the collaborative endeavor of eliciting a life on tape must not be limited to preconceived notions of narration or history, but instead representative of the fullness of the life once lived. Whereas it is unreasonable to expect that every recollection can be captured on tape, it is indeed possible to reconstruct a reliable version of a person's past.

The most important variable in producing an oral narrative is the relationship between the narrator/interviewee and the interviewer. The collaboration itself is problematic because the author/interviewee reveals self in the presence of an "other" rather than in the solitude prescribed for written autobiography. Thus, there is always the lingering doubt about how much and in what ways an interviewer influences both the process and the final product. Can an individual's account of her life be considered undiluted first-person narration if there is another person (i.e., interviewer) involved in the telling process? It is humanly impossible for an interviewer or any other researcher to be totally *objective* and entirely removed from the narrative process, just as it is for narrators to be absolutely candid about all of the details of their personal lives. Yet many readers and scholars react to collaborated life texts as if this is indeed true or even possible. Consequently, the value/purity of collaborated texts as autobiography is frequently judged according to the level of involvement of the interviewer. However, these artificial criteria only advance our own ignorance. Issues of objectivity/subjectivity and truth-fulness/falsehood are counterfeit dichotomies that are neither productive nor enlightening. Much more important is the extent to which author/narrator and interviewer can cooperate in constructing a text that is fully representative of the narrator's life.

WOMEN'S AND ETHNIC AUTOBIOGRAPHY: "MAGGOTS IN THE RICE"[2]?

Many long-standing theories of autobiography have been con-structed in such a manner that only white Western males are pre-sumed to be capable of producing "pure" autobiography. Women and ethnic minorities are thought to lack such a creative capacity, in part, because their sense of self is not grounded in the individualism characteristic of "advanced" Christian societies in the West. This slanted theoretical stance evokes images of the ancient and oppressive Chinese society described in Kingston's *Woman Warrior*. Women were so devalued in this culture that negative sayings or proverbs about them were common: "Girls are maggots in the rice" (43). Thus, as the title of this section suggests, the autobiography canon and its theoretical underpinnings are formulated and practiced in a fashion that resembles the same kind of antiquated despotic thinking, only this time ethnic minorities are included:

> Moreover, it would seem that autobiography is not to be found outside of our cultural area; one would say that it expresses a concern peculiar to Western man, a concern that has been of good use in his systematic conquest of the universe and that he has communicated to men of other cultures; but those men will thereby have been annexed by a sort of intellectual colonizing to a mentality that was not their own.[3]

These ideas not only restrict autobiography to a scholarly, single sex elite, but also establish and simultaneously alienate an "other" who never can be legitimately admitted to the canon: "but those men will thereby have been annexed by a sort of intellectual colonizing. . .". In essence, even if an "other" manages to compose an autobiography, its originality and worth is diminished since the product is a mere imitation of a Western invention.

Even though the preceding view of autobiography has been widely accepted, framing theory in such absolute and discriminatory language reflects a concealed agenda that is neither innocent nor harmless. Theoretical principles and scholarly analyses are not generated from impartial designs or methodologies, but are shaped by cultural values and canonical regulations. G. Thomas Couser warns that "sweeping dismissals" of particular texts from the canon are highly suspect:

> definitions of literary merit are ultimately grounded in extra-literary considerations: valorization of some texts as literary and denigration of others as subliterary . . . always reflects political and cultural agendas, whether conscious or unconscious.[4]

So whether or not we acknowledge it, accepting some texts as autobiography and others as not, granting a dominant group authority to write autobiography and not other groups, establishes a "tradition" in autobiography that is severely limited. It is probable that no healthy offspring, especially women's and ethnic autobiographies, have been conceived from this male model not only because there is no mother, but because the "tradition" indeed is impotent.

Finally, there is the related issue of literacy. In Western society language is split into two opposing parts: written versus spoken. Written language is valorized[5] and accompanied by certain privileges (e.g., access to authority, advancement in education, exposure to the literary canon, etc.). It is considered to be the manifestation of complex thought and a symbol of advanced civilization. On the other hand, spoken language is regarded as primal and limited to *basic* social/communicative functions. According to Jan Vansina, the lay person "fondly imagines that written sources reveal events of the past which can be accepted as fact, but considers that oral sources tell of things about which there is no certainty—things which may or may not have happened" (104).

As a result of this "mainstream" attitude toward written and oral sources, oral traditions (e.g., story telling, personal and group narratives, group histories, songs) in so-called primitive cultures generally are devalued. They are identified with "simple" folk ways, but not necessarily with literature or history. Thus, oral narrative becomes problematic because of its connections to oral traditions and separation from the prestige of written language. In actuality, values assigned to orality and literacy are culturally biased. So the decision to include/name an oral narrative as a work of literature, for example, is based on a cultural agenda that has little or nothing to do with literary merit/worth.

Oral narrative as autobiography is as complex as it is controversial. It is influenced by several factors such as the oppositional model of language (written versus spoken, orality versus literacy, literary versus nonliterary), canonical restrictions, and cultural biases. While there may be no simple or easy solution, searching beyond the confines of "acceptable" theory and practice is critical.

THE MYTH OF THE INVISIBLE WOMEN

> For despite the range and significance of our history, we have been perceived as token women in Black texts and as token Blacks in feminist ones. (Giddings, p. 5)

The study and interpretation of African American women's lives typically has been subsumed under African American issues and women's issues. The assumption is that norms for the larger groups are suitable for the smaller group, African American women. However, their unique experiences in history, language, and culture suggest otherwise. Membership in two oppressed groups alone sets African American women apart because they experience double discrimination as a result of their dual status. So what is true for African American men and white women is not invariably true for African American women.

When applied to scholarly research, the large group norm which creates a singular reality can be observed by the conspicuous absence of African American women from major studies in most disciplines. Margaret Andersen observed that several groups of women of color are "rendered invisible by studies that concentrate only on the experiences and perspectives of dominant groups" (8). This denial of alternate realities/experiences effectively maintains the status quo and excludes knowledge essential to the well-being of society as a whole.

As a case in point, most studies of women's and African American's speech have tended to focus on dominant groups: white women and African American men, particularly urban adolescents.[5] Conclusions drawn from these studies usually have been generalized without regard to possible discrepancies in the speech of African American women. In contrast, investigations of African American women's speech have been small in number and sporadic.[6] However, their findings suggest that there are unique features in African American women's speech. Once again the myth of a singular reality has contaminated scholarly research to the detriment of us all.

The notion that African American women are an invisible group on the sidelines that easily can be combined with other groups is a convenient fiction that conceals their power and importance. They have played major roles in all of American culture and continue to do so in spite of resistance and a variety of formidable barriers. These women have demonstrated repeatedly that change requires nothing less than the complete alteration of what we do and believe. *My Soul Is My Own* is intended as one of the many steps toward knowledge, transformation, and change.

PART I

N ARRATED LIVES*

*Partially edited, 45-minute segments of whole narratives.

1

NINE NARRATIVES

JANE

I did not take Mrs. Roosevelt's offer because I did not want to go into administration. I wanted to call my soul my own.

music composer; birth year 1914, B.A. 1938; M.A. 1945, 1954

I'm retired from schools. I've taught at several black colleges. The play I wrote was about the history a black community. And I wanted to know why the world before us was made before us in the first place. Why the community had grown the size that it was, there was of type of reality, organization in the place. Ah, that was common of other towns, and I wanted to know why it was never incorporated. And ah . . . having come from an all black town out west, I was born in an all black town. Then I knew what was what there. I knew why the town was there, why it was named, and everything about it. And we were very proud of our town. And ah, then I come here and find that everyone was very, very closed. It was as though, you were enmeshed in a sort of, ah oh what do you call it? You were enmeshed in a sort of a closed society that was closed because of what had happened not because of preference. And so ah, I wanted to know why. And then as I began to investigate I found out more and more things that were different. One person would tell me one thing, one would tell me another. And then I began to go through the record books to find out actually what happened. And, I went all the way to the state library. I went to the county historical society, the, the library here. I went through what I could find in the library in at the university and what was there from another local university library. And ah, I put all the facts together. It took me five years of research to put this together. I began researching this in 1979. And after I had put it together, then I began to write. So ah, this is how long it had taken, you see.

My home town. O.K. It's a old like town. And it's right at the edge of the Indian reservation and, Indian reservations for the so called, civilized tribes, the Creeks, the Cherokees, the Seminoles, the Choctaws. Those are the tribes that were near my home town. My mother is Creek. My father is a native of Africa. He went to school in England through the efforts of the missionaries. And then came to the United States with the missionaries at the time when the, the Italians took over the government of his country from the English. And ah, after going through, to a college, which I don't know even exists anymore, he went to Meharry, to a medical school for blacks in Tennessee. He finished there and then went to Wisconsin and ah, he was to do intern work at Wisconsin but, ah it was very cold to him and he came back to Indiana and he practiced there for a while. And then felt like he had to go back and do his internship somewhere ah in order to validate the state's requirements for his license, so he came out west to do an internship with the Indians.

No, I remember the year that he came from, from England to America, that was 1892. And ah, then ah, there was a run for property and that must have been around the year of 18, oh no, 1904, 1905, 1906. Where the people who wanted property ran to cover the land and the land that they covered by this running was theirs. And this was how they apportioned the land that was near the Indians ah for, native Americans and ah, so my mother's brother's ran and that's how they got the, the farms that were between two small towns. Now that's all I know. And that ah, it was somewhere between there and, my mother contracted pneumonia and my father went out to see her and thought that she was the most beautiful woman he had ever seen. That was in September and he went back in, at Christmas time and married her. So, that's how my parents got together.

You see my mother was 19 when they got married and my father I'm sure was near 40, because he, see he, had gone through school in England and when you came from his country you were very grown even there because I don't know what kind of missionary schools that they had there before you went to school in England. See? So, there was a large difference between their ages, I'm sure.

My father became Mayor of the town. One of the beginnings of the town was Mar, Marcus Garvey's ah, interest in taking people back to Africa . . . was the fact that he felt that there, was no way that black people were going to get a good deal in these United States. And he, along with ah, what was his name, the man for whom the town was named, along with another man who ah, was the son of one of the people that was with John Browns raid. And ah, they were trying to get water and they discovered that the water was very, very metallic and they kept sounding farther and farther down and they'd spent so much time there, that they decided, well maybe we better start a town here. And they started a town and they made a gin for cotton because cotton was a large crop around the place and ah, the Creek Indians knew a lot, quite a lot because they had been brought there from Florida. They kept them moving farther and farther west until they got them to New Mexico from Florida.

So, they were very, very, experienced cotton growers and ah, with the help of one of their, I don't remember what his name was ah, his English name, they called him . . . , but I don't remember what his real name was. But he, he was ah, over the gin and there was a Mr. Green and Mr. Tate they had the, had the gin and ah, then they went to the capital of the state at that time and got the place incorporated as a black town. And my father was the Mayor at the time. It's still there today!

It was almost like a college community. Because everyone there was committed to making their children be the best of whatever they could. So we were exposed to all types of music, all types of sports, all types of ah, intellectual things and ah, then we knew all about the word wholesome. So that when you, you never thought about competing really as such because when we played ball whoever could pitch well pitched for everybody so you, you just had groups of, of people that were on this team and that team. But, you couldn't, you couldn't very well have competition if you were gonna use the same pitcher all the time and same catcher all the time. So that, the spirit of ah, competition was not as it is in most of America, but everyone knew that when you went to school you got your lessons, you did your assignments, and ah, you know that ah extra work was a part of the school. For instance, when I was in fifth grade we were singing the Messiah and we were not singing just the part that your voice would do, Miss Johnson, who was the music teacher at that time would come in and say Jane, you and Vi are going to sing base today and, Mike you are going to sing soprano you know, and you read the part you were assigned, you read it, not in the ah, pitch that, but you read it according to the way you could, in your, your range. And you were graded on music just like you were graded in Math. You took watercolors, you took ah, ah, crayons, you took ah, ah, finger painting, you took ah, oils. You did this as a part of your regular work. Our town had an ideal situation as far as education of its children was concerned. Oh, we seldom had ah, any detention at school, because everybody was so busy trying to get what was there and the parents were always coming around to see what happens. We had ah, they had a Parent/Teachers club, but ah, I could leave home and ah, sometimes leave my mother washing and by the time I got to the second period of school, she was there, to see what I was doing. And ah, so, ah she wasn't the only one, people just did this. And ah, when, when you were assigned to your work you were given time at home to do it. Your parents checked just to be sure that you did it before you did your dinner. So you, you always got your work and, ah, people from our town went on to do great things. Course not many of them went back to live in the town.

But ah, they went on to do, to do great things because ah, you were inspired, you were inspired and ah, I'll never forget. One year the primary teacher who was also a Johnson, Miss Johnson had taught her children how to do some a . . . ac . . . acrobatic dances, for children. And ah, they had hoops for the stage and by some accident these hoops were left out and they had been cov . . . with ah . . . I mean covered with crepe paper and all and it rained on them and it ruined them and ah, when we got to the program that evening, I'll never forget, here was Miss Johnson standing up there in tears talking about her hoops for her children. And the principal of the school says, we'll have the program next week how many parents will stay and volunteer to do the hoops? And everybody, said, we will! So they stayed there and they had ah, ah had tea for the parents and they stayed and fixed the hoops so they could have the children do their things next week. And this is, I feel that this is what, what will happen when you can get black people to do things when they're not looking over their shoulder to see what somebody else is doing because in our town everybody seemed to cooperate! And when, ah, I'll never forget, one day a, a Mrs. Thompson whose husband was a, was a, a county demonstration agent, came to school. She taught somewhere but she was there to see what her two boys were doing that day and ah, someone said that, that James Thompson went out ah, he was excused from class and she says if he's if he was excused from class for any reason he's whipped already. I'll see to it when he gets home. Hahaha. She didn't wait to see, what the excuse was that he wanted but she just said that. So, you know parents cooperated with the teachers and the teachers cooperated with the parents. Whenever you couldn't get your work, somebody from the school visited the parents to find out if they could be of help, to help that child get that work. And, we were rather disappointed when the college was made the school for blacks in another city rather than having it in our home town.

At sixteen I had finished high school and then ah been to ah, to New York. I had been not to New York City, to Albany. And I had ah gone to school there two years and, I came back home. My father said, now you're ready to go to school, so then I went to Tuskegee. I finished Tuskegee in three years!

The church sponsored the school, so that ah even when you came here to teach, even if you were a member of the church, you were sort of out of your league, haha. And ah when I came here and this was in 1955, I was told you are an outsider. I had no relatives that were members of the church, so I was an outsider. And, you see it I, I don't know why the ah, climate didn't improve from 1865 to 1955 as far as cooperation was concerned. Now then they had ah, teachers here that were not members of the church but ah, they were, I don't know how, they sort of somehow got to endorse church thinking and ah, of course one of the, one of the a best examples was Mr. Groden. He had thirteen children; he was Catholic and he was over the history department but because he wasn't a member of that denomination, his salary was never enough to ah, support his family so he worked in the fields and the school. And some of the people who worked here who were not members of the church had three jobs. And that's how it differs from my home town. See we had one large church building and one smaller chapel and the different denominations took turns on having service in that one church. You see, where else would you get cooperation like that.

My father heard from his sister quite often and ah, he had been given a Christian name by, by the ah, by the missionaries. And he was called, he was called Clyde. Now his African name he, he, wrote for us a time or two but he told us, your are Smiths, haha. So we never, ah, you know, used an African name.

My father was very, very kind. He was all for anything that we wished to do and I think he was much more tolerant when it comes to that. He wasn't much of a disciplinarian because he was waiting to see how you're going to develop, why you did such a thing and why this. And my mother, on the other hand, would say, no that's not right you're gonna do so and so, so she was the disciplinarian in the family (haha) not my father. And that's interesting too because Indians have a way of discipline that's not quite like what we normally think. For instance if my mother told us ah, we, I want you to come in and sit down, and rest a while before dinner, and you didn't do it, she'd have you come in and sit down in a chair and she'd tie you in the chair. So you sat there until she got ready for you to come out. And ah, so, you know, and then one day ah, one of the violin teachers came by because she wanted me to play something, I don't remember now what it was and she came by and we were doing something and, giggling in the other room. Miss Schultz said ah, Miss Smith don't you whip your children? And my mother said, no, it's too much work. And then, Miss Schultz couldn't understand that but my, she, my mother could intimidate us in such a way that you never forgot what you do. For instance one day, I don't know how we were playing but we, she had left the ironing board up for us to iron some things and she went to a club meeting, and we had knocked the ironing board through the window and broke the window. And when she came back she said, how'd the window get broken and of course we all laid it on each other so she tacked a cloth over the window to keep out the out the, the wind. And then she went out and she was singing and we wondered why she was singing soft. So she went out and she made a large fire, in the, in the outdoors. And ah, so my brother went out and said, mama whatchu makin the fire for? She says well I think I've got to purify some kids so I guess we'll just have to skull 'em in dip. Haha! She wasn't gonna do that but we didn't know that. So ah, when the water got boiled in this big thing, she called her neighbor Miss Doren, she called her. Would you come over and help me please? Miss Doren said yes. Ha, so she came over, ha. And my mother said, you know my kids, they lied to me. They broke the window with the ironing board, and I don't wanna, I don't wanna wash their mouths out with lye because that'll mess up their tongues. I just think I'll just put some hot water you know dip, dip 'em, ha into it. And so Miss Doren said, well Smith, I'll go get some rope to help you tie them together. And when she said that, all of us started screaming and all of us said we'd be good and we never broke anything else. But you know they, the Indians have a way of doing things that you know gets the job done.

SIDNEY

In 1931 when I received my A.B. degree, I became the first black member of Phi Beta Kappa at that university. And my father had been elected to Phi Beta Kappa around 1895 when he graduated from one of the Ivy League schools.

professor of Romance languages; birth year 1909; B.A. 1931; M.A. 1935; Ph.D. 1942

I finished college at age 21, and ah, as it happened, I was elected as the first black to be selected at state university to Phi Beta Kappa and my father had been elected to Phi Beta Kappa around 1895 when he graduated from another university in the area. And so, ah, ah, interestingly enough when it came out in the papers that my name was among the ah, sixty or so, ah, seniors being elected to Phi Beta Kappa. I first of course, called home and my mother said to papa, you better go down and ah be present at that initiation service and he thought about it and he said, well maybe I will. Well it also came out in the newspaper that five of the Phi Beta Kappa graduates were inviting their parents, one of their parents to come to a bestow the key at the initiation banquet because they also were members of Phi Beta Kappa. And so then I went over to the secretary of the Phi Beta Kappa chapter there and ah, said to him, I would like to have my father be invited to the banquet, if possible and he said well Miss Ramsey we would like to do that but ah, you see the reason those parents are being invited is because they're members of Phi Beta Kappa too. I said well so as my father. Oh is that so, well very well. And so they did invite him. . . . And so of course he came and it was interesting because it was that very year that ah, a very liberal professor of sociology had been so bold to, as to invite his class from state which had girls in it, down to one of the black colleges for some function, some professional club meeting and ah, at the close of the meeting, they had a social and these girls danced, white girls danced with black young men at the college and when they came back and told their parents about that. The parents were up in arms and they insisted that the board of trustees fire that professor. And so he had been such an outstanding professor of liberalism and advancement in social studies that it was a tragedy. And so after the ah, we're getting back now to the Phi Beta Kappa Banquet when my father was among the five or six parents who came up and first bestowed the key before the other graduating seniors were to receive their little diploma and their little certificate and their key. The chairman presiding for the evening said would the following ah, I think it was six students, whose parents will bestow the key upon them first, please stand. And among those six was Sidney Ramsey. And so when I stood up, you can imagine the ah surprise on the faces of other people to see that among those six preferred ones, there was a black girl. And so when my father bestowed the key, he just said, it makes me very happy to do this for you Sidney. And he was quite dapper. He wore a tuxedo as did the other professors. And when one of the professors, ah, was a professor of French, Dr. Harlen was assigned to have him sit with him and he had met him at the elevator and hosted him and so that was a very ah, dramatically kind of historic event and the local paper which was a leading and daily newspaper took it up and ah, caught that point and said, and the title of the article, which was an editorial, was Forgetting Prejudice and he went on to explain that it was very interesting that in this year when the professor of Sociology was fired because of his liberalism, that Phi Beta Kappa had inducted the first black into Phi Beta Kappa State University. So there wasn't a picture there but it was a nice article.

So then here at this university, there was a new president who was only 36 years old and was the first black president of the university. And the reason he was appointed, he was an outstanding ah, minister and professor. He was appointed the first black president because the students at the university had been on kind of a strike. They had protested the fact that their white president was returning funds to the church association saying this college doesn't need these funds for this year so we return a certain amount of money, our students didn't need it. And when they, they were tired of that. So they protested and said they wanted a black president and the trustees did appoint this ah, very fine. And when he looked around to see what was happening here I guess he must have come maybe in June to assume his position, he found all these white teachers had resigned, even though they were missionary in spirit and had come down from New England to teach blacks. They had drawn the line when it came to working for a black. And so all of them disappeared except two. And therefore the president was hard put to it to rebuild his faculty, overnight as it were. And so he told me, that various applicants that were coming, most of them for their first positions after getting their master degrees, he had to decide that well here's a young lady who doesn't have her masters but she has a Phi Beta Kappa key. So I will take her. So I was the only one that came down to the university to teach at 21 without a masters degree. But ah, in a year or two I had some scholarships and I did get to finish the masters. He asked me to teach ah Spanish as well as French. Well I only had a minor in Spanish but I, I got busy and I taught both. Then I fell in love with Spanish even more than French and from then on, I ah, sort of majored in Spanish. Got a masters in French, but then later I doctored in Spanish. And the reason I got that doctors in Spanish was because my next job was to be at a teachers college which was a in Washington D.C. and I had met a man who was at another university. And he ah, had gone up to the teachers college which was supposed to be quite the ideal place to go in the city and ah he was looking around for a Spanish teacher. He had his doctorate in French, and he was a Phi Beta Kappa graduate. And he, and so he told me, he said, I want you to get your doctorate in Spanish so we'll have a balance here so I said yes I'm interested. So I decided to major in Spanish. So I went back to state on scholarship and ah, did finish the doctorate in time. And ah, so then my second job was at the teachers college. And I stayed there.

Now my next job was just teaching in ah, public schools in Dover. I think just a semester. So my sister and I decided we would go back to our home town and see what we could do there with our lives. So we went on back there. And then my next job was ah, just suffering in the junior high school, hahaha, for about a semester until an opening came at what is now State University but at that time it had another name. And I think because ah, there was a need overnight, the they thought the person they had hired didn't show and so they called me and said you come tonight to meet a 6:00 class. I said yes and I escaped from the junior high school.

And then another job came there at another university. So I was doing two jobs. And really for ten years I think I taught day and night at different colleges. I can't even count up how many different colleges I've taught in, maybe seven or eight. And I stayed there and enjoyed that teaching Spanish, lecturing in Spanish part time at both places until 1950. This was in 1931 that I had started teaching at the first university. And in those interim years at the teachers college. And then, having moved to Dover, then to Chicago. It was about 1946 or 7 I guess that I was teaching in Chicago. Then in 1950, my primary interest was growing more and more in serving my Faith . . . and my sister and I offered our services as pioneers [missionaries] . . . And the letter said, thank you for excepting this responsibility and, it will be pleasing if you will go for the summer [to South America]. Well we were so honored to have such support . . . and such inspiration and we said oh, we'll do better than that, we'll stay two years. We'll just be very, very sacrificial. Haha. So we went and we were back at the end of the summer. . . . The major reason was . . . that there was a clause in the country's constitution . . . which we discovered after we had stopped our housekeeping, sold our car, given up our jobs and gone to . . . to take the plane . . . and before we could go we needed to have a visa . . . and when we asked for it, they said . . . the counsel in the office said, you can read Spanish, yes, read this constitution, and there, there was a clause saying that socially undesirables would not be admitted into the country under any circumstances and listed some of these socially undesirables among whom were Negroes of the United States. Now to jump ahead a little bit, there was really a merciful restriction, but at the time it seemed so prejudicial and discriminatory that we were just heartbroken. But we had burned our bridges behind us. . . . But the reason for that clause was, as we discovered later, was to protect the slaves from being transplanted in the 19th century before 1863, 1865. Just being transplanting by their masters into Central American countries. And I understand there were many masters who managed to do that and get around that law but this was an aim to protect ah, blacks from slavery, continued slavery. But it looked so bad, it now applied to us in the wrong context but how could you change the constitution?

So here we were, young black women having to come back to Chicago with no jobs. And my dad ah, accommodated us in his house. . . . But ah, by the grace of God we managed to get two jobs within a short time that could keep body and soul together and we started up again in Chicago serving the Faith. And ah, you ready for the my next job? Haha.

Well, I had not had any methodology courses because my degree was from the college of liberal arts and I had maybe one course in educational psychology and one course in ah, general education. So I didn't know, how to teach. But I said to myself. I have a friend who only made C's in French when she was at state and she went down to a college in Mississippi and was very successful. So if she could do it, I could do it too. And I just set about teaching the way I had been taught but of course I was somewhat severe. I learned afterwards—students said, and they would go out of my class and say, she's trying to make Phi Beta Kappa out of all of us. We just want to learn a little Spanish. We don't want to be any Spaniards. But ah, it, it was gratifying because several young women and a few young men did, did decide to major in French or Spanish because of our inspirational approaches I guess and some people said I was successful. Haha.

The best students were the ones I invited to the Portuguese Program and this young lady . . . became director of a Portuguese Program for the government. And it was all she said because of my influence. And she's just a prize, she's just a beautiful prize as are some others. So yes ah, I did fall in love with ah Spanish, and then again with Portuguese and I've taught these subjects shall I confess, over 50 years.

But ah, at the end of the year I had an opportunity to go to State College as a Professor of, full Professor of Spanish and French. And ah, although this was supposed to be a temporary job, filling in for someone who was away studying, I took it.

Back into my more, more comfortable position as professor, and ah, after a year, I was appointed chairman of the department and stayed there and was even appointed chairman of the humanities division before I left. Now the reason I, if, I think I was there six years, and the reason I left that time, I seem to be prophetic, because I'm moving all the time but, the reason I left then was because I had a letter from the Faith. . . . We would like to know if you could go south and ah, help. . . . But I said, I wrote back and said, if I can find a position in the south yes I will do that. And so a very wonderful friend . . . had been watching my career a little bit I guess and she had been writing, saying won't you come to Louisville and speak for us sometime? . . . And so I did go, on this occasion to give a talk and to be entertained in her home. . . . And ah, after I had been there, this Mrs. Milton had given a reception. She had invited a number of ah, professors from the black colleges. And so one of the teachers who was there was the chairman of the department. At this reception, she was ah, she said to Mrs. Milton, I'm going to have an opening in Spanish this coming year, I wonder if your friend . . . would like to consider coming down to us. And so she very happily wrote me and I said yes if it can be worked out, I'll come. So, that's how I went to Louisville. And ah, stayed there four years.

Yes, I distinctly remember both my grandmother and my grandfather on my mother's side, they're the ones . . . who were slaves. But, my father's parents had died when he was twelve years of age. Therefore of course, we never got to know them. But, I have a picture there of him, my grandfather on his side standing ah, at full attention with a gun as he had been mustered into the Union army after slavery and was standing proud and free. And had ah, met the Yankee Army as they came down into Virginia where he lived and had ah, served them as a water boy, groomed the horses and stuff like that. And when they went further south and won the war, they gave him his freedom and mustered him into the army as a soldier. And so my dad has preserved that picture and I'm trying to preserve it for generation yet to come. But . . . my grandparents . . . on my mother's side, came to live with us in Chicago before they died. And ah, my grandfather who was obviously a son of ah, one of the sons of the master in the slavery period, because he was absolutely white in every respect, appearance and um, gentility and dignity and so forth. And he had been given a barber shop by that master when, when he married, so he'd never really worked ah, in any difficult situation and he was also a barber in Chicago. My grandmother um, had been what they call I guess a, a, little girl in the master's home, in the big house, and played with the little ah, ah, children of the master and his wife. And so her tastes were entirely in ah, that quality and she . . . she my mother told me many times how in the afternoon my grandmother would dress up and sit on the porch and she would say to my mother, Barbara you're still wearing your morning clothes and running around here and working and you should be sitting quietly on the porch in the afternoon. And then my mother . . . became a suffragette who was an activist to get the vote, get out the vote in 1918 and she would even march in parades and ah shocked my . . . her mother, distinctly and ah . . . My mother told me that they carried big banners and posters that said such a thing as, If a woman is good enough to be the mother of a president, she's good enough to vote. So that became my mother's type of life and not at all in line with the dignity and the gentility that, haha, her mother had given as an example.

I always think of my sister as my mentor, my guide, my best friend, and my model . . . my sister was a leader, a natural born leader because the oldest, as the oldest one in the family of four children, I have two younger brothers. My mother had said to her, now Linda you're going to have to be my helper and be kind to Sidney because her attitude toward me, since I was . . . I was a little scrawny something and pretty ugly. And she'd said to my dad, when he came home and would, had been in the habit of holding her on his knee or in his arms, she had said to him one day now papa, put that ugly little thing down and hold me!

ZORA

I don't think I've ever been truly discouraged in my life. If you're disappointed, then accept it as God's Will and with that frame of reference. I went on to do the next thing. I got a job in the WPA and helped to write the history of the state.

teacher/social worker; birth year 1914; B.A. 1940, Ph.D. 1992

What I most recall about my mother is her strength and her justice, her sense of justice. She had five of us and one could never feel that one was treated any more, carefully or better than the other. So, many times when you're in a family of many children one might say, oh you were the favorite but we never had that feeling in our family because of her sense of justice.

When she was the age five or six, in those days if you would like to know, she was born in 1890 so in those early days mothers didn't know what to do with their children on Sundays so they would send them to many different Sunday schools and she would hear from the Catholic and the Baptist or the Episcopalian or whatever church she went to, that that was the only way to God. And, it began to bother her at the age of six or seven as to why if, if, God would leave out so many people in the world that probably had never even heard of Jesus. And, so one day she asked her father ah why is it that unless you go the Baptist route you can't get heaven. And some say unless you go the Catholic route you don't get to heaven and she asked the question um, why is that so. Why would God leave out so many people in the world that never even heard of Jesus Christ? And he told her not to ask such questions that, that's sacrilegious. He really didn't have an answer for her. So from that tender age, she became aware that there was something missing in her life as far as religion was concerned.

My mother's foster father was also a poet and also the first black to have a white collar job in the statehouse. . . . He was a very delicate man, painting, you know that type of early um, wonderful character really. He was the first to, black to graduate from the high school in the year whatever. In the early 1800s yea, or mid-1800s I guess. Yeah. She [foster mother] she was educated too. To some extent but she was also a social butterfly type.

My father's mother came to this country I think possibly in the ah, before the 1920s. But she didn't spend a very long time, she wasn't very much happy with America. Ah, she went back to Barbados. And she passed there.

My grandmother on my father's side, she had, she was Carib Indian and so she had hair way down her back. She could sit on it. And she was a very powerful character according to my father's stories of her. She was very strong minded and very anxious that all her children be properly educated and that kind of thing. In those days that was considered quite advanced because um, and she, I think she was a businesswoman in addition to, you know, as a means to helping to support the children, and her husband also had some means of support which I, I have forgotten at this time. If you really wanted to know that history, my elder sister knows that more because she goes to the island every now and again and she picks up the family history from my uncle Carl.

We were reared in the country and we had kind of a big piece of land out there and a brook and a pine grove and all the good things that make your early childhood days really wonderful. And ah, and even from the beginning we were always surrounded with other children, the neighbor's children always came to play with us even though we were the only black family in the whole town of 2,000 people. The very first day we arrived the neighbor's children, now the nearest neighbor was about ah, like half a city block away, but they came up the very first day and brought us fresh vegetables out of the garden and that was like they were welcoming us but incidentally that was the only family that really welcomed us the first few days. But, after that people used to come by on Sundays to look at the people in the zoo, you know? They couldn't quite make out what blacks were like. And we had to overcome all of that. And incidentally my brothers even had to fight the town bully to prove that, you know, they could take care of themselves. And so we went through all that but my mother never allowed us to feel that ah, we were in any way inferior to anyone so that there was no way that ah, we came up and felt sorry for ourselves that we were black and other people were not black. Ah, although in those days we never talked about blackness anyway. Everybody talked about, mixed color or nonwhite or something of that nature which is kind of ridiculous anyway but I remember when we were kids . . . we're walking back home [from town] and we decided to go a different street than usual. That means to say my two brothers and my one sister at that point in my life. And, when we walked down this street which was an all white street, the kids began to call us nigger and we stopped dead in our tracks and said, we're not niggers. . . . And that's, that sort of startled them and we were so proud of ourselves, we went home and told our mother that. But as I say, in that town ah, what actually happened to get the people to regard us as human beings was ah, we had a fire in our house um, it was an electrical shortage in the wall or something. No one was at the house. My mom had been ironing before she went to a nearby city and took my youngest sister on ah, an errand and while she was gone and the rest of us were in school, the house caught fire on account of the short, electrical short in the wall. And the house burnt down. And, as a result of the house burning, nowhere for us to stay, certain families took in some of us and it was as a result of the fire that ah, the people began to realize that black people and white people are really the same when it comes to things like that. And it was the beginning of the change of the attitude of the people in that town, my mother ah, developed a um, an orchestra. She had an Italian play the violin. She had a Swedish boy playing the trumpet, she had the one brother on the drums, my older brother sang. We had um, I've forgotten the other nationalities but there were a total of seven ah, young men plus my one brother that sang and they roped me into singing too. And we used to go and play ah, music. . . . And we played at the hospitals, charities, and different things like that. And ah, she [mother] said that she had developed that orchestra to prove that, you know, all mankind is one. And they had a wonderful time. As a matter of fact, at my brother's funeral just a few weeks ago, some of those, one of the fellas at least, that used to be part of the orchestra came and was so happy to see us again after 50–60 years. And he remembered the orchestra. Haha. It was really wonderful.

Well she [mother] was ah, an achiever I would say, because not only, not only was she um, concerned about the achievement of her family, but even for herself. After she got us well on the road she went back to school herself and studied Law. And ah, then that was that was something. Let's see, that was, I think it must have been in the early thirties. Yeah, it was before I started col, college at ah, Teachers College so it was before then, I think it was the thirties. . . . She didn't [finish]. She did 2 1/2 years. She only had a 1/2 year to go but I have forgotten what caused the, the, her stopping. But, I remember something that was in connection with my grandfather's passing. He became ill while she was a student there and I remember her telling the story later that he had said that she could've come to look after him if she hadn't been at school and I don't know whether that had any . . . something to do . . . with making her stop or what it was that got in the way but something apparently got in the way because she never completed the work there.

And I think she [mother] thought knowing about it from the real legal point of view would help her in her life even, even if she never practiced it [law], I mean the fact that she would have some understanding would be good for her. See, she married relatively young because in her years, she married at the age of 19 and when she finished high school as I say she, she was the first black woman to graduate from the high school. Her father was the first black person, man or woman, to graduate from the same high school. She couldn't do any professional work until she became 21 and see she finished at 18 or 19 whatever it was. And ah my father came along you know before she became 21 and so that changed her plans. But it must have been in the back of her head all the time to go forward. She had wanted in those years to study nursing but instead, later on as she grew older and more concerned about what she really wanted to do with her life, she chose law.

I remember when, ah, when we were little tots oh, I must have been 5, 6, ah, we were children on the floor at a gathering in town somewhere and a lady who was very artistic and dramatic and beautiful soul, and she referred to us as, look at the beautiful black pansies among us. And, my mother came and explained to us that she meant no harm that she's trying to say that um, pansies are beautiful black, green whatever color and we accepted that. I thanked my mother for that because we could have been feeling that she was trying to speak in a derogatory way but ah, I was very happy that she [mother] had made, she had given us that answer.

Now my mother often had dreams or visions of some kind. I always thought of her as some kind of mystic or something like that, very unusual woman really. . . . As a matter of fact, later on she wrote poetry and she did a lot of different things: painted, she was a very talented lady really and, and in her later years in her 70s and 80s she um, she used to belong to the senior citizens club and she used to read her poetry there. . . . And they used to have, you know, like they have in these senior citizens card parties or something, and she would make little gifts but you'd always have it showing the oneness of mankind.

My father was a very quiet man and very loving. He had a very strong sense of, of morality. He was very protective of us, especially girls. Um, I can remember I used to think the boys had much more leeway than I had as a girl. I was always kind of strong-headed like, wanting to do what the boys did. Climb trees, jump out of barn windows and that kind of stunt. And so when the boys wanted to go, in those days it was safe to ah, get on the road and get a ride somewhere from a passerby. So when the boys used to come home and talk about their trips to town and how they would thumb a ride and came back with all these adventures, tales, I used to feel, oh why do I have to be a girl because I couldn't do all those things. . . . And so as I say, my dad was um, very careful about us and protected us and I'm glad because he brought us up in a way which you don't, I mean people don't bring their children up that way anymore. You got permission from your parents before you even consider doing anything and this kind of thing which is an upbringing I'm happy I had to tell you the truth. It's stayed by me well. . . . We used to sit as a family and decide family issues around the table. We had consultations as kids, coming up. It seems big things which would affect us as children, our parents communicated that to us and we talked about it around the table.

Well, when we first moved outside of town of course his job was in ah, the city so he had to commute and he used to just get home weekends at first and then when he got a car he was able to commute and get home every night. Um, and I imagine those first years must've been sort of hard on my mother 'cause I remember that the men used to come and whistle at her and she would become very annoyed and very angry about that and the way she dealt with that um, there was one doctor in, one white doctor of course in the town and she made it known to him that those men who are whistling might as well give it up. She's not the slightest bit interested in them and he could go right back and tell them that she's happily married with her family so forth and so on. And, it ceased as a result of that. So, I'm saying that was a brave woman to let him know with no uncertain terms that she wouldn't be entertaining any of that because see they knew my dad wouldn't be coming home until the weekend so they were going to do the usual, you know, interfere with her happiness.

Do you know that we didn't have TV and even when we got a radio it was a big event. And it was battery set and my uncle who had that ability to put the thing together, brought it down. It must have been in the late 20s early 30s, and gave us a battery set radio. So, obviously with so little um, means of entertaining we were within ourselves, creative. We used to have ah, plays which we created ourselves and dramatized ourselves and sing and dance and do all that kind of entertaining for ourselves. Play games, make them up, all this kind of entertainment for ourselves. We were very much ah, encouraged to be creative because we didn't have all this outside things to interfere, and then of course as I said earlier part of my father's, ah, temperament wanted us to make sure we ah, spent time with our religious and spiritual development so we had to read the Bible or read words from the writings on every Sunday. He made sure about that. He, you know, oversaw that so that we didn't leave out our, you know, our interest in, in God. We knew we had to cling to Him. And it was a good thing because when the Depression came along if it hadn't been for our knowledge that God was there to protect and help us we might have suffered more than we did. It was the Depression that changed his [father's] life-style to a great extent. That it was very severe, as you know, and um, I think, I don't remember the year but I was still in high school when my father ah, lost his job and that, you know, was a change in his life-style to a great extent. But, as I say, we had the faith which saw us through and ah, my mother too. She went back to work to look after us and that kind of thing . . . but that didn't deter the family 'cause all three of us went on to college just the same, worked our way through and all the rest of it. Because, we knew it was important.

He [father] was a very quiet person, you, you wouldn't be able to get much out of him except in retrospect, you know that he suffered because of it [the Depression], that he was no longer the bread winner and I'm sure that disturbed him to some extent. But, um, somehow he had been careful to the point that in the good years so to speak he had ah, invested in property so that for a while those properties paid a, little money until the tenants were also affected by the, the Depression and weren't able to pay their rent. So then the house became a white elephant and he had to dispose of it, things like that. So that kept him going for a little bit until things sort of sorted themselves out, but um, yeah, I'm sure a lot of people when they look back at those Depression years, I think they, they ah, if they had a good, strong religious upbringing they probably got through it better.

ELMIRA

I was continually having to prove myself, but I took all that in stride because you know you're a pioneer in the field and you have to go with the flow of it.

attorney; birth year 1908; B.A. 1928; J.D. 1930; two honorary doctorates, 1939

My grandparents on my mother's side passed while my, my maternal grandmother passed before I was born and my maternal grandfather shortly thereafter. I do remember some very interesting things about them. My maternal grandfather . . . was a member of the state legislature. He was elected during the ah, um, reconstruction period and he was a minister. My maternal grandmother ah, opened the first school for black children, in her home. And I have her certificate ah, to teach reading, writing and spelling with arithmetic crossed out because the, Board of Education for the state felt that it wasn't necessary for her to teach arithmetic. I have given her certificate and my grandfather's certificate of membership in the state legislature to an archive at a black college.

I know that my grandfather was a minister and ah, I suppose that he read and write, learned to read and write. And ah, my grandmother, I do know from my mother, learned to read and write while she was taking ah, the little white girl whose family she belonged ah, to school because it was against the law to teach blacks but this little girl taught my mother who was a little, grandmother who was a little girl, all the things she learned at school. And that's how she learned to read and write.

My grandparents on my father's side, I do remember a little more clearly because um, they lived in Kentucky and ah, they both read and wrote, and ah, my grandfather was a coachman on my father's side, for a very wealthy family in Kentucky. My grandmother did not work. And ah, there is a very interesting story back of them too. . . .

Well, the story as my paternal aunt told me ah, she told me one day when I was on home leave from work in Africa. And she said, "You know some of our relatives are in Africa." And she said that in the days of slavery in Tennessee, her father who was my, ah, paternal grandfather and her mother, here in Tennessee. And my maternal grandmother's father, belonged to a family who had been given manumission by their owner at his death in his will. And he had left them a certain amount of money so that they could leave the slave state and go to a free area. And at that time, they were organizing passage to the ah, to Liberia. You remember there was the, an organization for freed men to go and settle in Liberia and they were going to book passage on that ship and go to Liberia and the state of

Tennessee told them that the youngest child who was under age could not leave. They would not consent to his leaving.

And ah, he couldn't. The state would have to accept his inheritance and he would have to wait. So they went through the agony of deciding whether to leave this child or to give up their plans and face all the dangers of being freed in a slave state. They went on to Liberia and this youngest child was a boy went up into the Tennessee hill's and lived with a family of mountaineers who did not keep slaves. Eventually he grew up, he married a mountaineer girl and they came back to a city in Tennessee. I don't remember the city and my aunt, of course, did not remember. And there he raised, he reared his family. And my maternal grandmother was his youngest child. She was a very beautiful girl and ah, one day, as I was told the story, the son of the person who had freed them came back to this city, heard that they were there and came around to look at the family and a told them who he was and he saw Mary, who was the youngest, and saw how pretty she was and said, "I will take this girl and educate her and rear her." And her father said, "No, I will never give her up. She is my child, I'll educate my children." And ah, he [the man] was rather offended and he left saying you better have her ready because I'll be back for her in a week and ah, the father, Mary's father went to the person whom he worked for who was an official in some bank there and said, "Now I'm not going to give up my daughter because I have no confidence in this man rearing this girl and if he takes her, if he attempts to take her I will kill him." And the ah, official at the bank said, "you know that will cause an uproar. There will be a lynching and there will be all sorts of things. You just go home, keep quiet. I'm gonna give you some money. Tell your family just to take whatever they can carry and I will get you across the river to Ohio which is free territory. And ah, you can stay there and carry on your life. So that's what the family did.

My parents were very wonderful people. I have always praised God and prayed for their welfare in the world beyond because they gave us such a happy childhood and one of great security. We never felt that we were not loved or cared about. And that is true even though during my adolescent years my mother did work outside the home. She became a teacher. And my father was in military service most of his life and when he came back from the first World War, ah, he went into what they used to call unity service and then into insurance. . . . My father always was interested in taking us to see people and to see things. I remember visiting and meeting Marcus Garvey with him and he [father] told me what an important and historic man this was. And my father served in at least two wars. He died a Major and met a lot of discrimination and ah, had a lot of overcoming to do, but he was never bitter.

I have a letter from President Harding. Although my father had all the qualifications for Major ten years before he was granted it, the president wrote and said it was the policy of the United States Army not commission any more Negro officers. And he [father] kept fighting. . . . He came from that period and my mother also faced it in early Illinois which was not a very liberal state even though it was a free state. And I remember as a child hearing about lynchings and discriminations and I grew up incidently quite bitter.

When she [mother] came she entered the school and at that time Illinois did not have compulsory segregation of schools, but had districts. All the black schools were in the black districts and you didn't get anywhere else. And, the teachers used to have to fight for equality and opportunity. In fact, in her late years my ah, mother was a very active member of the teacher's union. And I remember also, because they had accepted the ruling about promotional rights being tied to your educational accomplishments. She went into college you see after I graduated and I used to help her with her homework. And I went to her graduation from the university. And I remember how proud I was to be sitting up in the stands watching my mother get her degree. And ah, all of those things meant that she was forever trying to improve upon life's situations for the sake of herself and her family.

She [mother] was a person that everybody loved her. . . . And she was a caring person. Ah, like most of the black teachers, in the black schools of that period, they realized what a handicap black children were operating under, motivationally and socially and economically and they did things to help children. And to help them find the dignity of being in essence a purpose in life and ah, I remember that very clearly. The city was interesting. It was the gateway to the south and during the great exodus of blacks from the south, many of them came as far as our home town and couldn't get any further . . . and it was the caring blacks in those areas who made a difference in a period of a decade. They really did.

I would say that, oh yes, during my early years she [mother] taught me at home. And ah, when I first entered public school I went into the fourth grade . . . they entered me in the fourth grade and I made it from there on. . . . She really taught me. I knew how to read and of course my father encouraged me to read and ah, really I, I was totally unprepared for public school demeanor but I entered it.

Oh yes, yes as the youngest of thirteen children, her mother sent her to Tuskegee, ah at that time was a combined normal and industrial school. And she entered Tuskegee and she was fiercely independent. She did not want her mother who was in her late years of life to put her through Tuskegee so she marched into Booker T. Washington's office and asked if she could have a job. And he gave her a job at the school. And she worked her way through. He took great interest in her, both he and Mrs. Washington did. And it was in Tuskegee that she met my father who was, who came down during the period she was there and was commandant. He was in charge of military training there.

Oh, she thought of them [Mr. and Mrs. Booker T. Washington] really as her family because she was very close to them and she loved Mrs. Washington and had a great admiration for what ah, Mr. Washington was trying to do with education. And incidentally, that tie was deepened because her mother died while she was in Tuskegee and um, naturally the ties deepened.

He [father] was charming. He was an engaging personality. And he was a rather handsome man. His hair grew white quite early in his years. And he was a beautiful talker, beautiful speech maker and an engaging storyteller. And ah, I used to just admire him. I didn't want him to know how much I admired him of course but I admired him very much.

Oh, it was a very interesting experience. It so happened that I was the first American black woman to enter the university law school. And I was pretty much a curiosity. But the Dean of the law school was very interested and very helpful. The rest of the staff had a sort of hands off policy. . . . The university had a very tough law school. They had a reputation for flunking people from Harvard and Yale and ah, they just let it be known that anybody who went to the law school had to really deliver the goods. There was no, ah particular charity or anything like that. You carried your weight and you got your grade. And ah, I'm very grateful for that because I had to shape up like everybody else there were at the time, only three of four women students in the school finished.

Ah, my freshman class numbered about sixty which in today's terms is small, but seemed very large to me. And um, I, I really gave it my best because at the end of the first year of law school, I had been offered an opportunity to write case review articles for the university law review. And ah, in my senior year I made ah, the Legal Aids group of the senior students who were chosen on the basis of grades and ability to work with the Legal Aides Society on a part-time basis, so I think I carried my weight.

I entered the law school in '28 when I was completing my Bachelor of Arts work and I went over and let my first of law school act as my last year for the Baccalaureate degree. And the legal course was three years so that I graduated with the L.L.B. which is now ah, Doctorate of Laws Degree, in 1930. There were three male students who had proceeded me. But I was the first black woman to enter and graduate.

I liked the study of law because I think it sets a standard for human relations and I also like the matter of applying a principle to human situations involving individuals and I thought that was most interesting. It was my second choice however because had I been able to take my first choice I would have gone on a stage . . . Sissle and Blake came to town. "Shuffle Along" played and Florence Mills came with what is called "Dixie to Broadway" I believe. And I saw each one of the shows three or four times and I was determined that I was gonna run away and go with the show. And I don't know how my father knew this but invited Mr. Sissle, who he had known in the army, to come to dinner. And all they talked about was how stupid it was for people, blacks, not to finish their educations and how so many ignorant women got into the show when they couldn't make it and then there was nothing else they could do and then ah, he turned to me and said, "I hear you're interested in theater. I said, "Oh yes." He said, "well you finish your education." I was then in the university, I wasn't in law school, and "you ah, come to New York if you still want to go on the stage. I'll help you." So, I backed down from my impulse to run off. I'd seen the show about three times as a member of the audience, about two times from behind the scenes. They just let me watch and I just thought there was no other world like it. But, as I matured and went on to law school, I saw how limited the chances were for really good black actors and actresses.

It wasn't as difficult in law school as it was when I came out, took the Bar, and started to practice. Because I had to overcome the tradition of a male, this being a male field. And I would go down to the courts and take my seat in the section which is reserved for lawyers and the bailiff would come over and say, "Young lady this is reserved for lawyers. You have to sit back there." And I was continually having to prove myself but I took all that in stride because you know you're in a pioneer field and you have to go with the flow of it, you know.

It so happened that I was with the first class of young blacks to enter the university and I had some rather interesting experiences there. All the girls were called into the Dean's office and we were all told that we should be as unobtrusive as possible on the campus, that we were members of the subject race. The university did not really want us, but as it was a city university it had to take us. And ah, we left that interview just about in a state of shock because we hadn't been prepared for that and we immediately met with the young men on the campus and told them about it and we all decided that we're going out for everything. That everybody in that freshman class is gonna come away with some distinction. We didn't burn any buildings down or anything like that, we just decided, we were gonna show them. And we all did. Every member of that freshman class had some distinction. And ah, the success of it was that the next year, the same official who had spoken to us called us back and apologized. He said, "I made an error and I want you to know that you are a credit to your race." That first year, we published a little magazine . . . and we ah, got contributions from any student on the campus who would give us a contribution and contribution from nearby universities. Poetry, short stories, articles. And ah, we sold it I think at either two cents or five cents a copy.

We were not given any residential privileges [on campus]. We had to take gym, but we didn't get to use the swimming pool. And ah, we were pretty much on the peripheral except for the way we made a live for ourselves together.

HARRIET

We all had to pass a French and German language exam. But that's just ordinary reading. It's kind of simple. But to go abroad to study required working in another language, so I went to Heidelberg.

historian; birth year 1911, B.A. 1933; M.A. 1938; Ph.D. 1946

I was born in Maryland in 1911. Attended St. Mary's school which is an Episcopalian church school from the kindergarten through junior college. From there to college in West Virginia where I earned the Bachelor of Art Degree . . . I earned the Masters and the Ph.D. in History, however, there were intervals where I taught.

I remember everything about my parents. My mother was a housewife, my father was contractor in building, having pursued his trade at a Normal Industrial school. Like most of these schools uh, of the south they taught trades, vocational trades, and that's where my father took his plastering and brick laying. And uh, my mother died first in 1941, and my, and my father in 1960. I am the first, the oldest and uh, the younger ones say I attempted to boss them all the time, and say I want to be the matriarch of the clan, but it isn't that, it's just that I have been down the road that they have to come over. So I give them some advice, some they take, some they don't, but they've all done very, very well. My sister has retired from teaching, my young brother who's living, now has ah, has taught at the university where I was for almost thirty-eight years. And he was coach and physical ed. instructor, and the brother who died followed the trade that my father had. And so that about sums it up, three of us in teaching and one followed the profession, the one who died in 1975, and so that's about it.

My typical days were filled with reading, studying, playing, that kind of thing. But you see I was at such an excellent school that we had something on the campus all the time, it's a private school. We had all kind of activities such as, I don't mean the athletic, because I wasn't in those except to take gym, as they called it in those days. But we had the Literary Societies, Sojourner of Truth, and the Harriet Tubman Societies, we had the debating club, we had a dramatic club uh, and all these kind of things. And those were the things that I participated in, more than the others.

I did everything with my parents. I learned to cook, that was one of, the main things. And my mother relied upon me. I never did do any cleaning, my sister did that around the house. But the cooking part I was assisting her early in life because you see my father in those days and for jobs he contracted he would have, he had twenty-two men working for him and we had to prepare the dinner and get it in the baskets. And he'd send the truck for it and we'd have to have that ready at twelve sharp. Nobody was eating like they are now you know, uh a sandwich or something like that. We had a whole dinner including apple dumplings and stuff for dessert. So my mother and I did that, and uh, she didn't call on anybody else to help, so the busiest part of our day in the summer was that. And in the winter time I was in school, but our busy part was to have that dinner ready by twelve, in those baskets, and plates, and they went right on to the men who were working.

I couldn't do what my father did for a living. I learned how to figure plastering uh, and he'd always try me out on that, 'cause you know, how many yards in a building, and what you do per yard, and how many bricks you'd need for thus and so, but no nothing beyond that. He kept his own books. He had a room in the house that he called his office room. I don't think it was much of a office room, but at least that's where he paid off on Saturdays, in that little room on the back of the house. And he was very good at that himself, and he made a very decent living uh, to the extent that uh, I suppose I never regarded us as being poor. Yet after the depression was over and I read all these books on the Great Depression . . . I said well maybe we were poor but since I, but due to the fact that we never had to miss a meal, we had three meals, comfortable place to sleep, the house was comfortable so uh, I didn't know until the books began to tell me that we were poor. But I know he didn't work from '29 . . . but uh, but not because he couldn't get the work. The depression had come but he also broke his leg, and uh, it was put back uh, improperly and uh, he had to have that done twice more, but uh we never felt any, any pressure because of that.

We, we, ate, we dressed, and uh, we were in school, and we had some place to board in. You see this church school required you to board in your last two years in high school, so we had to live on the campus, all of us, which we thought about it then we didn't think it was necessary, we lived right there in the town. But as I look back upon it, the activities that were on a campus and the friendships that were formed and the uh, activities that we participated in uh, made those two years most memorable, most memorable.

Well, my father worked from Monday to a half day on Saturday and what did we do on Saturdays? . . . But Sundays were his main days at home, except in the winter . . . and what did we do? We were among the few families that had a car, old fashioned T model Ford, and we would go on Sunday for rides around the country side, although the little town itself, and things like that. And uh, and that was about the main part uh, except as we grew older, then he'd take us to uh, far away places then. We went to the uh, the uh, world's fair in New York in '37 and Washington and places like that. Yeah, so that was the part but I guess that's the only time I'd call quality time because he worked every day and, and uh, when he'd come home at night he'd go to bed early during the week time, because he had a hard day the next day and he didn't want a lot of uh radio blasting and things like that. And he'd tell us that and yet he'd say he was going to sleep and yet if we were out of the house, he never slept, never slept until we got back in. As soon as he say so and so, and so and so, he'd call our name then he'd, my mother said then he would go off to sleep.

I'm sure that my father's father was white. I, I'm, I'm positive about that. He [my father] was uh, you could not tell that he was a black man till you saw him with my mother, and all of us. Not that, that was any big tribute, but he came from a area which had, as my mother use to say had the whitish Negroes up there. She said "I hate to go up there to meetings and family reunions, 'cause I'm the darkest one," she would say, "in the whole group." But she didn't really, I guess mean it.

The Episcopal church, yes St. Mary's where I went was just one. There are more . . . but those schools are now closed because the states took them over, but I'm, jumping ahead. . . . That's about the main thing I can tell you. I've always done public speaking, from Sunday school and things like that, and my mother would sit up there proudly listing, and she heard it one hundred times in the kitchen, but that was her joy, so that, that was a good time.

Now let's see, she [mother] was never shy, she was active in the church. Several times head of the women's auxiliary, and uh, she had leadership quality, because the women, the women uh, well course I shouldn't say that because she would laugh now if she were here. She would say "I don't know whether I had leadership quality or whether everybody else or every other wife was busy and therefore since I was not working in a formal sense," everybody put it on her. Yeah she'll lead that group, she'll take this group, she'll have this chicken supper or dinner, so it may not have been leadership, it may, she would laugh, "I'll tell you what," she would say, she'd laugh and say it wasn't so much leadership as it is the others didn't have time for it. So I think all of us take characteristics after both of them. However, she never talked as much as my father. My father talked incessantly. He kept up with things you know, and, and maybe I do much of that, uh perhaps with association with him, I don't want to say the genes did it but at least all of us are more like him on the talking side you know. Always talking, always having something to say. Mother was very quiet, but very firm. It would pain me more to see her cry, than uh, than anything I'd know. And I would know what sometimes, what she'd be crying about you know. Maybe uh, because her sisters didn't do as well as she did you know. I mean in marriage and children and family and all, like that. And she was always fixing up little packages to carry to them, you know, always. I don't know, but anyway I couldn't stand it. Now what else do I know.

I only remember my grandmother, her mother. Nothing much cause her mother lived with us. I was born in 1911, and she died in 1919. So I don't really know too much. . . . I just remember how she looked and things like that. She was dark, like all of us, like my mother, dark like my mother, dark like all of us. She was dark brown, that's all I remember.

St. Mary's was an all black school . . . I had one of the, I had a rich curriculum. I had a rich, a rich one . . . uh for instance, in high school we had to do uh, three years of math. We had to do uh, I'm talking about ninth grade now. We had I guess you'd call it algebra, that's what it was, and uh sophomore uh, ten, tenth grade we did uh, geometry and in the eleventh grade calculus. We had four years of Latin. Ninth grade we did general grammar, that kind of thing . . . and then for History we had ninth grade World History, tenth grade United States History, eleventh grade civics and twelfth grade problems in democracy. Uh, we had to do two years of Bible, ninth grade and the twelfth grade and we had to have uh, oh we took gym, just once a week, we had gym class all the way through. And you had a home economics class all the way through. I'm trying to figure if there's anything else, oh the sciences, yeah we had uh, I guess in the ninth grade, you'd call it Biology, tenth grade Botany, eleventh grade chem, chemistry and twelfth grade physics. I was never able to do anything you see, never, never. I laugh now because I tell, I tell my friends I relied heavily upon a man . . . he knew his physics you know. He could figure it out and all that kind of stuff. . . . We just went to church thirteen times a week you know, on the campus. You'd go in the mornings at uh, they had a program every morning from 7:30 until 8, then that night we had the Vespers. I think it was from 6:30 to 7, in the big, in the big chapel and that was five days, and on Saturday, we had no church but we had a religious service in the dining room, very brief one before the dinner meal. And then on Sunday we went three times a day, five, ten, and eleven. Yes we went to Sunday School at the church, eleven o'clock service and six o'clock Vespers, but that was required.

One dollar and a half a year [tuition]. That's all they paid in high school. Now when you get up to the uh, the last two years, when you went into the dormitory, yes I think that was about sixteen dollars a month. Something like that.

Let's not call it a well-to-do, let's just say fair, because I told you as I read the history later and we were not so well-to-do. (laughs) . . . On our street we had uh, uh my father put a water thing, a spigot on the outside of the house, but he put it there for, simply to wash the cars and trucks down, and all like that. But the neighbors did come for water and now I don't know what he charged them or anything like that, but I know uh, several families used the water there rather than go to a well. That was, that was way back in the twenties.

Our house was a big one, ten rooms. Everybody had a separate room, and uh, a reception room, maybe bigger than this and then a big kitchen, because we all have a great habit of eating in the kitchen . . . we did that, when more people came and they came in the living room, I'd take them right back to the kitchen and uh, because the kitchen's been a place for meals but not only meals, but for good talks.

I think my mother took care of the discipline, really. If you want to know the truth, I don't know if my father did a lot of discipline. She always said he gave in to us, so I don't know I'm trying to see now about any spankings, she may have switched us a little you know, but I, I don't have those memories. Everybody, I can't say everybody, but all of us were bent on doing right, you know, to a great extent you know. Nobody was stealing anything from each other. Nobody was doing this thing. Only problem we had was with the car. Now that was a big problem in the late uh, twenties you see, because my father had his car, well the family car I guess you'd call it and the uh, the trucks. Then he bought a second-hand car for us and that was a big problem. My sister, she's only two years behind me and William is two years behind her, so uh, we never could agree, and she would say uh, that I was taking the car because I was teaching up at St. Mary's. See I taught there later, this was a home school and because she [my sister] was teaching in the rural area. I took the car every Saturday and uh, to show off she'd say. When she didn't have anything and that after all I had used it during the week time, and Saturday should be her time, the biggest argument.

My mother never drove. . . . The ability to cook delicious foods and plenty of them makes me most like my mother . . . but I don't want to brag about what I, that's not important. 'Cause there are some things I can be very demanding about uh, I'd say that perhaps because they all talk about how I cook like her now especially when they come uh. I think my, my place is the, is now the home place of the gatherings when they [family] are in town.

Talking, speaking that kind of thing, holding the attention of a crow is how I'm most like my father. All that's my daddy. Yeah, that's what I'd say, yeah uh huh, and he was a quick thinker too. I perhaps don't think as quick as he does. I weigh too many factors and maybe because my training has given me more factors to weigh, you know maybe he didn't have that many to weigh to what, to what it was going to be you, you know, so he's a quick thinker in general. He was a mason, and had some position in the church and uh, you know P.T.A. and all those things. He did all those things, he did all that kind of stuff, uh huh.

Yeah, my father did P.T.A. . . . Once a month, uh huh. They had it at night, 7 to 9, and especially if they had uh . . . raffles to make a little money. Everybody looked to him to do the raffling, 'cause he could auction it off, and sell it. . . . Mother went too . . . they'd see him coming in and they'd ask him if he would raffle this off, and that off. It was about thirty five cents, fifty cents, maybe what they were selling you know, the foods and all that. Well we had a very good home, home life and we're very close.

FRIEDA

I was never stupid enough not to be afraid. But I always had faith in God and I was always careful. People would be easily persuaded for a few pennies. For example, someone would give somebody $50 to poison me.

union organizer; birth year 1924; H.S. diploma 1941

My father was a World War I veteran, and he went to the army and came back. And after he had been home 'bout six or seven years I think he met my mother and married her.

Well, I'm serving in the capacity as a counselor in some low income houses being (section 8). I mean, most of the people in there uh, indigent people. And uh, I have two that I work with, one in the mornings and one in the evenings. And I've been with the one in the evening since 1953. And I've been with the one uh, in the morning since last year but they're owned by the same company. Ummhmm.

I help people with their problems. . . . Because when the telephone bills have to be paid . . . and food stamps have gotten lost, have been stolen, food stamps have run out then they find Mrs. Locke and I do whatever I can to help in any manner by asking churches, organizations, individuals to share, you know, with some of them, funds with these people. And I also have what we call clothes barn . . . getting some clothing from some, some neighbors and some friends of mine, now that they'll be out for three months this summer and they're cleaning out closets and getting things clean and washing things for me, and they give them to me so that I may give to . . . these people in these complexes. . . . Well, I don't find it too difficult to . . . one of the complexes where I work in the morning, it has been named by the, police department and the sheriff's department as one of the worst in the city. Now where I go in the evening, when I first started then '83 it was [the worst], but I've been told by the police and the sheriff's department that it is, that it's different. And I would like to think that I made the difference. At least they said so.

Not only these things, but I encourage them to go to church, and, I go to school sometimes when parents have problems with the principals and with the teachers because they said I know everybody in the city. Not that I do, but I know quite a few because I have some of my neighbors and, my family works uh, in the field of education. So that kinda gives me an entry into the city school system. And I claim the school superintendent as one of my children. Ummm hmm.

Oh, there's so many things. In every aspect as far as I'm concern is rewarding because when I see kids uh, come from areas like these low income houses, and they go to school and they come and show me their, report cards and they have A's and B pluses. To me that's, rewarding.

But this, small project [helping high risk teens, especially teen mothers, go to college] I said that uh, myself and a group of people from, group of people from various churches across the city and, other people that I can encouraged to come in and work with us. . . . I've been successful in getting several of them [to go to college], if don't get but one, if it's just one person, I'm happy about that, in getting them back to school. . . . Some of these are young mothers with two and three children. . . . I've been successful for the past three years I've gotten two, but I'm happy about those two as if I gotten two hundred, to get back in school. That's the most important thing, if I can help them understand the importance of getting education. . . . And by the year two thousand, if you don't have some type of technology, and uh, some type of skills rather, what I should say, the there won't be no jobs for you. . . . But uh, I'm trying to encourage them to get back to school, and to learn a skill so that they can be able to support themselves and their families.

Well, I was born in Alabama. . . . And my parents, my mother and my father separated when I was about two months old, and she moved back to where her home, where she came from, from Arkansas. . . . And uh, she left Arkansas when I was two or three years old, and she migrated to Mississippi with her family, with her parents, my grandparents.

And, of course I uh, graduated twice because, with the year that I graduated in the 40s you would have in graduation exercises from the eighth grade here in the city. And I graduated from Fulson Grammar School. And from Fulson I went on, back to Menton School. I had gone to Menton in the, about the fourth the fff, and the fifth grade. And then my mother married again and moved to the other district. And then that's when I began to attend Fulson Street School where I graduated from the eighth grade then went back to Menton to high school and I graduated from Menton High School.

I didn't see my real father, not until I became thirteen years old. And that's the first time that I can remember seeing my father. When I was thirteen years old I went to Alabama where we were born, where I was born, my mother, excuse me, had one sister that lived there. And uh, we went to see her, to visit with her and that's when I met my father. . . . I was excited. I was excited because this is my father and, and my mother's sister, she had two younger sisters, and they all said you just like him, you just like him . . . you don't look like your mother. . . . They all said, your mother is pretty. . . . I said, I look like my daddy? They said you look like your daddy, but you're a pretty girl. And I can remember quite well, I was uh, overjoyed to see my father for the first time.

I kept in contact with him and we had a very good relationship. And in '62, he called me and all doing the struggle of civil rights struggles he was concerned about me 'cause he had heard, 'cause someone told him that I was crazy. Excuse me, and I said crazy? He said yeah, you're involved in the middle, in the middle of everything that's happening down there in Mississippi. They tell me you're making part of that happen. I said, well, you know, they can say anything. He said of course I know you're in the middle of everything that's happening because we get the newspaper clippings . . . so my father was concerned about me. And he called once in a while, and I called him and let him know I was okay, that I knew how to take care myself. Of course I let him know that, I'd seen inside of, of a few jails, but I'm okay. Yeah, but I'm okay. Ummmhmmm.

Yeah, I brought him [father] to live with me, in '83. And he expired in 84. Ummmhmmm. And he [would] sit around and tell the stories about things that happened to him in service and, the places that he had gone, and where he had been. And he could speak a little French, yes. And it was just amazing to me that at ninety-four he could remember that all those things. Ummmhmm.

I had a sister, my sister got killed when a cabinet fell on her. My father wouldn't let my mother take my sister. She was a year older. And one of those old fashioned cabinets fell on her. She was trying to get up on top of the cabinet get some, something. So they said, and the cabinet fell on her and as a result from that they said living in the country as a rule black people didn't have such good medical care, at that particular time. And uh, she expired and they buried her at the age of, I think it was seven. Seven or six I think it was when they buried her, but she was a year older than me. Yeah, so I had a sister. . . . My mother went back to the funeral and he [father] wouldn't let my mother have her. He wanted to take me but, I was a little bitty baby and my mother ran away with me. Uhhuhh. So uh, my sister he kept her . . . and then he [father] remarried again, and he had those two girls. He kept those two girls, he stole them away from their mother. . . . I don't know, my father was very jealous I've been told and my mother was very pretty.

At the age of four I saw my great grandmother on my father's side. She was a, full-blooded whatever Indian, kind of Indians in that area. But I was afraid of her because she was, I wasn't used to seeing white people. Yeah, and uh, I was afraid of her, and I wasn't used to seeing anybody with that much hair and I was afraid of her.

Well, my mother was a very good looking woman. She was a smart woman. . . . She went to school. And at that time, you know, you got to tenth grade and that was it. And she did go until tenth grade. . . . And uh, my mother I don't ever remember my mother eh, ever having said that she had gone to the doctor. You know, most blacks at that particular time, didn't have too much of uh, too much medical attention. Didn't get too much medical attention. So I don't remember my mother ever saying that she had gone to the doctor. She wasn't ever sick. She died suddenly.

But my mother was a woman that she always wanted me to, go to school. She says get an education, do the best that you can and I'll do whatever I can to help you . . . but we just were too poor, for me to continue in school. I won two scholarships . . . but we just couldn't afford [college]. So when I came out of high school, I worked. It was disappointing 'cause the person who had worked so hard to see that I would take the, the, the test, it was the exam. Well, I passed, I missed one word, everybody else missed three and four out of ten questions. I missed one. And I should never forget that [word] . . . But see, I made the highest score. I just missed one, and I it hurt me because I wanted to make the perfect score. And the teacher told me, she said, nobody is perfect. Nobody makes a perfect score. She said you made an excellent score.

Yeah, well first of all, my mother worked at a laundry, then she left the laundry and she went to work for a company. They were downtown and she decorated their windows and kept the furniture dusted in there. And uh, she kept, well she didn't really keep and make out the receipts, but she kept the receipt books in order. . . . Well, when my father was in the city he worked for the government. He worked at the post office. Ummhmm.

I would go spend time with my grandmother. I was the only grandchild, for twelve years. My mother's sisters nor her brothers had any children so I was the first and the oldest grandchild.

Oh my grandmother was four feet tall. She was, dark skinned, very pleasant. . . . When school was out in the evening you would come home and study, get your lesson, then do your homework whatever you had to do around the house. And everybody had to wait for my grandfather until he came home before we all wash up and clean up and eat. That's one of the things that surprises me now that people let children just come to the dinner table and eat. But we had to wash up and clean up before we got to the table. And my mother's baby sister, was the baby, my grandmother's baby. She always liked the corner of the corn bread. . . . My grandmother made corn bread in a long pan and she [my mother's sister] liked the corner of the corn bread and we would have an argument about that. And my grandfather said there won't be any argument at this table. She [mother's baby sister] is gonna get one corner and you get the other one. I said I'm not particularly interested in the corner daddy. And he said well, that's okay. This is the way it will go. But my grandmother always insisted that we go to school and I was the oldest and the only grand baby. And they said I was always calling children dumb because they couldn't get the lessons and I would get my lesson and was always the teacher's pet.

And uh, my mother's sister, she's seventy-five now. She said we would be coming home, and she was down in grade school. She said I'd run home and start fights, calling children dumb. They start to fight me and the others would take up the fight and fight for me and I'd run home. And my grandmother, we called her mamma. Mamma said where're the rest of the chil, children. . . . She'd say where are the rest of the children? [I said] they're coming. She said what are they doing? And I said, I don't know mamma I left them back there. And by the time they would get home, they would start after me, and I would hide behind my grandmother. And she would say what's the matter? My aunt said, that old crazy girl started to fight mamma, and we always have to take it up and fight for her. My grandma said what did she do? She is always calling somebody dumb and she knows she can't fight. She said, because she gets a lesson and doesn't have to treat the other kids that way. But uh, it was fun growing up in that town.

The men [looking for me] were in town. They were at the motel and I happened to pass by the door, they were in the room next to me, and they didn't know it was me because I wasn't there when they came and it was dark when I came in the house. And I was going around the corner to get some ice, she [the manager] had an some ice box around the corner. . . . But they were there, they were talking about what are we going to do about this black woman. And they said well we can't find anything wrong . . . we can't find, what can we do? Said we can't get to the union records and one says yes we can, so we can get to the records, said but you don't need to get to the records because everything is alright. He said well I don't know whata hell we are gonna do about her. So they said well just let her alone. And then the other said well you know we've been called 'bout how the union looks after her too. So he said hell, let's forget about what the other side's doing. Let's look after her. So I overheard them and I didn't say anything. When I went to the office the next morning, the uh . . . office manager says to me . . . "So

we had some strange men here last night." So I said "yeah, who?
. . . I said, "what were they doing here?" 'Cause see sometime
anything I want to learn I could learn it . . . because we got to be
very friendly. I could learn whatever I wanted to, but I had no
information to give.

MARGARET

I didn't get angry when patients called me nurse. I don't see the
point, why get angry? The traditional role of women in the hospital
has been that of nursing. If that's what people expect, fine. All
you have to do is inform them.

physician; birth year 1915; B.A. 1937, M.A. 1938; M.D. 1943

Uh, basically of course I've always been involved in the community. . . . Well, I'm, I sit on several boards, uh, if I haven't been
tossed out since my surgery in January . . . and then I work in var,
uh, in various groups . . . it's one of the things that I find that instead
of being able to do two or three or four things, I do more . . . uh
so that uh, I find that I may make plans and then have to, have to
cancel them.

Oh! I was born in the best place in the world!. On the island of
Manhattan in New York City. And I uh, it's the one smart thing,
two smart things that I did. I picked the right parents who had me
born in the right place. The only two things I've done right in my
life.

And uh, uh I'm an only child. Uh both, of them although they
didn't know each other, uh, both of them were born in St. John,
under the Danish flag, of course. Uh because they were born before
the islands were bought by the United States. Well, and Uh, they
came to this country as, as, as very young people. Uh my mother
had much less formal education than my father but up until, within
18 months of her death she read all the newspapers that came into
the house. She was a mystery novel reader, uh very much interested
in the news on, on TV, uh and, and that kind of thing. Very, very

much interested in what happened in the community. Uh, my father had some high school training but didn't, was not a graduate. He was probably the first black man on foreign mail in, the, New York City post office. And that's why I could spell Czechoslovakia when I was five and nobody else could. Both my parents felt that there was more to life that just eating and drinking in the sun, and, their interests were in quality. And they both felt the mind was somewhat of a very important, part of the body and that you developed it as best you could, to its fullest extent. And uh, never was I, told that I must do so and so. The only thing that they asked me to do was to do the best I could. There was really nothing that existed in the immediate environment, by the environment I don't mean the street where I grew up essentially, but ah, everything that existed on that island [Manhattan] was made part of my childhood: the zoo, the aquarium, the Metropolitan Opera, the concerts. And you, you did this on the cheapy-scale, you know. You didn't have season tickets to the Met, but in those days, the Met would have, if I recall, about two or three weeks at the Met, not the way they do in the park now, but it was a similar philosophy. Then the uh, uh, the tickets would be cheaper, and that sort of thing. You know, the Metropolitan Museum was my home. Museum of Natural History, all of those places that uh were available, and just the streets, the public buildings. Um my father would be aghast if I didn't know, couldn't identify the public buildings, from a distance, you know. Course now they're so changed in New York, that, that you, except for City Hall you can't recognize 'em. . . . But uh, uh they both felt that you, you had to, you should have a close association with your, with your city, regardless. For example um, there was no question that there, there were some places where we were not welcome. And one was a chain of restaurants called Child's . . . and um you're aware of this, but you don't let this so color and so upset you that you forget all the other places that are available to you and that are more important. Uh to my knowledge I don't think Child's exists at all any more. Course I lived to see that particular problem broken down. But uh, the uh, I was pretty well shielded from the nastiness of, of life, as I grew up.

Um I went to public schools and then um one day they asked who were interested in taking the exam for high school. I had no more idea what a high school was than nuclear physics. And so, one of my friends was going so I raised my hand too and uh we were given slips and told when to go and so forth and so on and passed the test and was accepted. The uh, and, and there I was, uh, and of course we again, it was uh, the community. By the community I'm not talking about the large community, but the community of families with whom you associated: your friends, your parents' friends and what not. These were people who had fundamentally the same principles of living. In other words, quality was more important than quantity. Uh, no one was interested in conspicuous consumption. You wanted always to present a good appearance, but, you know, there wasn't uh this, this fantastic business of every body had to have a mink coat, or whatever. You had good things. And I, I was very fortunate of course, my, my mother sewed. That, that's what she did uh, before she married. In those days, which you, you see we're talking turn of the century, um, wealthy people employed a seamstress. And that's what you did. You went in, and you made, you sewed clothes, and that's what my mother did, she did all the fine sewing. So that uh, I didn't realize until I was more than an adult the kind of clothes that I had been wearing, because my mother made the smocking and the embroidery and the lace and all of those good things and I didn't realize . . . the kinds of clothes I was wearing in terms of quality. And, you know, that nice silks and so forth, lovely cotton, and whatever.

We were not wealthy people, uh my mother did not work after she was married. I uh, I can't, I absolutely still cannot understand how we did the things on my father's income. Um, and uh—not too many years ago I was opening some old uh envelopes and here were uh little, and of course this was done in longhand in those days, these little merit notes to him saying that um he was getting his merit increase, the merit increase for the year was a hundred dollars . . . and out of that small salary, um he saved. And again it's amazing because that was a great deal of saving in terms of not having to buy uh, clothes for me because I grew very fast. Uh, but nevertheless I'm still amazed. I don't know how they, how they did it, but they did it, and so did everybody else!

Yeah, uh, I can remember the . . . in my group of friends, not talking about family, my group of friends, I can remember the first car that was bought by uh one of our, families. Uh and again this, these were, these were not people who were millionaires or who were trying to put on any airs uh, we bought the car. This could've been maybe um, late 20s, 30s, early 30s. Trying to think uh, where I was. This, this was before high school, so it, it would be maybe late 20s, and I can see the car, but I can't recall the [make]. It was a, sort of burgundy and you know that, you know what they call a touring car? . . . And then one of the uh, single men, a cousin of one of our friends, he got a, he got a Ford . . . it wasn't a Model T, it was Model A. And it had the rumble seat, oh gee, you know, such a thrill! And the fact that my parents allowed me to go in the car, flying, flying down the road at 20 miles an hour.

Both of my parents, even though they didn't have the, formal training, had intellectual curiosity. And uh, we had books and papers, nothing unusual. My father read Shakespeare, read it to me and had me commit it to memory, things like that . . . my parents always got the New York Times . . . we always got the Evening Sun and the New York Times General. My father had me read something from the New York Times General every morning, well every day. We were doing these things uh not to improve anything, but because they were there to be done . . . one of my friends became an orchestra conductor, one a professor of psychology, one a pediatrician, so those who did not go into as extensive careers as we did still were brought up with the same kinds of quality and uh exposure. So that um this, this was not unusual, um the uh, emphasis on excellence and education and integrity were just taken as a matter of course.

School was uh, that was sort of a breeze, because I went to school reading and writing, and uh I didn't go, and . . . but that wasn't all good, in the sense that I did not go to kindergarten, and never developed hand skill, tying bows and cutting out things and that kind of thing. Um, I went right into first grade and uh, uh, that was a breeze. I began to realize that I really didn't know everything there was to know as I got into what we call junior high school.

In college I majored in Chemistry and Physics. No, no. Physics was a minor because I, I, you see, I was in a pre-med program. . . . This was the largest college for women in the world. . . . Put it this way, I don't recall being stared at. . . . Nobody said, "Oh, you can't do that". And I think part of the reason I didn't pay much attention 'cause I had the support of my parents. . . . And not only that . . . I had another friends going in the same direction. It didn't appear to us to be a big deal.

Ah, after undergraduate school, my father felt that I should be sure that I wanted to go to medical school. So he suggested that I do a year of graduate work. So I did a year in Psychology.

When I applied [for medical school] my father had a great, great respect for the university. One of my father's bad habits was that, if he liked you and admired you, you could do no wrong. If he did not, you could do no right. . . . And it never occurred to him that I was not going to get a position in surgery at the university. The dean told me in plain English, that first of all, the class was filled for this year, that he didn't wanna promise me for the next year. If I were around, if I were around next year, maybe. It just so happened for no reason I had applied to another school and was accepted. . . . You know I think it was more sexist than racist. I'm sure that race had something to do with it. But I think it was more sexist than racist. I think that he [the dean] did not think that women needed to go to medicine school, and certainly not a black woman. But I think that the emphasis was more on the sex.

At school at another city . . . suddenly I'm confronted. . . . There's nothing wrong with rules and regulations, but I'm confronted with these things, regulations that they put on, you know, on town girls. And along about Thanksgiving . . . I was invited to ah, one of the fraternity parties. . . . I had a master's degree, but I wrote home and asked my parents. . . . So . . . at midnight there is a tap on the shoulder. It's time to go back to the dormitory. And I say dorm? . . . And of course in New York City, at that time you won't think of going home without eating. I mean you know, that was part of the thing. You went to a party, then you . . . when I said that I'm not talking about house party where you're served . . . or something like that. Then you always stop some place [to eat]. And of course when we got to the dormitory, we were confronted by the house mother. . . . I wasn't about to back down. And I said that I respected rules, but I say . . . even though it happens to be three o'clock in the morning and so forth my parents knew where I was. . . . And then I say, so I have no problem with that. . . . I didn't like an atmosphere where you were locked up. So they throw us out. Thrown out. Absolutely. . . . Everybody left the dorm. I mean, the whole group. . . . But ah, some turned tail, and they went back.

At the black college where I went to medical school, as a matter of fact there was a couple of white students in, you know, in class even then. But no that, that was no problem, because I happen to like people. . . . The color of your skin, the curl of your hair, is not, was never a big thing. . . . But you have to remember that at time Washington was still a very segregated city. . . . The interesting thing about, prejudice, ah some of the ridiculous things that happened . . . a chain of department stores, very nice department stores . . . they weren't about to seat you [blacks], you know. And I wasn't even going to try to pretend, to stand up to drink a Coca-Cola, because I just, I wasn't gonna do that. I'd rather die of thirst than stand. Not because I necessarily wanted to sit, but because I was not allowed not sit.

Oh well ah . . . they [patients] called me nurse. But ah, the, the reaction was not negative. . . . Some patients were so sick they did not care who helped them. No, I, I, don't get angry for that. I don't get angry because of things like that. I just say well, now I'm not a nurse I'm a physician. I didn't get bitter. Now there are a lot of women who do . . . but I, I don't see why. The traditional role of a woman in the hospital has been nursing. So if that's what they, people expect to see, fine. All you have to is inform them.

But again ah, you can't prove all those things [sexual harassment] by me because I don't, I'm not looking for it. And ah . . . you know, some men, some of the men would try to get, a little closer than they should and that's all. But, you, you handle it. You don't have to make a big thing out of it. And then at the end everybody ends up, well.

Well, I think, I think the most, I would hope ah, that people would think not so much in my being first, in this and first in that. That's, that's fine, but I want to be remembered as a careful, caring, compassionate person. And this is what I try to be with the patient. Ah, the most, probably the most difficult time, was in the beginning, when the, the prejudice was so bad . . . I couldn't admit patients to the hospitals.

MAGGIE

> I had to stand up to white people, to authority based on race. It was difficult because I knew I was jeopardizing my own career. On the other hand, if I hadn't I would have lost the respect of my troops. I always figure if you're going to die, go down fighting forcibly.

Lieutenant Colonel–Women's Army Corps; birth year 1918; A.B. 1938; M.A. 1947

I was in the Army service almost four years! . . . Ah, it was a wonderful four years, very valuable four years, ah, because I'm sure that I, I got a great deal of my training in people skills in, in the military. Because of the assignment they gave me, you know. And, ah, it is just a part of it [my life]. I've done lots of other things. I've had lots of different careers. Ah, but that [the army] was a short part of my life, just a brief part of my life, but a very important part of my life.

And the reason I wrote the book, was that, ah, I was afraid they were gonna close the history on World War II and not even mention that black women had been in the War. As a matter of fact, you didn't hear very much about women period, being in World War II. So, I thought it was one of those cases, well, if you want something done, then do it yourself. So, I, I did. And ah, of course now, lots of other people are writing books and asking me where they can get published and so forth, and I don't know the answer to that.

Ah, so that's why I wrote it. Because I thought it was something that should be recorded in history, at least it was something good that our young people could hear about.

You know, somebody else asked me that question. "How did you feel making history?" You don't know you're making history. You only know you're doing a job. It was a job. Remember, I left one job to do that job. So, ah, it was doing a job. You don't know it's a start. You don't know things are history until after they are already done. And I don't know, I don't, if I ever thought about it as history until years after that. And, ah, no, I guess, the thing that kept me going was that I had always, I think I say that in the book in some place there, I had always been expected to do well, and so I decided to go ahead and do well. See, the other point [option] is not to do well. And, ah, I guess my sense of humor helps me through almost any situation. I can always laugh at myself. A little bit, you know.

Well, good grief, who wouldn't laugh [I fell down marching backwards looking at my troops]! Remember, I had been to a candidate school, and I had been in the training of officers too, and I could imagine what would happen if one of those dignified officers . . . and I could see one would laugh at one of those dignified officers falling down. No problem at all. And I could see they [my troops] were dying to laugh. You know how you get that puffy cheek look when you wanna laugh. So I said, "Let's hurry and get off the marching ground so I could get these people to laugh." Get that over with. Next, you see, one the the things about working with people is, is that I knew that if I let them laugh, there would be no more further talk about Mamma [my nickname] fell down. You see, if I hadn't let them laugh, they would be good and say, "Mamma, she's trying to make us keep quiet, and Mamma, she fell, and." But now, it stops, you know, it's just another little incident. You can forget all about. And so it worked that way. Yeah. So that's the way you do.

If I thought that I ever was going out and making application for a job anywhere again, I might not do that [tell the truth about racism and sexism], you know. Although, I don't know, I might not be as thorough with it as I was, except for the part that had to do with going in the military. There was just no way you could get around that. It was, first of all the military has been macho. And, as I always say, back when David killed Goliath. It was a macho army. Armies are macho. When Hannable went over the Alps with the elephants, it was a macho army.

Now, the decision to put women in the Army was made by Congress, not by the military. That was made by Congress. And, of course, they must have had some levels of approval from the military, but in general, the troops themselves and whatnot, didn't have anything to say about it. And here we were, you know.

And then, of course, there was a problem of racism. This country was . . . this country was very, very segregated, and very, very prejudiced, and discriminating and bigoted, and all of those things. . . . But anyway, there was that part I couldn't skip over . . . the other thing that made it easier to write about things, and very truthfully about the way they were, there are so many young people who don't know what in the world this world is like. . . . I really don't think they know. And, as a result of not knowing what things used to be like, they don't know what things are like today. Many young people think, "I got it made, and I'm integrated." You're not integrated. You may be desegregated, but you're not integrated yet. And, I think they need to know what it was like. Maybe that will explain to them when something, when they bump against one of those hard knocks they're gonna get.

Well, I grew up in the south. My parents, my father is a, was a minister and a teacher. And earliest recollection of him was he was pastoring ah, two churches or circuits . . . when you have two churches, you go to one on the first and third Sunday and the other on the second and fourth Sunday.

I never did know what you did with the fifth Sunday, but that's beside the point. But anyway, and he was principal of a rather large high school. . . . I had a brother . . . next to me. He was born while we were living in Woodville. And I have some recollection of that because it was there that I had diphtheria, and, ah, they had to take me from this little town to another town . . . and I was very ill, and

I stayed with my grandparents. . . . They wouldn't take me to the hospital. They wouldn't take a little black baby to the hospital because they didn't have any room for black children, at the place there where I had to be treated. So, my grandparents would alternate. One would take me one morning, and the other one would bring me in the next morning. And I remember all that period of my life. I was very miserable. I was being fed through my stomach and I couldn't stand up. You know, because my stomach was sore. But anyway, I was only three, I guess, when that happened.

I was born in Tennessee, but my family moved there when daddy was Vice President and Dean at a small college in there. But then they moved to Brighton before I learned to walk. . . . And then, ah, daddy, oh daddy was Dean of the Theological Center at another small university. And then he went back into the pastorate, and that's when he went to this town where I was for a time. Then he went back to Woodville when I was four years old. And that's ah, that's when I, where I lived the rest of my life. That's what I consider home. I was raised there. We lived in the parsonage, ah, in the parsonage right downtown.

My father had a bachelors degree from a southern black college. And lots of honorary degrees, you know. My mother finished high school in their hometown. She had a degree in teaching, in education. That was like a junior college degree. It's almost like what we call an associate degree now. But she was, uh, quite a good student. Just, that was good enough for her time when she came along.

Grampa, we went to visit Grampa Herman and Grama Liz, that's on my father's side. And I'll never forget, we always slept on a pallet at the foot of their bed. That was Frank, the brother next to me. The two of us were very close. Always together. And we always had to sleep on the pallet at the foot of that bed. Then we went, when we went to Big Papa and Big Mama, that's the other set of grandparents. We did because there were lots of cousins over that way, in that section of the area, community. So I could sleep with a girl cousin, and my brother would probably sleep with a boy because there were cousins about, about our own age. The cousins on my father's side were a little older, mostly, and except the family, the one that had lots of children, they never had any room for anybody. It was, it was all right, and we visited them every summer. And, ah, but we nev, we never lived on the farm except then, and when I was at grade school I remember every summer we spent two weeks on the farm. And had to work. I remember that very well. Hoe cotton. Had to pick cotton if it were late in the summer.

When I got old enough to go to school, I could already read and write. My mamma was a teacher and daddy was a teacher.

My grandfather on my mother's side was the principal of the Black School, Negro School where they came from. So on my mother's side of the family has . . . they had more inclination toward education, you know. Yeah, so I started to school and I was all ready. So they tested me and put me two grades ahead.

I was the oldest child. There were four of us all together, two girls and two boys. . . . And, ah, we'd get home [from school], and I had chores, and I had to do my homework, and then we used to have lots of fun time. You know, the whole family did. Ah, go on trips, Daddy played baseball with us, and, you know. We told, we told jokes to each other, and all. We'd do, we had good times. . . . We either had grits or oatmeal every day of your life for breakfast. That was when I was very young. Later on, we'd begin to get cold cereal and what not. But when we were little, I can remember that so well because I swore I'd never cook grits when I got up. And so I got a daughter who loves grits and a son who loved oatmeal.

In our family we grew up knowing we were going to school [college]. Why, I don't know. I guess they, the seeds were planted somewhere during that time. And, ah, we knew we were going to school. And I went to a black college. And I was Valedictorian of my high school class so I had a choice of the scholarships. And the three prime scholarships at that time were Fisk, Howard and Wilberforce. They were the three big schools at that time.

I majored in math and physics. I wanted to major in math and history, but they told me they didn't go together. So I minored in history. I had two majors, and my minor.

I wanted to be a civil engineer. And a lawyer. I didn't tell my family because by this time my brother who is next to me wanted to be a lawyer, and I thought, I took it on myself to presume that daddy couldn't afford to send both of us to law school. So, but, I took the math to get ready, in case, and I never did, but, ah, no, that's what I wanted to do at that time. The chances of that working out at that time were very, very slim. I know. That may be part of what influenced me not to, to worry about it. I could have been a lawyer. And, um, but I just figured that at that time, you know, it was more important that the man get the education. I took that on myself. I didn't, I should have told my family I'd rather been a lawyer.

When I finished college I taught junior high school. I liked teaching, I just didn't like the rules that went with it. . . . As a math teacher, I thought it my duty to teach kids the advantage of saving to buy something. Whatever, a dollar down a and dollar a week. So, I would have, we set up these, we would buy things. You know, make up things, and pay on them. And we'd clip the things out of the paper, and we'd have a chart, you know, and you'd pay, and nobody ever bothered to add it up. They would not realize they had paid twice as much, you know. So, I did that, and it must have caught on with a few people because the next thing I knew I had to go see the superintendent. There was a merchant or two had complained. So, I didn't stop teaching that. I just . . . called it something else, you know.

I was there [at the junior high school] for four years. And then that when I went into the military. I guess I was becoming rather bored and unchallenged by jobs teaching 8th grade, 9th grade, math, you know. Other people were so narrow-minded, you know. I saw, I just wanted something else to do, and this [joining the army] was a job opportunity. That was part of it. And we were at war. And, ah, I was always patriotic. . . . And so, ah, I was really going for two reasons. It was my next job, and I was patriotic. And I wanted to go fight the war. I wanted to win the war.

Well, Congress passed a law that we could have women in the military. They decided that they would hand recruit, hand-pick and recruit the first class. Because the first class were to be officers. And so they wanted what they called the highest caliber people. So, I was recommended by my Dean of Women at my alma mater. . . . I took all the exams, and the physical exams, the military exams, and psychiatric exams, and the interviews and whatnot. And I was one of the ones chosen.

I had an interview the day I was graduated from officer candidate training and was told that they didn't know what they were going to do with me. That was Saturday, and then on Monday, they made me company commander. That's the Army for you. But, ah, I, I guess I was probably best qualified for that because I watched what my own company could do when I was in training. The other officers redid everything, sort of collectively.

It was most difficult, I guess, when I had to stand up to white people. Stand up to authority, based on race. . . . It was difficult because I knew I was jeopardizing my own career, you know. But, on the other hand, if I hadn't, I would have lost the respect of my troops. And that was important. I always figured, if you're going to die, go down fighting forcibly, fighting for something, you know. I guess that was really the most difficult. But the ones where I had to stand up to a superior officer, that was difficult.

Well, I guess the most blatant act of racism was actually the one at the beginning when we got to the training center. We were all in there together, and they had us [black women] sit in some special separate chairs, and then called everybody else by their names. You know, it seemed that they could of called us by our names too, and separated us that way. I guess that was really it.

Job-wise, I enjoyed being a company commander more than I did any other thing. And, therefore, I enjoyed being a battalion commander because at least I was back with the troops. I wasn't especially happy when I had an assignment to get me in the office. . . . No, that was not the happiest time. But I just liked being with the troops. Working with the people.

Before the war started, it had been assumed by the general populous that anybody who's in the military is bad. . . . And I can remember that ever since I was growing up. So that the men were soldiers and the women went in the Army with those bad men. They must be in there for something bad. So they thought we were prostitutes. And, it didn't last very long, though. It just was a short period of time . . . but then you can't worry about what people think about.

MAE

When I was a little girl, I told my father that I was trying to kiss my elbow because the other kids told me that if I could kiss my elbow, I would turn into a boy.

university administrator; birth year 1916, B.A. 1937; M.A. 1945; two honorary doctorates 1985

My mother tells me that one of the first disagreement that she and my daddy had happened to be about me and swimming. He believed, he's West Indian, and they swim when they can toddle out to the ocean. They learn to swim. . . . So he believed that his child had to know how to swim. And I was just barely walking and he took me out and he was six feet two, and he walked up to his neck, and just dropped me. And my mother . . . yes, just shooooot. Because we lived in New England. I was born in New England. And, ah, the water was cold, and mamma said she was standing on the beach, screaming bloody murder, "Gimme my child!" And daddy said, I came up and I came up snorting, blowing it out of my nose, and I looked and I saw him, and, ah, and I grinned. And I started when he was telling me, "Baby do this," and so I did the dog paddle, and that's the way I started. And I dog paddled right on back with him, right by my side. Of course, you know he did not have me out of his control at all. So, I started swimming after that, and then he gave me formal lessons and I became an examiner, a life guard examiner, and, ah, I wanted to be on a swimming team, but they didn't have too many girls. . . . Black folks don't like to swim, and I think it's a hair problem. I used to beg my friends to go . . . my girlfriends to go swimming. "Oh, no, I don't wanta get my hair wet." Well, you know. I guess I can understand that. I didn't then, but now I guess I can understand that.

And, so I keep myself fit, as fit as I can be at 74. I'm 74, I'll be 75. I'm going to have a big bassssh. . . . I was born in 1916.

And I love to entertain. I was just brought up like that. To entertain. My mother was very shy, and at a very early age, I was my father's hostess because mamma was so shy, mamma would do the work, and tell people what to do, and get it all together, but when it came up to meeting people, she would withdraw.

Now, since I have retired . . . well, some of the things here are mementos from my retirement, awards in the hallway, and I have a room in here which I'll show you where my grandmother and my grandfather, and my mother and father and I are on the wall. And the trophies that my husband and I won bowling.

If I stayed still, I'd go crazy. I think one of the low points in my life was, um, some years ago when we had come back from an important meeting where I had to go to defend the accreditation of the university. We had been granted it unconditionally, but they [accrediting association] did not then know that the . . . er, the chairman of the board was trying to get rid of me. I didn't tell them that. And when they discovered that he had put out an ad that they were looking to fill my position, then they got nervous. So, they said . . . they insisted that, um, we come and defend the decision, um. Now, we had, I had done all this work, had written, with my staff, had written a study, and I had been there five times since I've been at this institution, you see. . . . And, so I knew the ins and outs. So, we took the new administrator [my replacement] with us, and he made, he was smart enough to make a brief statement that he'd only been in the position a few weeks, and, ah, so on, so then he turned the rest over to me. And I answered all the questions, and they asked me, did I think we needed a committee to come down every now and then, and tell what was wrong with us? And I said, with all due respect, we don't need anybody to tell us what's wrong. We know what's wrong. We need mo– . . . ney, lots of . . . of . . . it. . . . Now, if your committee can tell us how to get money, that's fine. But as I said, this study shows you that we know what our problem is, and I, I think that, I think the programs will go on, and things will be as they should be, and I'm certain this administrator will follow through, and so on and so forth.

So, we were scared, scared to death. We went upstairs to get some coffee, we had to go up and wait until they made the decision. When I just poured a cup of coffee, and they said, the man who was the chair, came up, and he said . . . You made it! I said, "Ooooooooh, all right!" I came home from that. And the next morning when I woke up, the only decision I had to make was when to get outta bed. And that was trauma. It was absolute trauma. I kid you not.

My doctor talked to me about retiring. He's thinking about it. I said, "John, don't retire." If you, when you have worked all of your life, and I came up wrung by wrung, nobody threw me into something, made me an administrator from nowhere. . . . I worked my way, bit by bit, wrung by wrung, up that ladder. And every day was competitive, and complete with problems that I had to solve. I'd wake up in the morning and I'd say, oooh, I wonder what's gonna happen today. Because it was always something. and all of a sudden you wake up, and you're alone, you and your cat, have nothing to do, and no place to go, no one asking you any questions, it's dreadful. And for a few weeks, I was as low, as . . . I'm a moody person, very moody, but I'm not, I don't get low.

I've learned to live with myself as an only child, grew up alone, and being alone wasn't the problem. The problem was having nothing to do. So, I said, "Shooooot, I had to get outta this mess. I can't stand it." So I prayed, and I worked my way through prayer. And it was winter time which meant that you can't do too much traveling, and I couldn't get to the pool, and do all the things that gave me great pleasure. I read. I guess I read that whole row of books there. I read all the time anyway. And, I um, started working on my memoirs, and that wasn't suiting me because I said I can't do these mem, this memory thing while I'm down because that isn't me, and it will reflect itself in what I'm saying. And, it just seems I, oh, I guess it lasted a good six months. A good six months. I didn't want to see anybody, I didn't want to go anywhere. I just sort of felt like somebody had thrown me out with the dishwater. And, um, it was a horrible experience. Particularly, the way, the way it was done. I was put out, see by a man who does not like women, and who the chairman of the committee thought a women should not be a high level administrator.

Yeah, he came to my office, and he told me that that was the time he was gonna get me out; he felt that I should go, and that they needed a man, and this was between the two of us in my office. And he told me the only reason that I was in this position was because of nepotism. And what did he say that for? I have an awful temper, literally. and I let lose on him, and I said, "Do you mean for over thirty years that I worked here it's been someone else's position that's been evaluated? Is that what you're trying to tell me?" . . . And I said, "That's not the reason the board elected me. And you have no right to say that." I said, "Now they may have felt that it would be different, and something unusual, to grant me the privilege of being in this position, but it was with the knowledge that I was capable of doing the job."

And I think until I write all of this up, and get it published and let the world know. . . . Then I, I, I think that after I do that, then I'll be at peace with myself. But I still, I still have not had the ambition to , to, to get to do it. See, I retired several years ago. But, it takes a little time, and I have to get my head straight. And, um, get some perspective.

This man just felt women had no right, to be in positions of authority. . . . But see, he has to retire in two years. . . . And I can't wait. . . . I have a few things I wanna say to him, that I didn't say at any other time. Um, but while he's in that position here, we have to run into one another, and there isn't any need in showing animosity. And I'm the better for it because the people look at me and they say, "Geez, I wonder how she can let him hug her?" And they don't know that I'm saying "Yeeuuuuuk!!!" Control like mamma. Control. Control.

So, that's a bit of that silence, and part of which I believe is a part that is essential to almost every woman's life who has achieved something in a man's world. . . . I am sure there are incidents . . .

they were not all terminal as mine was, but certainly, there were incidents that they [other women] had to go through. And the little strings that they had to pull, and little insults, and little hurts, big hurts. That they had to deal with. Ah, as a result, it's [life] not, it ain't no crystal stair. And my father told me that it wouldn't be, but he taught me, and I was very young, about five years old, sitting on my porch, trying to do something here. I was contorting myself. And daddy came home, promptly, always at 5:00 he would come home for dinner. He had a routine. Daddy would always come home [on time].

I used to run down the street to meet him. And I didn't run down the street to meet him that day. I was sitting there concentrating. He said, "Baby, what are you trying to do?" I said, "I'm trying to kiss my elbow." So, he said, "Why are you trying to kiss your elbow?" I said, "The kids told me, that if I could kiss my elbow, I would turn into a boy." So, you know, in those days, five-year olds are innocent. Nowadays, they tell you how you get babies. But, um, He said, "Baby, why?" His major concern was, why do you want to be a boy? And we talked about it after I grew up. He said, "Mae, you reeeally blew my mind." He said, "I didn't know how to talk to you because I didn't know why it was you wanted to be a boy." He said he didn't know if I should ask you, whether it would be too heavy for you to handle, or just what. But he said, finally, he said, "Ooooh, you don't wanna be a boy, anyway," he said, "I like you just as you are. You see, I couldn't pick a boy up and hug him and kiss him the way I'm kissing you." So, he let it go at that. But it festered and festered in his mind.

Finally when I started to school. I guess I was about seven. I made my first public speech for him when I was eight, telling people to run, to vote for my daddy for the school board. So this, I was about seven then. So he said, "Do you still want to be a boy?" And I said, "Yes, more than ever." "Why?" I said, of course by now I knew I couldn't do it by kissing my elbow. But I said, "Because everybody who comes in the house says to you, "Doctor Brandt, what a shame, you don't have a son." "Doctor Brandt, "Ooooh, well this is all you want, is just one girl, no boy?" "Oh, too bad that you don't have a boy to follow in your footsteps." I'd hear that all the time. It was true. And you know it's true. You've heard it yourself. People have girl children, and people will say, well, that's a shame. And if a woman can't have any more children, ooooh, what a shame you didn't have. . . . And people fill their house up with girls just to get a boy to satisfy that man's ego. So, here, I'm hearing this, and I'm thinking there's something bad about being a girl.

That's when he [daddy] sat me down. And he told me constantly . . . how much he loved me, that I could do and be anything that my brain would let me do, and be, never mind that I'm a girl. Be proud that I'm a girl. And he explained to me about womanhood and what it meant. That I should be proud that I was a woman. And that as a woman I could do whatever I made up my mind to do. But make sure, that I train myself for what I was doing, and did not live in fool's paradise thinking that I could do things that I could not do [because of lack of training]. Try it, work at it, if it doesn't work, move to something else. . . . And that's the way I was brought up. To use what I have, and I turned out to be really, really smart.

It turned my whole life around. I stopped worrying about being a boy. And I kicked them in the pants. I would beat them playing tennis; I'd beat them at everything. Other little girls hanging there. They wanted to beat the boys. . . . And my mother used to say [to my daddy], "She'll never get a husband. Oh, you're just bringing that child up like she's a boy. No man will ever marry her. She's gonna be too strong." Daddy said, "I want her strong! She's got to be strong to survive. And survive she will! Go out an beat them." He used to play tennis with me every Saturday, and boy, he was a good tennis player. And he played me hard. He never held back on me. I'd go out there with the fellows and beat the socks off them. And, of course, I could out swim all the men that I ever swam with.

All of my best friends right now are men. I don't have any women friends. And I was thinking about that today. Somebody asked me, somebody said something about how nice it is to have a best friend. . . . And I said [to myself], who is my best friend? I could name me five men. But I can't name me one woman. Not one. And I guess that's a fault in my life. . . . So why that is, I don't know. Maybe some psychiatrist will analyze it.

Well, I only remember my grandfather, because my grandmother died, I think, when I was just about three years old. . . . But I certainly remember my grandfather because he lived to be 92 years old, and I was his favorite grandchild. . . . He taught me how to play cards, he taught me how to make loud noises with cocoa shells. . . . What we used to do is take the shell and boil the shell. And it makes a drink that tastes like cocoa, and looks like tea. And they always had a big pot of that on the stove when my grandfather and I used to see who could slurp the loudest. And my mother was very picky, very, uh, glove wearing, hat wearing, proper. I don't think she ever figured out where she got me. And, ah, my grandfather again, treated me like a boy. And he took me to ball games with him, and so on. . . . And we'd set up at the kitchen table playing cards. . . . Mama came, and she was appalled.

"You're teaching my child how to play cards." Grandpa said, "Dorothy, go to bed, go upstairs." And I loved it! Nobody ever talked to mama like that. And I said, "Oooooh, I just love this man." . . . But anyway, she let him alone with me.

But my father was a good pastor, not just a preacher. He was a pastor. Yeah. And people loved him. So they took care of his family. So I had what I wanted. I had everything I wanted. They used to give me dolls. And I hated dolls with a purple passion. I'd go and cut them up and see what was inside them. I don't know why I didn't like dolls. Just didn't like dolls. I'd rather have fire engine trucks to play with, a truck of some sort. . . . Left-handed, being in those days. . . . And they used to tie my hand behind my back, refuse to give me things with my left hand, and as a result, it made me ambidextrous. And so I use either one of them. But they sent my cousin off. He began to develop little fits. But that's another story.

PART II

INTERPRETING
A WOMAN'S LIFE

2

"THE EXCEPTION OF THE EXCEPTIONS": AFRICAN AMERICAN WOMEN IN HIGHER EDUCATION

The participation of African American women in higher education has been punctuated by exceptional individuals who were active in their communities and major contributors in their respective fields. These women have been forging paths of distinction in American education since Mary Jane Patterson became the first African American woman to earn a baccalaureate degree.[1] Fanny Jackson Coppin (Oberlin, 1865), Anna Julia Cooper (Oberlin, 1884), Mary Church Terrell (Oberlin, 1884), Lucy Laney (Atlanta University, 1863),[2] and others followed Patterson's lead bravely and without apology. Their departure from prescribed servile roles marked a new era in American education.

Earlier societal views of women as homemakers and African Americans as servants ensured a thorny path for African American women who dared to go beyond "basic" education. Solomon observed that in the late nineteenth and early twentieth century, "the black college woman was the exception of the exceptions" in that neither black nor white colleges wanted her (76). Yet, in spite of these imposing barriers, African American women were not to be deterred. Progress was slow but steady. According to Perkins, only 30 African American women had completed B.A. degrees by 1890 compared with more than 300 African American men and 2,500 white women (77–78). The trend reversed in the early 1900s. Noble found that African American women earned more college degrees than African American men in the twentieth century with the exception of the decade between 1920 and 1930 (89). However, before we take comfort from statistics, it is important to understand that these figures in no way reflect the conditions of African American women's college participation. Were they accepted as equals or were they relegated to the same second-class status that they experienced outside of the university? How did they cope with being the "only one" in a particular class or program? What were their strategies for survival?

LIFE CHOICES

Before we examine African American women's experiences in higher education, we first must understand their reasons for attending college under the circumstances previously described. Undoubtedly, African American women's decisions to pursue a college degree can be attributed to a variety of factors, but certain patterns warrant close attention. Jeanne Noble, for example, suggests that the mission of racial uplift continued to be a dominant philosophy of the African American community well into the twentieth century (89). Young women and men were encouraged to attend college not only to benefit themselves, but to better the race as a whole. Consequently, many of the women from this period were second-generation college graduates intimately familiar with the charge to improve self and simultaneously to serve the race.

Thus, it was no surprise that several women reported that college education was a family tradition. Harriet, a 78-year-old historian who completed her undergraduate degree in 1931, remembered that her family anticipated college education from the very beginning:

> I don't know how to answer that question 'cause nobody in my family ever thought he would stop after high school, I don't know . . . that's all we ever talked about, going on after high school . . . uh . . . I don't, I don't know. Uh . . . so I've never been pushed in any way, except that I know the extent to which I was going on. Whatever the height it was, that was the direction I was going . . . so I can't say that my parents pushed me to go to college because I was cryin' at night and wonderin' [how I could go to college], and that kind of thing . . . now many of them [classmates]

did go there [S. A. College], and many of them took the two-year
program and, started teachin'. (30:2, p. 3)[3]

It is interesting to note that the family expected the children to rise
to the highest level possible in their chosen professions. Perhaps this
approach encouraged achievement without pressure. The goal was
general enough so that each child could fulfill his or her own
ambitions and at the same time satisfy family expectations. Also, this
attitude of excellence indicates that the lift and serve mission was
not a lock-step philosophy to be followed blindly by all families, but
rather a way of living and instilling values in the younger generation.

A family tradition also was motivation for Ellen, an 87-year-old
musician who graduated from college in 1938. She said that her
family knew no other alternative:

> Well, uh, it uh, yes, that's interesting uh. It was I always knew I
> was going to college. It . . . uh . . . that was just part of our family
> . . . my . . . uh, mother went to Howard. She graduated from
> Howard, My aunt went to Howard, my uncle. . . . In other words,
> what I'm saying to you is that it was a tradition. It never occurred
> to me that people didn't go to college, but that was . . . everybody
> went to college in my . . . in my family. (5:1, pp. 14–15)

Ellen's situation illustrated the ultimate benefit of earlier generations
of college graduates. Many African American families throughout
the country were able to build on the experiences of those who
graduated before them.[4] Family discussions, letters, stories, and
other sources provided children with information about college as
well as role models.

June, a 65-year-old editor who completed her 2-year certificate
in 1944, responded to her family tradition even though she was the
only girl. She too was expected to earn a college degree:

> In fact, we all knew that we were supposed to go to college. I mean
> there was . . . that was just an on-going thing. We all knew that
> we were supposed to be somewhere productive in life. And . . .
> there were two brothers and myself and the good thing about my
> dad was that he had expectations for me as well as them [brothers].
> And I . . . I guess now I can appreciate that. (52:1, p. 14)

June's background confirms Perkin's observation that many African American families especially encouraged their daughters to pursue a college education. Not only did they feel that their daughters needed to be able to earn a living in the event of widowhood or a failed marriage, but also women were the first educators of their own children. Several families went to great expense and sacrifice to educate their daughters including moving across the country. Such was the case of Mary Jane Patterson mentioned earlier (71). So the imperative for African American women to attend college was taken very seriously.

Whereas the family tradition was extremely important, it was not the only reason that some women pursued a college degree. Individual women felt the need to seek knowledge beyond secondary education even though few could afford such a luxury. Others sought to improve their quality of life through education. Lula, a 71-year-old foreign diplomat completed her 2-year certification in the late 1940s and joined the foreign service in the 1950s. Her decision to attend college was based on economics and living standards:

> Because I wanted to improve my standard of living. And ah . . . there's just no way of getting a better job without an education. . . . (34:1, p. 12)

Lula went on to travel throughout the world, especially the Far East and Africa. She met and socialized with dignitaries from various countries, learned to speak other languages, and was honored by several foreign officials. Her quest for an education led her beyond the classroom to places where few Americans had ever ventured.

Another woman, Anna, a 70-year-old educator graduated from college in 1956 and later went on to earn her Ph.D. at the age of 50. She felt that it was fate that led her to college:

> It was just inevitable for me because I just loved books. You know, it was just that simple. It was always in my mind to do and I was not interested in getting married early . . . nor working early . . . but, just going on to school was just inevitable to me, as breathing. (18:1, pp. 16–17)

Anna's rejection of "traditional" expectations (i.e., marriage, work) allowed her to indulge in a love of books and learning. Although she did not have to choose between education and marriage, she strongly felt that she could not adequately support those two interests at the same time.

Finally, Edna, a 71-year-old educator, began college in the 1940s. However, circumstances such as raising a family prevented her from completing her undergraduate degree until 1962. She credited her mother for encouraging her to go to college:

> My mother was one of these mothers that um . . . she missed her education . . . well let me go back and tell you how she learned to read. . . . So, she ah . . . um . . . having taught herself to read and then she read everything she could get her hands on. We had the *Crisis* magazine in our home and the newspaper and she followed . . . Booker T. Washington. We had their pictures on the wall and um . . . so she encouraged education. (16:1, pp. 18–19)

Even in situations such as Edna's where there was no family college tradition to call upon, there remained family expectations. In spite of the fact that her parents were not college graduates, they advocated a college education and supported each of their children in attending college. The parents felt that their children had a chance of accomplishing what they could not. Success of the children meant success of the family as a whole.

The content of these narratives indicates that for most of the women in my study, going on to college was a family decision. It was not the individual isolated from the group who made this decision, but the individual in the context of the group (family, race). Usually, family involvement on this level also meant family support, moral and/or financial, throughout college and beyond. It is interesting to note different families' strategies for preparing their children for college. Some used informal, but regular discussions (i.e., at the dinner table or bedtime); others told stories and/or shared their own or others' college experiences. These narratives of college life, in turn, became part of a child's outlook. The result was a generation of young people who valued and expected to earn a college education.

SPECIAL PROBLEMS

Sometimes college attendance had to be delayed because of age. Several women reported that they were not permitted to attend college after graduation from high school because they were too young. Jane, a 75-year-old music composer, finished high school at 15 and was not allowed to enter college at that age:

> I had finished high school and then ah . . . had been to a . . . to New York . . . I had gone to school there two years and . . . I came back home. My father said, "Now you're ready to go to school." So then I went to Tuskegee. I finished Tuskegee in three years! (27:1, p. 16)

Loretta also graduated from high school early. The 78-year-old teacher went on to complete her B.A. in 1938:

> . . . I finished high school very early. But at that time I went to high school, there were no public high schools in town. And so I had to attend the university for high school. I went there for six years to the university and finished a normal, normal course. Uh, after that my daddy sent me to a university up north from which I received two degrees, my bachelor's and my master's degree. (26:1, pp. 2–3)

Early high school graduation presented a dilemma that many families had not anticipated. Most parents, however, appeared to find good use for their child's time in the interim. Some opted for their daughters to work, whereas others sent their daughters away for further education on the high school level.

Coupled with the issue of early graduation was that of choosing a career. Sidney, an 81-year-old professor of foreign languages graduated from college in 1931. She remembered that her father guided all of the children in choosing high school courses in anticipation of their later college education:

> I think it's interesting that a . . . when we were going to high school, all of us were told by my dad who really was the ah . . . well both of my parents were scholars, but my dad seemed to advise us just what subjects to take. He wanted all of us to take Latin, which we did, all of us, all four of us. Because he felt that

> Latin was the root of language. Not only of English, but of so
> many Romance Languages also, all of them. (3:1, pp. 21–22)

This kind of mentoring by a father was a very significant influence
on the children, especially the girls. Sidney and her brothers and
sister excelled in college as well as their careers. Although a father's
influence is not necessarily the most powerful constituent of a child's
success, these early women especially benefited from their father's
interest in their well-being and advice on education and career.

Similarly, Elmira, an 82-year-old attorney, described a close relationship with her father. His guidance was sometimes indirect as can
be seen in his elaborate plan to dissuade Elmira from becoming an
actress:

> I liked the study of law because I think it sets a standard for human
> relations and I also like the matter of applying a principle to human
> situations involving individuals and I thought that was most inter-
> esting. It was my second choice however because had I been able
> to take my first choice I would have gone on stage, but my . . .
> That year "Shuffle Along" played in town and Florence Mills
> came with what is called "Dixie to Broadway," I believe. And I
> saw each one of the shows three or four times and I was determined
> that I was gonna run away and go with the show and I don't know
> how my father knew this, but he invited Mr. Sissle who he had
> known in the army to come to dinner. And all they talked about
> was how stupid it was for people, blacks not to finish their educa-
> tions and how so many ignorant women got into the show when
> they couldn't make it and then there was nothing else they could
> do. . . . He [Mr. Sissle] said, "Well you finish your education
> . . . and you ah . . . come to New York if you still want to go on
> stage. I'll help you." So, I backed down from my impulse to run
> off. (36:1, pp. 20–21)

Elmira then pursued her second choice and finished law school in
1930. Ironically, she later successfully represented an actress in a
suit against a touring company. Although Elmira recalled that this
was one of her favorite cases, she did not regret her choice of career.

Again, as was the case in deciding to attend college, choosing a
career was often a decision arrived at in consultation with the family.
However, it was fathers who were reported as having the most
significant impact on career decisions. Often they served as mentors

for both their male and female children. Many were said to have given equal time to their daughters. This kind of attention may have influenced these women to achieve goals beyond the typical expectations of women in general, and African American women in particular. Women in my study who reported a mentor relationship with their fathers were more likely to select nontraditional fields such as law and medicine, and/or excel in a given field or profession. While this subsample is too small to warrant generalizing to a larger population, undoubtedly, emerging patterns of fathers' active participation in family decision making and child rearing was extremely important. By no means should this be misconstrued as a diminishing of mothers' roles in the family; rather it is evidence that fathers could offset the negative impact of sexism on their daughters' lives.

TEACHING: A WOMAN'S PLACE

Selecting a career was not a simple matter of choosing from unlimited possibilities. Societal conditions limited African American women to restricted areas of service. According to Noble, black women could teach, become home demonstration agents, or perform domestic work for whites such as cooking or cleaning (90). Furthermore, college curricula targeted for African American women emphasized home economics and training in "nutrition, tailoring, home management, invalid care, laundering," (90) and other domestic subjects. The objective was service within the confines of home, community, and family.

Many women lived out this role of service, not in deference to the wishes of the community, but in response to their own talents. Zora, a teacher and social worker born in 1914, knew in early childhood that she had an aptitude for teaching:

> I went straight into teacher's college because I had a scholarship there and of course you know in those years which was the early thirties most black women went into teaching. And I had the proclivity for it. In any case it wasn't hard to go into teaching. Whereas, I don't know if I would have even thought about another

choice at the time 'cause even when I was a kid, at the camp we
ran, I always enjoyed teaching the kids. So it was kinda natural
for me. And I started out in early childhood education, of course
we didn't call it that then. We used to call it kindergarten and
primary education. (37:2, p. 11)

Zora's early recognition of her special teaching talent turned into a
lifelong commitment. She was not concerned that teaching was a
preordained career for African American women, but rather focused
on how she could best express her gifted teaching ability. Other
women were not as fortunate and entered teaching as a direct result
of pressure from the African American community and occupational
restrictions imposed by white America.

Margaret, a 75-year-old retired physician, at first tried to honor
the teaching tradition. Even though the course work well prepared
her for a career in the sciences, she initially thought teaching should
be her professional goal:

I had a year of biology, actually had five years of science in high
school, and then I took an extra semester or two of botany and
zoology. Yep. That was when I decided. First I was going to be,
as I mentioned, a physical education teacher, 'cause my mother
and my aunt had been phys. ed. teachers, but, then, as it turned
out, my talents were not in athletics. But I really didn't realize
that in athletics, you didn't have to be a good athlete in order to
be a phys. ed. teacher. On the other hand, I was intrigued more
by science and the microscope. (53:2, p. 7)

As science began to compete with her teaching interest, Margaret
no longer felt certain that she should become a teacher. However,
she continued to pursue education until after her student-teaching
experience:

But I did some student teaching in the north and decided that was
not gonna work because there were discipline problems and I have
a very short fuse with reference to discipline while teaching. And
I decided that was not for me. . . . I can't imagine having to tell
people to keep quiet to learn. . . . That, to me, was something I
did not want to be involved with. (57:3, p. 12)

Even though one could argue that one student-teaching experience
does not necessarily represent the classroom experience in all

schools, it was enough information for Margaret to conclude that this was not to be her life's work. Consequently, she turned to her love of science, went to medical school, and became an outstanding physician. Had she not tested her teaching skills, she may never have had the resolve to go into medicine.

Returning to the question of career choice, as the African American community moved further away from slavery, the mission to uplift the race shifted from emphasis on group support to an unequal pressure on women to serve rather than to lead. Specifically, Perkins interpreted this change in attitude to mean that African American women could best uplift the race by teaching the young (76). Thus, many of the women who entered college in the late nineteenth and early twentieth centuries were motivated by a teaching mission[5] which would ultimately advance the entire race. Those who were not inclined to teach, regardless of their own personal aspirations and talents, were expected to teach anyway. Consequently, this prescribed teacher track left few other choices available to black women. Not surprisingly, many women struggled with this dilemma.

Some women did not initially plan to teach, but eventually became teachers because of so few alternatives. Loretta, for example, viewed teaching as a prelude to marriage, a temporary occupation that she would give up when she assumed the full-time role of wife and mother. Teaching would allow her to utilize her college degree and was compatible with the antebellum notion that "education for black women should be moral education primarily as preparation for motherhood and marriage" (Perkins, p. 76). So in this context, Loretta's lack of commitment to teaching was entirely understandable:

> I just kinda gradually went into it [teaching]. Because when I started teaching I said, "Oh, I'll teach for two years and then I'll get married" . . . I just kinda slipped into teaching . . . Because he [daddy], he just thought, I'd just become a wife and mother. Just like my mother. You know, but I was always independent and aggressive. I was never like my mother, I was never a home body. You could eat off her den floor. Because she kept an immaculate house. But, see, I'm not a house keeper . . . I'm an outdoor person you see. Generally, I'm not like my mother . . . But my daddy,

always taught me to be independent. He always said, "Now listen. See, I want you to be independent, whether you marry or whether you don't marry. I want you to be independent." And so that has stayed with me too." (26:2, p. 5)

It is interesting to note that by becoming a teacher, Loretta was actually going against her father's expectation that she should follow in her mother's footsteps and become a homemaker. At the same time, Loretta's father also wanted her to be independent and seemed not to realize the contradiction in his expectations. Also, it is significant that she takes great care to distinguish herself from her mother and describes herself as "independent and aggressive." Loretta knew instinctively that she was not suited to teaching, at least not young children:

Well, I . . . uh . . . now, I started teaching first as an ele . . . elementary teacher. I did not like it at all. I really strove to get out of the teaching profession. But then after I went back to school and only because I had finished a normal course, as I said at the local university before my daddy sent me to the northern univ. Because see, the . . . the . . . the students that I . . . in whose classes I was in, at that time, had gone on, and I wanted to go too. I mean he [daddy] wanted to send me to a . . . another university. Then when I came back from there, I was given a high school. Put into a high school. And I loved teaching then because the students were on a higher level and we could . . . I mean we could discuss, we could discuss things that would ah . . . man to man, you might say. (26:1, p. 5)

Once her intellectual needs were met in the classroom, the narrator was willing to commit to teaching as a lifetime pursuit. She found older, more mature students more suitable to her teaching style.

June rejected the idea of teaching even before she entered college. She finished her two-year certificate in 1946 and recalled that the suggestion of teaching came from her father:

My dad wanted me to be a teacher. He . . . really kept telling me. There weren't a whole lot of options (laughs) O.K. And he thought that I would make a good teacher. And . . . I just rebelled that. I . . . it jus . . . I kept saying "No, I don't want to be a teacher. Uh children don't like to go to school, and I want to do something that people want to participate in." And uh . . . so I decided that

> I wanted to be a social worker. And ah . . . ah . . . when I was
> in school [high school] I had this ver . . . very well meaning
> counselor who kept trying me . . . to . . . to get me to go into
> secretarial work. And I thought, "I don't . . . I *know* I don't want
> to go into secretarial work. I mean . . . I like people . . . ," you
> know (laughs). And uh . . . um I guess he just didn't know
> anything else that a black person could do. He . . . he meant well,
> you know, but. . . . (52:1, pp. 49–50)

As can be seen from her discussion, the narrator was encouraged to
take up professions reserved for women and particularly designated
for "service." Her idea of social work was also one of service, but it
was her own idea based on her own interests. The fact that two men
steered her toward the "service" occupations is significant.

Some mothers also pushed their daughters toward teaching. Edna's mother repeatedly told her to go into teaching:

> Every time I had lunch with my mother, she would stop and she
> would say that "I want you to be a teacher. I want you to finish
> your education." And she did this so much. . . . (16:1, p. 22)

Although Edna wanted a college education, she was not convinced
that she should be a teacher. Before Edna could work out the
problem, she married and her career plans were interrupted almost
indefinitely. As previously mentioned, even though most African
American families could not afford it, the predominate ideal, based
on white American values, identified the proper place of African
American women as the home. So it was expected that marriage
would automatically terminate the employment of most working
African American women. As an extreme example, Loretta recalled
a particularly unpleasant incident in her community:

> See, there were so many graduates every year. And the only thing
> they could do was to teach so consequently when women got
> married, the black ministers went to the board of education . . .
> they kept saying that when a black teacher married they should
> have to give up their jobs. Because there were so many others
> [men] and there was nothing else for them to do. . . . Because I
> know when I married they didn't even allow the pension to be
> received by the widow. See it was really discrimination. (26:2,
> p. 2)

While teaching was a benefit, it sometimes was a liability. Conventional societal standards often required women to give up their teaching jobs when they got married and/or pregnant. This, in turn, created an artificial incompatibility between career and marriage/family. Some women quietly abided by the rules, and others assessed the situation for what it was in reality—sex discrimination.

For some women, teaching was the only way to obtain a college education. Anna recalled that due to lack of money, she had few alternatives:

> I went first to the junior college for two years, and then I wanted to transfer to go to um . . . the university . . . but we couldn't afford it and . . . um . . . so I went to umm . . . State Teachers College at the time, which is in the next little town, . . . uh . . . and uh . . . but I wasn't interested really in being a teacher, but I didn't want to stop college. . . . So, I went . . . and was really put in the wrong 'cause they put me with a . . . the kindergarten, first grade which wasn't my interest at all. But I didn't know enough at the time to say this is not what I'm interested in. And I didn't do well . . . (18:1, p. 17)

Although she did not pursue the matter further, the narrator may have done poorly simply because teaching at that level was not her strength. Like Loretta, she may have been teaching the wrong grade. It was not until later that she discovered that adult education was her most fulfilling level of teaching.

Teaching was a respectable occupation and extremely valuable to the black community, but the subtle pressure to teach diverted many African American women from equally worthy callings. Some readily accepted their predetermined mission and plunged into teaching full force. Others challenged the status quo by venturing into "nontraditional fields such as law and medicine. These fields were not more important than teaching, but they were professional alternatives that few women or African Americans had adequate opportunities to explore. However, the most important issue here is that the majority of African American women who pursued a college education at this time could not avoid having to give some consideration to teaching as an "acceptable" career choice. It was not by any means all they could be or do.

THE COLLEGE EXPERIENCE

In spite of barriers to higher education, African American women enrolled in colleges and universities in ever-increasing numbers. What was the quality of college life once they arrived on campus? Clearly, experiences varied. Some of the variation was due, in part, to the environment. Those African American women who attended historically black colleges were more likely to report positive experiences than those who did not. Women who ventured into traditionally male professions such as law or the foreign service were more likely to recall racist and/or sexist incidents. This does not mean that sexism did not exist at historically black colleges, but women in this environment usually did not regard it as a hindrance to their success.

Many women were "firsts" as Elmira discovered when she entered law school in 1928. Again, it was a situation that had both benefits and drawbacks:

> Oh, it was a very interesting experience. It so happened that I was the first American black woman to enter the university law school and I was pretty much a curiosity ah . . . but the dean of the law school was very interested and very helpful. The rest of the staff had a sort of hands off policy . . . (36:1, p. 18)

Accompanying the feeling of being on display was the benign neglect, "a sort of hands-off policy," treatment that was common to many African American students, especially women. Elmira, however, was able to discern who was helpful (e.g., "the dean of the law school") and who was not, and she acted accordingly.

A more direct form of discrimination was found in university housing. On most campuses, African American students were prohibited from living in dormitories. Again, Elmira observed that:

> No, ah . . . we were not given any residential privileges. We took gym, but we didn't get to use the swimming pool. And ah . . . we were pretty much on the peripheral except for the way we made a life for ourselves together. (36:1, p. 18)

The "life for themselves" was an important coping strategy. It meant developing a supportive community among themselves and outside of the university. African American students were truly outsiders in academe, but they refused to accept the condition as inevitable and/ or permanent. They banded together and created a rich, nurturing, social and intellectual environment which allowed them to be in control of their own educational growth.

In some cases, the restrictions on campus housing were quietly removed as African American students and their parents worked with college administrators to make fair accommodations for minority students. June vividly remembered her first year of college:

> I had made arrangements . . . our family made arrangements for me to go to the university . . . And . . . my aunt, my uncle's wife uh . . . in another town knew the dean of women at state. And uh . . . she . . . we asked her . . . at that time they were segregating housing. And uh . . . we asked her if she couldn't get me in the dormitory. Otherwise, I'd have to live way out in the community. There was a place for . . . for the young men to live near the campus. They couldn't live on campus, but there was eleventh street, was adjacent, but there wasn't any place for the young [black] women. So um . . . she [aunt] went up and talked with the dean . . . had lunch with the dean of women an . . . made arrangements for three of us to be ah . . . living in the dormitory. . . . And then they brought in another young lady from another town. . . . And uh . . . it was . . . they asked us to remain if we would ah. It was a freshman dorm but we didn't want to remain in a freshman dorm so we moved out ah . . . at the end of that time. But that did break the ice. . . . (52:1, pp. 61–62)

So housing restrictions according race were lifted, somewhat. The administration's inclination to house all African American women in the freshmen dorm, regardless of status, was yet another unfair regulation. Thus, progress was slow and not without cost. In addition, making some sort of housing available exclusively for African American men effectively disenfranchised African American women. These uneven campus practices and policies weighed very heavily on African American women who were disadvantaged by both sexism *and* racism within the university.

There were some actions at other campuses that were even more conspicuously biased. Elmira never forgot a talk with one of the deans:

> All the [black] girls were called in . . . to the Dean's office and we were all told that we should be as unobtrusive as possible on the campus. That we were members of the subject race, the university did not really want us, but as it was a city university it had to take us. (36:1, p. 23)

Singling out women in the first group of African American students to enroll at this university sent a clear message. African American women were the most undesirable of the undesirable. They were expected to be grateful for being there and to keep quiet. They did neither:

> And we left that interview just about in a state of shock because we hadn't been prepared for that and we immediately met with the young men [black] on campus and told them about it. And we all decided that we're going out for everything. That everybody in that freshman class is gonna come away with some distinction. We didn't burn any buildings or anything like that, we just decided we were gonna show them. And we all did. Every member of that freshman class had some distinction. And the success of it was that the next year, the same official who had spoken to us called us back and apologized. He said, "I made an error and I want you to know that you are a credit to your race." (36:1, p. 23)

The dean's explicit racism inspired the African American students, led by the women, to challenge racial barriers by excelling in several aspects of university life, especially course work. Instead of creating quiet, docile students, the dean's "talk" incited campus activism among the African American students who enrolled in every possible course and club activity. As a result, the individuals in this first class of African American students graduated with honors and continued their quest for justice and excellence throughout their lives.

Sidney, who retired as full professor of foreign languages, remembered that the discrimination she experienced was more subtle. The university administration was sure that it could get away with being "selective" (i.e., excluding African Americans) until she brought the facts to the attention of school officials:

> Interestingly enough, in 1931 when I received my A.B. degree, I became the first black member of Phi Beta Kappa at the university. And ah . . . the background story about it is that I read in the

> paper that five ah . . . four or five parents were going to be invited
> to attend the initiation of the Phi Beta Kappa recipients in that
> year and I went over to the secretary of the chapter there . . . and
> asked if my father could be invited. And ah . . . this man looked
> at me and said, "Well, we'd like to do that Miss Brown, but you
> see the only reason we can invite those particular parents is because
> they are also members of Phi Beta Kappa." I said, "Well, so is my
> father a member of Phi Beta Kappa." Whereupon he was sent an
> invitation and my dad came. (3:1, p. 25)

In this instance, Sidney's defense was straightforward. She informed
the official that her father, who graduated from college at the turn
of the century, was also eligible to be invited and the university acted
appropriately. Calling administrators' attention to the facts did not
always work, but, in this case, the student and her father could not
be ignored.

On the other hand, women who attended historically black colleges and universities had different stories to tell. On the whole, they
were more positive about their campus experiences:

> Tremendously great. I went there, majored in history, was a
> student assistant. . . . I went to state in thirty-one to thirty-three
> and this is in the very midst of the depression. But uh, when I got
> that little job up there . . . that paid, I think, twenty dollars almost,
> or eighteen, I think it was . . . I worked and that made my . . .
> I think I got eighteen, at least twenty dollars . . . I think room and
> board was eighteen. (30:2, p. 5)

Harriet's education was not disrupted by the Depression because she
could find work within the university. She felt that the university
provided a nurturing environment and was interested in the well-
being of each student.

Similarly, Jane's years at Tuskegee Institute were filled with histo-
ry-making mentors. Dr. George Washington Carver knew her older
brother as a student, and later befriended her; "little Miss Tennessee"
he called her. Dr. Carver would take Jane and a few other interested
students through his lab during visiting hours. Near graduation, she
composed a class tribute to him. In addition to her friendship with
Dr. Carver, Jane also had the benefit of the wisdom of some very
important women. Her practice teaching, for example, turned out

to be a truly memorable event. Not only did visitors appear in her classroom unannounced, they also were quite impressive:

> So in the group, there was one woman who was walking around looking at all these people and she stopped and talked to every child. She didn't miss a one. And I wondered who she was and I wished she'd hurry up and get out of there. And the others were . . . had looked over the place and were out . . . standing outside talking. And she was still going around looking at all the kids and asking 'em what they were doing. . . . Then she came in and told me that I was an excellent teacher . . . and told me that her name was Eleanor Roosevelt. . . . And that's how I got to meet Eleanor Roosevelt. She asked me if she could come back . . . and I told her . . . I said yea. So . . . when she . . . came back she had Mary McLeod Bethune with . . . with her. And they came in to see my play . . . and it rained and it was leaking all through the house so I had to give 'em umbrellas. They're sitting up in there, looking at my play with umbrellas in the house. . . . (27:1, p. 43)

This single incident led to a lifelong friendship with Eleanor Roosevelt. Sometimes when Mrs. Roosevelt offered advice, the narrator very graciously declined to accept those suggestions which were contrary to her own personal goals. She said, "I wanted to call my soul my own" (27:1, p. 43).

The range of African American women's experiences on college campuses reflects, to some extent, institutional views of African Americans and women as students. Until proven otherwise, universities tended to embrace stereotypical images of this "special" population of students. Similarly, discriminatory practices aimed specifically at African American women were sobering testimony to the double discrimination that these women experienced both on and off campus. Yet, they did not waver. They confidently accepted the challenge and not only survived, but prospered even within the academy.

LANGUAGE IN CONTEXT: TELLING IT LIKE A LADY

Thus far, the discussion has focused on the content of oral narratives. Exploring common themes of storied lives as well as important differences provides us with a greater understanding of the unique experiences of educated African American women. However, content alone cannot reveal all of the information present in an oral narrative. It is equally important to look at the structure of a narrative. The very words and phrases selected by a narrator give a distinctive shape and meaning to her story. In essence, the language of oral narratives is not random, but is rather a well-defined pattern of personal communication on various narrative levels.

One of the most interesting linguistic features, for example, was that of dialogue or reported speech. The narrator's voice may change in tone or pitch and there is a shift from past tense to present tense. In this group of narratives the majority of women tended to represent the words of men, especially their fathers or some other authority figure, in the form of reported speech or direct quotation:

My father said, "Now you're ready to go to school."

He [Mr. Sissle] said, "Well, you finish your education . . . and you ah . . . come to New York if you still want to be on stage. I'll help you."

Ann ah . . . this man looked at me and said, "Well, we'd like to do that Miss Brown, but you see the only reason we can invite those particular parents is because they are also members of Phi Beta Kappa."

He always said, "Now listen. See, I want you to be independent, whether you marry or whether you don't marry. I want you to be independent."

These small segments of reported speech usually came near the very end of each response. It may have been a means of telescoping or focusing information so that those particular words would be given the most importance, or it may have been a way of highlighting the significance of a particular person. As previously discussed, many of the narrators shared a mentor relationship with their fathers and, therefore, would regard their advice as high priority. On the other hand, this tendency to reproduce father's words and those of other authority figures in the form of reported speech also reflects the disparate social roles of men and women. In general, women are socialized to "talk like a lady" (i.e., no profanities, obscenities, or swear/curse words) and to listen to men (Coates, p. 108). So it would not be unusual to find the same deference to men's speech in women's oral narratives.

Finally, one other aspect of language by and about father is also striking. Fathers' positive involvement in their daughters' lives usually was reported in the context of decision making and advice:

> And . . . there were two brothers and myself and the good thing about my dad was that he had expectations for me as well as them [brothers]. And I . . . I guess now I can appreciate that.

> Uh . . . after that my daddy sent me to the university from which I received two degrees . . .

> . . . all of us were told by my dad who really was the ah . . . well both of my parents were scholars, but my dad seemed to advise us just what subjects to take.

> My dad wanted me to be a teacher. He . . . really kept telling me. There weren't a whole lot of options. And he thought that I would make a good teacher.

The fathers' advice was not always followed or welcomed. However, many of the women reported their fathers as responsible either for the decision to attend college or to enter a particular profession. Notice too that the words "dad" and "father" were usually placed in subject position (actor). This syntactic marking had the added effect of portraying fathers as causal agents: "my daddy wanted," "my daddy sent," "by my dad." Even in segments of speech where there were no instances of reported speech, the term "daddy," "father," or the personal pronoun "he" occurred frequently and in dominant sentence positions. Lula, the 71-year-old staff officer in the U.S. foreign service, demonstrated this pattern in a description of her father's activities with the family:

> He played ball with my brothers, went on picnics and we were very, very poor and I remember my daddy used to, every other Sunday would take us for a street car ride. And that was, oh that was a big thing for us. And then he would take us shopping and ah, we each would have like five or ten cents to spend. And he would cook dinner on Sundays and he used to bake cookies and

we had a large dish pan and he'd fill that dish pan full of the cookies that he made. We had a garden in back and he would give each one of us a little plot so we could plant our popcorn or our tomatoes. (34:1, pp. 7–8)

Lula's father was a brick mason by trade and she remembered him to be a very quiet man. Yet, even though he was not verbally expressive, he demonstrated in other ways his love for his four children. Structurally, "my daddy" and "he" are central to this segment of speech. Most clauses began with one or the other term and all information clearly highlights daddy as agent.

Sometimes even grandfathers were especially influential. Jane took pride in telling a very touching story about her grandfather:

And ah, I remember so vividly that sometimes I would go out and there were some peach trees, they were native to the state and, I would always want to go and get a peach off from the tree. And one year it was too late for me to get peaches off the tree but my grandfather somehow tied the peaches on the tree so I could pull them off. (27:2, pp. 35–36)

Unlike previous patterns, here we have a telescoping effect. The term "grandfather" is not used until near the end of the segment, and the preceding information in the sentence serves as a means of foregrounding the agent. Again, this does not suggest that mothers were not important or had no influence, but that some women were especially receptive to their fathers' input.

In sum, African American women's varying college experiences were bound together by a double-edged reality. On the one hand, they were regarded as self-sacrificing stewardesses who would usher in a new generation of educated African American youth and then fade into the background. On the other hand, they were treated as undesirables, incapable of thinking or working beyond domestic concerns. They were neither, yet it was within this paradox of reliance and distrust that African American collegiate women carved out productive lives for themselves in the academy and in the world.

CLIMBING THE LADDER OF SUCCESS FROM THE BOTTOM RUNG: AFRICAN AMERICAN WOMEN IN THE PROFESSIONS

The completion of a college education opened the passage way to new frontiers. Having decided against teaching as a career option, African American women were now faced with seeking employment in a professional world rarely or never graced by the presence of an African American woman. Yet, this anomalous condition did not discourage some African American women from entering various fields. As early as 1887, the first African American woman had passed the Bar and, by the turn of the century, there were approximately 160 African American female physicians, 7 dentists, and 10 attorneys (Giddings, p. 75). In fact, the first female physicians in the South were African Americans: Dr. Matilda Arabelle Evans in Columbia, South Carolina, and Dr. Hallie Tanner Johnson in Alabama (Lerner, p. 75). These bold strides into uncharted territory signaled a milestone in African American women's lives. No longer confined to the bottom rung of the employment ladder, they could now explore career opportunities previously off limits.

Preparation for a specific career was not an easy task since many women could not predict what direction their career might take after the completion of a baccalaureate degree. Restrictions on career advancement due to racism and sexism, while not necessarily impediments, certainly demanded some attention and planning. However, the most effective strategies for professional success began in the home and in the community. In particular, active mothers and participation in extracurricular activities were some of the most influential factors that shaped the direction of these women's professional lives.

MOTHERS AS DOERS

According to an early study by Epstein, successful professional African American women grew up in the care of mothers who were doers (919). These mothers worked outside of the home at various points in their lives, held professional or semiprofessional positions, and were "aggressive" in seeking out the best for their families. Although the mothers in my study did not match Epstein's profile exactly, they indeed were doers in every sense of the word. Some took active roles in their respective communities, and many explored their own talents while providing a nurturing and supportive home environment for their children.

A medical technician named Vivian was born in 1923 and remembered her mother's outgoing attitude as well as the various kinds of people she invited into her home. This hospitality not only created an "international atmosphere," but exposed the children to different points of view and life-styles:

> My mother was the type that all kinds of people would come to my home. My mother saw to that, 'cause I used to ask her if she went to the train station to meet the Africans so she could bring them all to the house. She had a way of rounding up people. I remember an English woman teaching my mother how to make tea. I remember German women teaching my mother how to make Borscht. (29:2, p. 12)

Exposure to diverse cultures allowed Vivian and her younger sister to develop an appreciation and respect for others that might not have come about in a more sheltered environment. Later in life, Vivian moved to the Caribbean islands to live and had little difficulty in adjusting to the culture.

Sidney, the university professor, affectionately described her mother's active role in the community. She went beyond her duties as a school teacher and vigorously participated in both district and neighborhood events:

> Well, my mother was such a kind person and so beloved by
> everyone who knew her . . . People of distinction, mostly whites
> . . . who had seen her in civic service and seen her in educational
> circles, a devoted worker with parent–teachers organizations and
> so on . . . came as a committee and asked her if she would allow
> them to run her name as candidate for the board of education . . .
> She was elected the first, second and third times . . . She was the
> first Negro to be elected to the board of education. (3:1, pp. 2–4)

Sidney explained that this kind of popularity lasted throughout her mother's entire life. Upon her mother's death, hundreds of people attended the funeral and later the community named a school after her. All four children in the family were college educated and held professional positions. Also, true to the pattern established by the mother, the two daughters carried on the mother's tradition of community activism.

Zora, the teacher/social worker discovered that her family was the only African American family in town when they moved to New England at the turn of the century. This special situation helped Zora to understand her family in a particularly insightful way. She regarded her mother as a uniquely gifted individual. Zora's mother put a great deal of effort into helping others and she also regularly took time to develop her own personal interests:

> Well, she [my mother] was an achiever I would say, because not
> only, not only was she concerned about the achievement of her
> family, but even for herself. After she got us well on the road she
> went back to school herself and studied law . . . As a matter of
> fact, later on she wrote poetry and she did a lot of different things,
> painted, she was a very talented lady really. (37:1, pp. 10, 13)

In addition, she made a point of joining organizations that focused on helping others both inside and outside of the community. Zora's mother was able to merge her concern for her family and others through several noteworthy activities including using music to promote racial harmony in the community:

> My mother developed a [local] orchestra. She had an Italian play
> the violin. She had a Swedish boy playing the trumpet, she had
> the one brother on the drums, my other brother sang. I've forgotten
> the other nationalities, but there were a total of seven young men

> plus my one brother that sang and they roped me into singing too.
> We played at hospitals, charities, and different things like that . . .
> And she [my mother] said that she had developed that orchestra
> to prove that, you know, all mankind is one . . . (37:1, p. 7)

Zora felt that her mother, more than any one else she knew, not only lived what she believed, but also was very creative in publically demonstrating her ideas.

Like other women in my sample, Margaret clearly recalled her mother's unusual and diverse interests. Margaret believed that her mother was refreshingly different:

> She [my mother] was a very interesting woman. She was a fan of
> Isadora Duncan, the dancer. And she [my mother] was what we
> call an interpretive dancer, which would be like modern dance.
> She was active in civic work for a number of years and was involved
> in a number of different activities associated with her interests.
> For example, she took boogie-woogie piano lessons once. That
> was the rage at the time. She also developed a line of cosmetics,
> but she didn't know how to market them. She was a little ahead
> of her time . . . She was on the committee for evaluation of films
> for the city for a long time . . . And she did work during the days
> of W.P.A. She taught folk dancing and things of that sort. Very
> interesting woman. (53:1, p. 4)

Margaret's mother seized opportunities to cultivate her own interests and did so without neglecting her family. Formal education was another of her concerns and she eventually fulfilled her dream of completing her college education:

> My mother went to high school and then began college in the
> school of physical education. And then she did not finish there
> though. Like many women of her time, she delayed her education
> once she was married and had a family. She came to Washington,
> began doing some teaching and had a dance school for children
> and that's when she met my father who was in medical school
> . . . And then when I went to college she started back to college
> and she worked her way through college . . . and got her bachelor's
> degree the same year I got mine. She was 52 and I was about 20.
> (53:1, p. 4)

Finally, Margaret described her mother's contact with "interesting" people during her childhood and youth. It was as if she were immersed in a community of rising stars:

> And down the street from her [my mother] lived the Robesons, Paul Robeson and his family whom she knew. She grew up with Paul Robeson. He was a little younger than she . . . And when her father died . . . my mother had a couple of people who roomed with her. A Madame C. J. Walker was one of them. And my mother said she remembers Madame Walker putting her hair on the ironing board and it was of course Madame Walker who invented the straightening comb. (53:1, p. 5)

Growing up in the midst of history in the making provided role models as well as a sense of pride. These stories no doubt increased in value over time and enabled Margaret to pass on to younger generations of her family a keen awareness of African American history and culture.

Similarly, Elmira's mother also returned to school after her children were grown. Elmira explained that her mother was motivated to return to school in part by a board of education ruling that tied promotional rights to a teacher's educational accomplishments:

> She went into college, you see, after I graduated and I used to help her with her homework. And I went to her graduation from the university, and I remember how proud I was to be sitting up in the stands watching my mother get her degree . . . She was forever trying to improve upon life's situations for the sake of herself and her family. (36:1, p. 4)

Again, Elmira's mother portrayed an image of balance rather than of self-consuming sacrifice. She gave her best for her family *and* for her self. It was understood that anything that improved the mother in turn improved her family.

In general, these mothers were not content to sit at home or to be consumed by household responsibilities. They gave priority to their families while at the same time enhancing their own personal growth and intellectual activities. All did not work outside of the home, especially after marriage, but all were concerned about education. Their activities in the community exposed their children to broader world views and a variety of interesting people. These women were not long-suffering victims of overwhelming family obligations, but rather dynamic achievers/doers who discovered opportunities in many aspects of their lives.

Club Activities

During this time period, club membership for young African Americans was more than a hobby or a way of filling spare time. These activities were in many respects a way of maintaining cultural identity, a vehicle for establishing social ties with other like-minded individuals, and a means of off-setting the harmful effects of racism. In many cases, parents set a positive example by their own extramural activities. Sidney was fluent in several languages and attributed her interest in other languages to both parents' involvement in foreign language clubs:

> In the early days, it became fashionable, I guess in all cities and in all social circles for adults to study a foreign language. There were French clubs, and Spanish clubs, and German clubs and my parents were members of that kind of a society and they studied French and enjoyed it very much and they also studied Spanish. And then in their schooling they had taken German . . . And so all of us grew up in a family speaking a little bit of French, a little bit of Spanish, and a little bit of German and so forth. And we would be told to sit down in German or get up and go to the piano in French or study something in Spanish. And we even made up our own language. (3:2, p. 20)

Sidney's parents' interest in languages was integrated into their home life and eventually produced some small semblance of multilingualism in their children. Although Sidney was the only child in the family to translate her love of languages into a profession, her brothers and sister developed a genuine appreciation of different languages and cultures.

Even when parents were not directly involved in club activities, some women took it upon themselves to develop interests outside of home and school. Vivian, the medical technician, as did many others, became involved in religious or church-related activities:

> I was very active in the Junior Youth at the Bahá'i Center, and I was the main reader; I was very active. (29:2, p. 12)

Again, the reader's theater-type activity not only provided an extra-curricular outlet, but actually enhanced Vivian's ability and interest in reading. She later explained that this social connection was vital in her adolescent development.

Zora became involved in a small club primarily made up of two large families: her own family, and the second and only other African American family in town. It proved to be an enriching experience that bonded the two families for the duration of their children's education:

> By that time my mother's early childhood friends had children our age and we had formed a club called Les Amis . . . So it was among that group of blacks that we had this club . . . And we visited each others homes once a month and you know went the rounds and so always, at least twice a year in the winter a big weekend and the big summer weekend they would all come to our house . . . These were my dear friends during my high school years . . . So even though high school colleagues [white] were a little more warm than others, it didn't matter because I had my other friends that were meaningful friends. (37:2, p. 6)

Banished from the social life of the school by unfriendly white classmates, the African American children found solace in their families and in their tight-knit social club. Zora further explained that club members spoke only French during meetings to enhance their fluency in the language. In addition, she felt that an added benefit of club activities was the formation of lifelong friendships among children of the two families.

In another instance, Margaret acknowledged that segregation imposed by Jim Crow laws led to the creation of a high school club for African American seniors. Barred from most public facilities, the African American students combined their efforts and created their own social activities:

> We had a club, all of the black graduating seniors across the three high schools where black kids were. We joined together in a club, sort of a loose group . . . We decided to have a prom together because white students had their prom but we were not allowed in the hotels . . . to go to these events. So we had our own prom. (53:2, p. 9)

The unity generated by this endeavor became a sustaining force for the students. They were successful in solving a serious problem and began to understand that they could make a difference in their own lives. They learned how not to accept the negative consequences of racism.

June's experience was similar. Since integrated social gatherings were prohibited, some African American youth fraternized in mixed sex groups. Young men and young women got to know one another in a friendly atmosphere free of racial tension:

> We dated in groups. We would go out in groups. We had a lot of fun. We'd go to all the games. We'd go away on the buses and ahh, we'd go to YW functions, and uh the YMCA had a teen group that met every Sunday afternoon so it gave us all kinds of chances to get out and do things, and have proper guidance . . . High school was probably ninety-nine percent black, the YMCA was probably ninety-nine and four tenths percent black, but they did things that you didn't get in high school, your mothers didn't talk about . . . and gave us the option of doing what we really wanna do and what we **should** do in our lives, and I'm **quite** grateful for that. (52:2, pp. 48–49)

What the youth did not initiate themselves was provided by the community. The "Y," for example, offered wholesome activities, guidance, freedom to express themselves, and exposure to different and, sometimes, unusual ideas. These activities generated bonding among the youth and helped to develop their self-esteem. In some respects, they may have gained more from these kinds of gatherings than from integrated social groups.

Thus, club involvement carried with it extra incentives for success. On an individual level, club activities fostered the development of personal attributes such as self-confidence and self-esteem. On a larger level, these young African American women gained leadership experience through their club activities and, equally important, realized that they could enact positive action for social change. For many women, this early pattern of community involvement and activism lasted a lifetime.

WORKING IN REAL LIFE: AFRICAN AMERICAN WOMEN IN A WHITE WORLD

In many respects, the real world of work consisted of the same problems/obstacles that were found in high school and university environments. Racism and sexism did not disappear once an African American woman completed her college education and entered the work force. In fact, the discrimination often intensified as a woman advanced to higher levels in her profession.

Prior to entering the work force, preparation, usually in the form of education, was the first testing ground for upcoming professional women. The last stages of preparation, such as student teaching or a bar exam, were especially critical and sent a definite signal to the white establishment. The warning or signal was not ignored and, as a result, many women found themselves struggling to overcome yet another obstacle imposed in the late phases of their career preparation. Zora, for example, was allowed to student teach under strenuous conditions:

> I did my practice teaching in the same school where my favorite teacher was principal and she gave me every facility. I worked like a dog mind you. I didn't do just what I learned later that my other colleagues had done when they were practice teaching. I was writing lesson plans and teaching four grades and doing all the rest of it and having projects and so forth and so on. But, you know, even as a black person having to do more work than whites do when you're going through school it doesn't hurt you. It makes you even more advanced because you are more prepared. (37:2, p. 6)

Zora was aware of the extra effort that she was expected to put forth and turned it into a positive by learning from the additional work. However, this was not the first time that the educational system had tried to impede her career plans. Even before practice teaching, the board of education made it difficult for Zora to find a school that would accept her as a student teacher:

> When I was getting ready to do my practice teaching, I had to write a special letter to the superintendent of the very town I lived

> in to get permission to do practice teaching in the school I had
> been a student in earlier years. Because I was the first black person
> to come and practice teach, and of course being the first black
> family in town, that wasn't hot . . . And even after qualifying
> there was an opportunity, there was a vacancy for teaching, but
> they refused to respond to my application. (37:2, p. 13)

Zora's long-time residency in the community was not an asset when
it came to student teaching. She was denied several student-teaching
positions based solely on the color of her skin. However, Zora refused
to take no for an answer and persisted until she was placed in the
very school that she had initially requested. It never was easy, but
she was determined to reach her goal.

From a different perspective, Georgia, a 66-year-old high-level
college administrator, discovered that white graduate school officials
were suspect of her undergraduate degree from a historically black
college (HBC). She was grudgingly admitted, but was made to feel
that her preparation at an HBC was substandard:

> So once I got there and I had been there for a semester and was
> doing good, and then he saw, they saw me in live flesh that I was
> not perhaps an ignoramus or some strange critter from a black
> college, he actually suggested that I become a teaching fellow.
> See, that's an example of racism, perfect example of racism.
> Because there were other students there who were given teaching
> fellowships from college, no questions asked . . . So anyway, I
> had five years as a teaching fellow. I received my Master's which
> was in original research and my Ph.D. which was in original
> research. (61:2, p. 13)

Georgia could not finance her graduate education without assistance,
so she complied with the request that she become a teaching fellow.
As indicated, she was well aware of the fact that lesser-qualified
white students were given similar teaching fellowships without much
scrutiny. Again, like other African American women of her generation, Georgia's determination and persistence paid off. Her five years
as a teaching fellow earned her a solid reputation as an excellent
research scientist and paved the way for uncontested admission into
a doctoral program.

Margaret generally described her medical school experiences as positive except for one incident. Ironically, the prejudice that she encountered came from white women:

> It [medical school] was also a very good experience. Very good experience. The ah, the big trauma there was the sorority, that is, medical sorority. I noticed all these white envelopes in the [mail] boxes of women. So I asked about it. And, there was, really no one had to tell you about this but, these were bids to [join] the sorority. And I was not bid. And ah, that was really ah . . . But uh, that, that was really a big, a big trauma. Not that I particularly wanted to join the sorority. That wasn't the important thing. But the fact that I would be discriminated against because I was black. And ah, it took me several days to get [myself] together. But I did. (53:2, p. 2)

The other irony of this incident is that Margaret was going to become a member of the country's most prestigious profession and yet she still experienced discrimination within those sacred boundaries. On the other hand, discrimination may have been more likely to occur here because Margaret was breaking into a field usually off limits to women and African Americans.

Once fully prepared for a career, African American women were not necessarily readily admitted into their respective professions. Many had to work other jobs, sometimes unrelated to their fields, while waiting for an opening that did not always materialize in a timely manner. Zora, a teacher by training, held a variety of jobs:

> I've had many different variations in education. As a matter of fact, I was a social worker in Canada and that's another aspect of education. And I was a psychiatric social worker in England for twelve years. And then I worked as an administrator in a nursing home. So I've had lots of various activities which are connected with education in one way or another. Most recently . . . I've been studying nutrition, and that's what I did in India, was a nutrition project . . . And then I went back to an earlier occupation and did guidance and counseling. Just before going to Uganda I finished my qualification in guidance and counseling. And that's how I got a lovely job in Uganda having gotten qualification just in time because three months after I got there, I was offered a job as director of guidance at a school. (37:2, p. 11)

True to her nature, Zora did not regard these jobs as a detriment to her career. Instead, she considered all of them a form of education.

She was patient and willing to wait for an appropriate opportunity such as the position in Uganda. Like all professionals, she experienced setbacks, but even when out of work, Zora maintained a positive attitude:

> I don't think I've ever been truly discouraged in my life. I think I can say my parents helped us then in terms of, if you're disappointed, then accept it as God's will and with that kind of frame of reference. Of course you have little disappointments, you know it's true, but you don't dwell on it and let it be a stumbling block to your progress. No, I would more or less go and do the next thing. And with the depression and all . . . I got a job in the W.P.A., the writers project . . . So that's how I spent some of those years, not teaching, but doing something with some of my skills. (37:2, p. 13)

Zora survived by utilizing as many different skills as possible in the job market. If she could not teach, she would do something else until she could return to the classroom. Zora recently completed her Ph.D. in education and hopes to teach school in a third world country.

Frieda, a 66-year-old union organizer, was a housewife for many years. When her husband moved the family North she had to work because the cost of living was so high. She assumed several different jobs before devoting herself to union work:

> No, I did not work outside of the home, no. Not until I got to New York then I began to work in New York for a large department store chain in the office and I worked for Consolidated Retail Stores as assistant buyer . . . I worked in Chicago as a clerk in a store. I worked for the telephone company too. (56:2, p. 6)

Frieda believed that she did her best in all of her jobs. She was sought after by management, but really did not commit to a lifelong occupation until she was recruited to work with unions in the South. Up to that time, doing *good* work was more important to her than the *kind* of work/job. Frieda was satisfied to do her best.

On the job experiences were both challenging and rewarding. Most of the women found that they were the first African Americans and sometimes the first women in their particular positions. Consequently, racism and sexism on the job were to be expected. Lula found that she had to take a qualifying exam in a room separate from the white applicants who would be applying for the same job:

> So, I received a notice from the State Department saying that they had an opening . . . So when I got the appointment from her at the State Department I came up and took an examination in a separate room [separate from white applicants]. I was the only black in that recruitment in the early '50's and I don't really think today they knew I was black until I got here and . . . then of course they had to accept me. And I was kept here almost six months before I was given an assignment. (34:1, p. 15)

Lula explained that she felt that the long wait for an assignment was directly related to the fact that she was an African American. However, the different and unequal treatment did not stop after she received her assignment. Once at her post she found a kind of polite, benign neglect:

> At the embassy in Osaka, it was a different thing. I couldn't say there was a lot of racism because it was very subtle and everybody treats you coolly, politely. And on weekends you were left on your own so had it not been for the Japanese friends I would have been a very unhappy, lonely person. (34:1, p. 16)

Even though it was difficult, Lula believed that had she received friendly treatment at the embassy, she would not have ventured out to explore Japan and, therefore, would have missed the opportunity to learn more about a different culture. Being somewhat at ease in speaking the language, she found a whole new world opened up when she spoke Japanese:

> I learned enough [Japanese] to get around and I could hear their reaction to me without them knowing that I understood. And the first reaction was that I was so large, "Isn't she tall?" But I never heard any mention of my color, it was always my size. And then when I would respond in Japanese to them, to their remark, then they would just turn handsprings and practically give me half of the store. (34:1, p. 17)

Osaka was just the beginning for Lula. From there she went on to Korea and several countries in Africa. In retirement, Lula's life is not much different, she still travels around the world.

On the other hand, Elmira experienced success almost immediately after graduating from law school. She was the first African American female to graduate from that particular law school, and she found several opportunities for employment:

> When I came out, I came out the same year that one of the male students, one of the black male students came out and we formed a firm and I practiced with him for I guess about a year and a half. Then I went to a lawyer's convention and met a very energetic and enterprising young attorney from another state. He was running for the state legislature and he suggested that he might have an opening in his office . . . So I thought I would try it. So I went up and took the state's bar and passed it and I stayed there practicing law in his office for about two years. (36:2, p. 9)

Her reputation as an outstanding attorney was established quickly and solidly. Later, Elmira went on to become another "first:"

> So I came back to my home state and went into partnership with Mr. Brown and Mr. Mallory. Then a gentleman who had been very active in the campaign came to town and called on me. I didn't know him and he said that the Attorney General had promised him an appointment of a black. And he said that he had followed my career and he wondered if I would be interested. So I said yes I would. So I became the state's first black assistant attorney general, first female because there was also a young man appointed. (36:2, p. 11)

Although Elmira seemed destined to become many "firsts," she was neither threatened by nor impressed with her own accomplishments. She took it all in stride. She knew instinctively that there always were difficulties that accompanied each new rung on the ladder of success:

> That office was a tremendously interesting experience. There was an elderly man who had been with several administrations and I think that he was annoyed for several reasons: that I was a woman and that I was a black. There was only one other woman, a Jewish lady from another part of the state. And he went out of his way to help the men, but when we asked him a question he was very curt and acted as if he really didn't want to be bothered. So I only asked him a question once. After that I decided I'd have to educate myself. So I did some research and then I prepared my assignment.

And when I submitted my first opinion as a result of a request, it went through. . . . My assignment passed and I was very glad I hadn't asked for any help see . . . and it was the same sort of experience in a sense that law school was. You worked and you made it and then you got confidence that you could do it, you see. (36:2, p. 11)

The experience, while initially disappointing, served as a means of empowerment. Rather than succumb to unfair treatment, Elmira found a way to help himself. She never looked back after that.

LIVING AND WORKING IN REAL LIFE: AFRICAN AMERICAN WOMEN IN A MAN'S WORLD

In many instances, career choices outside of traditional roles for women automatically called male dominance into question. Most women were not actively seeking to usurp control, but rather to express their own talents and abilities. That they happened to venture into a male-dominant field was coincidental. Nonetheless, by so doing, African American women professionals reaped the rewards as well as the penalties. Elmira discovered early on that she was regarded as less capable of making fair judgments than her male counterparts:

I got my first criminal case and had to go to the jail and interview the person who was in jail and find out his side of the story, what witnesses he had, then I had to go and contact all those witnesses and find out if they were willing to appear and I was just convinced that the man was telling me the truth. He was a victim of a chain of circumstances . . . the prosecuting attorney unloaded all they had on him . . . The court found against him and afterwards the judge called me up and said, "Now I want you to understand that you're not to believe everything anybody tells you. You'll have to develop the ability to know when people are lying." I was really very upset about that because I said, "Well, your honor, I believe that he was telling the truth." (36:2, p. 11)

Elmira stood her ground in spite of the patronizing attitude of the judge. Later, when he was released from jail, the client visited

Elmira's office, thanked her for her help, and once again declared his innocence.

Georgia found that male employees constantly challenged her authority. Sometimes the one-up-manship backfired:

> It had reached a point where this was the only thing to do with someone who was trying very hard to use his power to exclude my activities. So when I read the riot act [to him] he said to me, "I resign." And I said, "I accept it," quickly before there was any debate in his mind." (57:3, p. 7)

She expressed no regret about the departure of this particular employee. There were no suitable alternatives and Georgia was neither willing nor interested in maintaining the status quo. She astutely summed up the issue/problem of being a woman in a man's world:

> There was some awkwardness about, I think, being a woman. There's one other woman in that position. And you know, there's always a feeling that the old boys want to get together at lunch and if a woman is there they can't cuss as much or they can't speak in certain kinds of ways. So there was some hesitancy about inviting me to join them when they walk across the street to have lunch. But it was more by omission. It's very hard for men to decide how to interact with women on a professional level. (57:3, p. 10)

Georgia understood her outsider status, but did not let that hinder her from doing her job. She performed as well and better than some of her male colleagues.

Harriet also was aware of the attitudes of her male counterparts, "Now with me I'm sure some of the men couldn't stand me . . . because they just weren't accustomed to women being the head" (30:3, p. 49). She regarded this kind of attitude as an occupational hazard, something to be acknowledged and resisted. Equally striking was Harriet's strong opinion of the impact of sexism on her career:

> I think that I would have been president of my university had I uh, not been a woman. I'm sure in the sixties I would have been uh, at that time it was felt that each university president had to go before the state legislature and plead his budget and in their minds was the question as to whether a woman would be effective with those white state legislators when she appeared before them with a budget and they couldn't cross that line, they could not . . . So

> I felt . . . that yeah, I would say that uh, had I been a man, I would have been a president of a university as early as 1940, no 1945. (30:3, p. 50)

Harriet was clear about the possibilities and limitations of using gender as a measure of worth. She knew that she had more to offer than that which was requested. Furthermore, it is interesting to note that in the beginning of the segment she frames woman/female in a negative context, "had I *not* been a woman." However, near the end of the segment, she uses a more positive framing, "had I been a man." This specific phrasing eliminated a third possibility, "because I was a woman, I was not offered the presidency" and, thus, a euphemistic means of verbalizing a disturbing reality.

Lula, a 20-year veteran of the foreign service and world traveler, thought that she had seen it all. She constantly had to be aware of cultural differences as she interacted with foreign dignitaries and did so without difficulty. Yet, it was her own countryman that habitually and jokingly badgered her about her interest and stand on women's equal rights. On one particular occasion, his luck ran out:

> And the next day . . . we were invited to the University of Kwanju' 'cause Tom was teaching there. The chancellor of the university said he was giving a luncheon for us. Food was very scarce. We must have been about twelve people and they had one chicken. They cut it in little pieces . . . and we all sat on the floor oriental style and the chancellor gave us a wonderful welcoming speech. He said they were very honored to have an American lady for the first time visiting their university . . . And he [the chancellor] said in honor of the lady we're going to give you the choice piece of chicken which was the chicken head with the eyes still in it and they put this on my plate. And, and Tom then nudged me in the side and said, O.K. you women's libber, what are you gonna do about this? So, I, I made polite overtures I guess toward the chancellor and I said, "Well, I'm in your country, I honor your traditions and your customs, and I would like to continue some of those traditions," and I gave my chicken to Tom. So I put it in his plate. And the professors applauded. They thought it was the greatest thing. Tom . . . not only had to eat it, but it is tradition to burp afterwards. (34:2, p. 9)

In the end, Lula felt that justice had prevailed. Following another culture's tradition allowed her to concede to a male and simultaneously illustrate her point that women were as intelligent and clever as men.

Unfortunately, sexism permeated all levels of existence, including the private lives of professional women. Jane relocated to another town when hired by a university, but her good fortune was short-lived when she found that no one would rent to a divorced, single parent. So she decided to build her own house, but even that presented some problems for a single woman:

> I wanted this house as it is. And when I said that I wanted to build a house because nobody wanted to rent to me, I wasn't in the church, and all that sort of thing. And I got Mr. Smith to take my money which he would not take until I had Dr. Green O.K. it, even though I had the money to buy the lot. I designed the house. Contractors said, "We don't build a house like this." I think he would have taken it [design] had I been a man, so, ah, then I tried to find another one that would take it. I couldn't, so I paid Mr. Brent to put my basement in. And when he put the sleepers on it, I paid him off and Mr. Jolly, a retired carpenter and I put this house together. I don't think I would have had that trouble if I was a man. It took me three years to build it, but it's what I wanted. (27:3, p. 58)

Jane's unwillingness to conform to the social conventions of that particular African American community meant that she would not benefit from the advantages of the community. So she was on her own. Out of necessity Jane created her own alternatives. This behavior met with resistance, but it was something that she could and did overcome. Although money could not override the builders' prejudices, she refused to accept anything other than what she wanted. Jane persevered and built her house, her way.

SEXISM VERSUS RACISM

It is tempting to speculate about whether or not sexism *or* racism most influences an African American woman's life, especially a woman professional who steps outside of the boundaries of women's traditional roles. However, the underlying assumption that life can be divided into discrete components without overlap or interaction is both reductive and misleading. As women in this study have demonstrated, more often than not, *both* factors have an impact on their lives.

Becoming aware of differences between the sexes usually occurred within the home. Early on, many girls realized that there was a noticeable distinction between themselves and their brothers. Zora, for example, did not think that it was fun to be a girl:

> My father was a very quiet man and very loving. He had a very strong sense of morality. He was very protective of us, especially the girls. I can remember I used to think the boys had much more leeway than I had as a girl. I was always kind of strong headed like, wanting to do what the boys did, climb trees, jump out of barn windows and that kind of stunt. And so when the boys wanted to go, in those days it was safe to get on the road and get a ride somewhere from a passerby, so when the boys used to come home and talk about their trips to town and how they would thumb a ride and came back with all of these adventures, tales, I used to feel, oh why do I have to be a girl because I couldn't do all those things. (37:1, p. 15)

Zora said that she made up for this later in life when she traveled to foreign countries and became involved in her own adventures. Also, she admitted that she appreciated her father's protection, "People don't raise their children up that way anymore . . . It's stayed by me well."

Mae, a 74-year-old university administrator, was an only child, but she learned from neighborhood children and family friends that there was something tragic about being a girl. Adults constantly remarked that it was too bad that her father did not have a son who could carry on his name and reputation as a university administrator. Eventually, Mae decided that she would correct her status in order to please her father:

> I was five-years-old sitting on the porch. Trying, you know, I was contorting myself. And my daddy came home promptly. Always at five o'clock. He would come home for dinner. We had a routine with that. Daddy always was home [on time]. I used to run down the street to meet him. And I didn't run down the street to meet him this day. I was sitting there concentrating. He said, "Baby, what are you trying to do?" I said, "I'm trying to kiss my elbow."

> So [he said], "Why are you trying to kiss your elbow?" I said, "The kids told me that if I could kiss my elbow I would turn into a boy." So, you know in those days five-year-olds were innocent . . . But he said, "Baby, why?" His major concern was why I wanted to be a boy. Finally, he said, "Oh, you don't wanna be a boy." "Anyway," he said, "I like you just as you are." He said, "See I couldn't pick a boy up and hug him and kiss him the way I'm kissing you." So, he let it go at that. But it festered and festered in his mind. Finally when I started school, I guess by this time I'm seven, he said, "You still wanna be a boy?" And I said, "Yes, more than ever." [He said], "Why?" I said, "Because everybody who comes in the house says to you: 'Dr. Blank what a shame you don't have a son,' 'Too bad you don't have a boy to follow in your footsteps.' " (56:1, p. 9)

This poignant experience was etched in the memories of both father and daughter. There was little the father could do to ease Mae's feelings about the disadvantages of being a girl. Ironically, education and circumstances provided opportunities for Mae to follow in her father's footsteps anyway. She even assumed the same job her father held when he was a university administrator.

In contrast to gender differences, racial differences and the accompanying discrimination tended to be discovered outside of the home. As an example, integrated school environments were excellent training grounds in race relations for many African American women. In elementary school, Vivian discovered the extent to which racism had contaminated even childhood innocence:

> My mother tells this story all the time . . . [about] when I first realized there was black and white. I had a very good [white] friend named Mary Adams. This was at the Christian school when this happened . . . One day she [my friend Mary] came to school and told me she couldn't play with me any longer. I was in about the first grade, and I said, well why can't you play with me? So she took my hand and she told me, it's because you're black . . . I said, "Oh, I'll fix that," I said, "When I go home, I'll tell my mother to wash me real clean." (26:2, p. 13)

This was a serious disappointment for Vivian. She not only lost a friend, but she found the ugly face of racism. Her mother helped her understand the dynamics of racial prejudice and the importance of self-pride, but Vivian never forgot that day.

Similarly, Zora's family's experience as the only African American family in an all white town in New England for several years was full of surprises and frustrations. It was in this context that Zora learned of the destructive impact of racial prejudice. Her family gradually had been accepted to some extent by the white community. Children in the family had white playmates and school friends. However, their interaction changed when all of the children grew older:

> But, oddly enough all those young [white] girls and one who was supposed to be my really closest of friends, as soon as she turned thirteen, she came to me one day and said, "I can't be your friend anymore." And I said, "Why?" "Well, because you're black and I'm white." But she didn't put it that way 'cause, those days we weren't talking about black and white. I forget how they said it. You're colored or something. And I said, "It's alright with me." But she continually came to my house to see my brothers. Now isn't that ridiculous? Ha! She didn't want to play with a black girl but she couldn't resist playing with black boys. (37:2, p. 6)

Zora felt a sense of loss, but would not show it because she was also deeply hurt by the racism that had touched her life. She credited her mother for helping her cope with this difficult situation. Furthermore, through this experience she became aware of the double standards often applied to both race and gender differences.

In both instances, Vivian and Zora were caught in a pattern most probably established by adults, not children. It is as if white parents felt it was necessary to separate their children from African American friends and playmates at critical points: the beginning of elementary school or the onset of puberty. Yet, in the majority of cases, children would not chose this course of action for themselves. Prejudice, like acceptance, is learned behavior. For African American women like Vivian and Zora, this was one of the first opportunities to develop strength, insight, and a means of coping with the kinds of biases that they would encounter for a lifetime.

Therefore, African American women entered the work force, not as rookies unaccustomed to bigotry, but as veterans with fine-tuned skills perfected over time. Within and outside of the home, and with the help of others, they recognized the assets and liabilities of being different. There was no place for African American women professionals, so they made their own way. Loretta, for example, became more active on her own behalf when she discovered a discrepancy in her paycheck:

> I know a man that was teaching and who was not the chairman of the department. I was the chairman of the department. And it so happened, that I saw his check, and I know that salary should have been mine instead of his. And so I called the board of education, Mr. Stricker I think it was, when he was superintendent. And so, I say now, I'm chairman of the department. But he [Stricker], he let that man keep that same salary and just raised mine to be the same. So that shows, that's discrimination between men and women. See as a black woman you have two obstacles to overcome. Being black and then being a woman. (26:2, p. 2)

She was not happy with the board's action, but learned a valuable lesson. Loretta realized that she was not willing to have the title and not the salary, so from that point on, she demanded appropriate compensation.

Georgia also had "trial-by-fire" experiences as she rose in the ranks of university administration. She had done nothing wrong or inappropriate, in fact she was an excellent administrator, yet when it was time for promotion to even higher levels of administration, doors were mysteriously closed to her:

> I have had two experiences which are pure sexism and racism . . .
> I was voted by the regents unanimously to become dean, but two high ranking officials objected strenuously because they had their own candidate in mind, a southern white boy. And they proceeded to sabotage the process and they succeeded . . . A year later their candidate was selected and [later] he went on to another university where he is now championing minority causes right, left and sideways. And that was the first experience. The second one was I was selected as clearly a candidate with all the right credentials . . . And the head of the board was for interesting reasons not interested in my being in that position. And there was a woman on the board . . . who said a black woman couldn't raise money for the college even though I had raised tremendous money for another college [when I was there]. And [it] turns out that the reason they were so much against me was that they felt there were

too many blacks already [one other one] in that position. So, they proceeded again to do things . . . the chancellors selected me and the bottom line was when they got to vote after all this political maneuvering, they decided, well, they had to open the search again . . . See they were trying to find a candidate who was as good as I was on paper. . . . (61:3, p. 17)

Georgia was angry about these experiences, but did not give up. Later she was hired for the same position at another university. Ultimately, she was thankful for not being selected because those particular positions were unusually controversial within their own campuses. As a result of these experiences, Georgia commented, "I do not believe that politics and education belong together. It is a terrible mix, and it's an insult to higher education and to knowledge."

In both situations, Loretta and Georgia encountered prejudice from several directions at once. Although it was apparent that they had been the targets of discrimination, it was not obvious that either racism or sexism was the singular cause. In all probability, it was both. For African American women, sexism and racism are intertwined and intimately connected. It is difficult, if not impossible, to separate the two. Under ordinary circumstances, African American women cannot delete gender or skin color from their personal identities, so any research methodology or interpretation of their lives must take this into account. Georgia best summed up the predicament of African American women professionals:

Well, it's always been, difficult being an achiever, high achiever in a singular place, you know. As a woman there's that problem. Second, being black, there's that problem. Both of those become very weighty responsibilities and awarenesses. (61:2, p. 3)

RETIREMENT: THROWN OUT WITH THE DISHWATER

Voluntary retirement gave many women the opportunity to concentrate on the personal interests they had developed over the years. They were no less busy, but now could focus on self-selected tasks. It sometimes was a welcome reprieve. Margaret explained that it was the appropriate decision to make at that time:

> They threw me out in 1985 (laughs). You see, I was seventy. This was longer than most people. I mean this had nothing to do with the company, it was my personal [decision]. I realized that we were getting heavily into the computer age. So let somebody come along who is much more interested. So I recommended my position to another woman and she is there now. (53:3, p. 3)

Margaret realized that technology was rapidly reshaping medicine and although she loved the profession, she did not wish to become seriously involved with computers at this point in her life. So she settled into retirement with the satisfaction that another woman had taken her place.

Forced retirement for some women, however, was as disturbing as prior confrontations with sexism and racism. Many viewed mandatory retirement as an unnecessary interruption in a successful career. Georgia expressed frustration with trying to confront a system that would make no exceptions:

> I would have liked to have stayed another year or two but the person in charge of our system decided that people should retire at sixty-five and I was caught in her decision. And then she lied about it and said that it was a board decision as well as hers. And then the board found out after she had said this to me. And that was the final straw that caused them to ask her to leave. (61:3, p. 5)

Due to her sudden retirement, Georgia had to move to another town and reorganize her life. The disruption was stressful and time-consuming. Yet, Georgia was productive and extremely busy. The university had lost one of its greatest assets.

From a similar perspective, Mae expressed the trauma that accompanied forced retirement. Her sense of loss was poignant and she did not hesitate to say as much:

> I think one of the, one of the low points in my life was when I retired. We had come back from an important meeting. We had been successful in our proposal, but they did not then know that the chairman was trying to get rid of me . . . I didn't tell them that . . . So I came home from that meeting and the next morning when I woke up, the only decision I had to make was when to get out of bed. And that was trauma. It was absolute trauma. I kid

you not. My doctor talked to me about retiring, he's thinking about it. I told him not to retire. When you have worked all of your life, and I came up rung by rung. Nobody gave me anything . . . I worked my way, bit by bit, rung by rung up that ladder . . . And every day was competitive and replete with problems that I had to solve. I'd wake up in the morning and I'd say, "Um, I wonder what's going to happen today?" Because it was always something. And all of a sudden you wake up and you're alone? . . . And nothing to do, no place to go, no one asking you any questions. It's dreadful . . . I didn't want to see anybody. I didn't want to go anywhere. I just sort of felt like somebody had thrown me out with the dishwater. And uh, it, it was, it was a horrible experience. Particularly the way uh, the way it was done. I was put out see, by a man who does not like women. The chairman felt that a woman should not be in this position . . . I raised a million dollars a year for the 3½ years that I was in that position. Except the last year. That half year he was giving me so much flack till I, I, I couldn't . . . every meeting he would call me just before the meeting and tell me that this was the meeting he was going to get rid of me. . . . He came to my office and he told me that he was, he was going to get me out, and he felt that I should go, and uh that they needed a man. And this was between the two of us in my office. . . . (57:1, p. 4)

Mae's vivid description of the first morning of retirement is haunting. She not only lost her position, but also lost face. The challenge of problem solving on the job had been stimulating, but now she only had to decide "when to get out of bed." It seemed that her hard work was neither important nor appreciated. The manner of her dismissal was equally troubling. She was harassed by a man in power and abused by a system that could not tolerate a woman in charge. Under these circumstances, forced retirement would be difficult for anyone, but especially for a dynamic high achiever accustomed to success.

Retirement was both a blessing and a curse. It opened the door to new opportunities while closing the door on others. The struggles and successes of these African American women in the work place were not in vain. Their confrontations with the system of white male privilege frequently resulted in a change in policy and/or the decision making process. Their presence paved the way for others.

The impact of race and gender on the lives of African American women is especially evident in the work force where they traditionally have been limited by artificial ceilings and double standards. Entering a profession was as difficult as staying in the profession, and there were no easy choices. Stepping outside of the occupational mold of "service" attracted rewards as well as discrimination. Society could not tolerate African American women out of place. Yet, as these women have indicated by their lives and their words, it is entirely possible to break with tradition and make your own place in the world.

AFRICAN AMERICAN WOMEN'S ORAL NARRATIVES AS AUTOBIOGRAPHY: THE CARE AND FEEDING OF "MONGREL OFFSPRING"

In a discussion of issues associated with collaborative life writing, G. Thomas Couser observes that because "collaborative authorship" ultimately "crosses autobiography with biography: the squeamish will shun the mongrel offspring" (118). Even though he acknowledges that this uncompromising position excludes most people of color from the canon, his choice of words highlights the stringent nature of "true/pure" autobiography theory. Couser's use of the term "mongrel offspring" negatively connotes something animal rather than human, anomalous rather than standard. Such linguistic framing of the concept of difference implies that variation in the forms of autobiography is not only unacceptable, but also stigmatic, tainted with the shame of illegitimacy.

In particular, most early autobiographies of African American women can be found in this gray area, this middle ground between subject (autobiography) and object (biography). These women arrived at autobiography through a mongrel form—the slave narrative, many of which were "as told to" or ghostwritten accounts. Dismissal of these texts because of their collaborative authorship would have permanently lost to obscurity crucial aspects of American history and culture. Narratives of women like Nancy Prince, Mattie Jackson,[1] and others put into place missing pieces of the sociohistorical puzzle. So to categorically deny the validity of these texts because they are deemed neither literature nor history hints of an attitude of intellectual superiority and cultural bias. Otherwise, there are no features inherent in the texts that automatically render them inferior to single author autobiographies. Such a decision about worth or merit is essentially a value judgment, but whose value and who judges?

Rather than expand the argument about what is "pure" autobiography and what is not, more basic and less prescriptive issues must be addressed. According to Couser, "The questions of authorship and authority . . . are difficult but fundamental: to challenge the texts' authorship is to ask whether—or how—they can be read as autobiography" (26). Thus, if we ask "how" instead of "whether," a text can be read as autobiography, then these concerns can be recast into two central strands of inquiry with regard to oral narratives: (1) Who is the primary authority of a collaborated text, and (2) does collaboration contaminate both the process and products of autobiography? Answers to these questions will be based on analyses of (1) the narrative of Louisa Piquet[2] (1861), (2) a contemporary oral narrative, and (3) a comparison of an oral and written text.

AUTHORITY AND CONTROL: WHO'S IN CHARGE?

Before undertaking an analysis of Louisa Piquet's narrative, it is important to understand the history of the problem. From the slave narrative, the earliest form of African American autobiography, throughout the nineteenth and twentieth centuries, African American women's participation in autobiography is shaped almost entirely by issues of race and gender. That is, perceptions of their stories/experiences and their authority appears to be influenced more by their race and gender than by the quality of their writing.

Critical appraisals of Zora Neale Hurston's *Dust Tracks on a Road* and Frederick Douglass' *Life and Times,* for example, demonstrate that autobiographies by women and men are treated differently by scholars and critics alike. Douglass does not discuss in detail key personal relationships in his life such as his first wife and the role that she played in his escape from slavery. Hurston also does not discuss the personal details of her life such as her third marriage.

However, Douglass is seldom taken to task for missing and "recon-structed" information in his autobiography.[3] In contrast, Hurston is accused of lying and deceit for the same offense.[4]

Additionally, there is the related issue of integrity or truthfulness carried over from slavery. Do we expect/want African Americans to be honest about the circumstances of their oppression when speaking/writing their lives? According to William Andrews there was public suspicion of authorship/authority from the very beginning of African American autobiography: "speaking too revealingly of the individual self, particularly if this did not correspond to white notions of the facts of the black experience . . . risked alienating white sponsors and readers, too" (6). Thus, the first African American autobiographers were not expected to be authorities of their own "slave narratives" and usually had to have a white "sponsor" validate (in a foreword or an appendix) their identities and the facts of their personal narratives. This kind of colonial/imperialistic approach to African American autobiography has continued to influence the criticism and interpretation of African American life writing, especially those texts written by women.

Harriet Jacobs' *Incidents* is another example of the difficulty involved in women owning their own writing. This "antebellum autobiography" was published pseudonymously in 1861 and was one of the few "major" autobiographical works by an African American woman that received public notice at that time. Fearing public condemnation for her sexual indiscretions, Jacobs did not initially acknowledge her authorship of the narrative and by so doing, unknowingly initiated a controversy that was not resolved until the 20th century. Up until Jean Fagan Yellin's extensive research uncovered that Harriet Jacobs was the actual author, the narrative was dismissed as either a fabrication or an "as told to" account written by editor Lydia Maria Child abolitionist, and friend of Jacobs. In fact, Yellin observed that "by the 20th century both Jacobs and her book were forgotten" (xxv).

So Jacobs spoke to her audience through a slave narrator named Linda Brent and not her own name. It appears that Jacobs' sensitivity to public disapproval of her moral character was so strong that she was willing to undermine her own authority by publishing her narrative under a pseudonym. However, when the reader understands the silence that she was forced to endure, then her position is not so difficult to explain:

> My master met me at every turn, reminding me that I belonged to him, and swearing by heaven and earth that he would compel me to submit to him . . . The light heart which nature had given me became heavy with sad forebodings. The other slaves in my master's house noticed the change. Many of them pitied me; but none dared to ask the cause . . . and they were aware that to speak . . . was an offense that never went unpunished . . . I longed for some one to confide in . . . But Dr. Flint swore he would kill me, if I was not as silent as the grave (28).

Jacobs' silence was conditioned by a history of abuse. Even after the fact, she could not bring herself to publicly acknowledge her own life story. In one way, this pseudonymity may have spared her societal ridicule, but in another, perhaps more subtle way, it sabotaged her personal power. She required that a reader accept her story, but not her authority.

In contrast, Zora Neale Hurston's autobiography is criticized *because* the writer exercises authority over her own life story. She reveals some details and conceals others. Robert E. Hemenway, Hurston's biographer, begins his critique of *Dust Tracks* by remarking that it is "one of the most peculiar autobiographies in Afro-American history" (ix), and that it "presents an image of its author that fails to conform with either her public career or her private experience" (ix). Immediately the reader is aware of one of the criteria Hemenway has used to form his opinion—one's private experience and public image *must* be consistent *and* must be accurately represented in life writing. Is this a fair measure of a *good* autobiography? In addition, he observes that the 1942 version of *Dust Tracks* "was substantially altered during editing to remove Hurston's criticism of Western imperialism in Asia" (ix), and that these remarks are inconsistent with those that she made elsewhere. He points this out as one of the first examples of the divergence in Hurston's public/ private image, but does not tell us if the editing was done by Hurston herself or by an editor from the publishing house. Even if he knows for certain that the editing was Hurston's idea, was she not entitled to change her mind?

Hemenway dwells on what he refers to as a pattern of "paradoxes" throughout his thirty-one page introduction to the 1984 edition of *Dust Tracks*. He describes Hurston's autobiography with words and phrases like:

"makes little attempt to confront or explain . . ."

"ignores . . ."

"confusing . . ."

"fails to discuss the public events of Hurston's private life . . ."

"diverges from the private reality of her public life . . ."

"deliberately ambiguous about her birth date"

"sacrifices truth to the politics of racial harmony"

What reader would be enticed to read a book introduced by such negative language, especially when Henenway concludes on the very last page of his critique that, *"Dust Tracks* fails as an autobiography because it is a text deliberately less than its author's talents . . ." (xxix)?

Although Hemenway admits that "autobiography is not history" (xii) and excuses Ernest Hemingway from telling the truth, he judges Hurston by a different standard and accuses her of intentionally distorting the facts of her life in order to fashion the book into a "document intended to further the progress of American race relations" (xiii). If this is true, is this deed so horrible that readers should dismiss the entire autobiography? Is Hurston the first and only American writer to ever have manipulated her writing for a particular purpose other than or in addition to telling her own life story? In the instance of American race relations, we should praise her instead of condemn her.

A more recent example of a similar situation can be found in an oral narrative by Bessie Jones entitled, *For the Ancestors: Autobiographical Memories*, collected and edited by John Stewart.[5] In the introduction, Stewart provides an historical context for spirituals that Bessie is noted for singing and arranging, and goes into some detail about his relationship with Bessie. In discussing this relationship, he observes that " . . . she was constructing a text by which she wished to be remembered—not necessarily reconstructing the actual record of her life. It is the limitation of all autobiography" (xxii). So why bother to mention this particular limitation? How does the interviewer know/judge that there is a discrepancy between Bessie's oral account and the "facts" of her *real* life? Is she not to be believed? Certainly Bessie Jones' authority is suspect if the editor/interviewer calls attention to what he perceives to be discrepancies between text and reality.

In all three examples, African American women's autobiographical authority has been undermined by "others" directly or indirectly involved in the telling of their lives. Many women told their life stories anyway, while some were silenced or muted by a cultural agenda that required strict double standards. This does not mean that African American women were helpless victims, but that they represent what Smith and Watson refer to as "colonial subjects," marginalized selves outside of the boundaries and privileges of Western autobiographical theories/practices.

LOUISA PICQUET AND THE VOICE OF AUTHORITY

The issue of authority in any text, especially in a collaborative text, is complicated by a variety of factors including purpose/intent, interviewee/interviewer relationship (i.e., status, rapport, gender, age), and situation or condition of elicitation (i.e., setting: home, jail, etc.). The narrative of Louisa Piquet is an excellent specimen for investigation because the person who elicited the text is also credited with being the author of the text according to the title page: *Louisa Picquet, the Octoroon: or Inside Views of Southern Domestic Life* by H. Mattison, Pastor of Union Chapel, New York (1).

The twofold purpose of the narrative is not immediately disclosed and then only in the last few chapters. The first and perhaps primary purpose was to sell the narrative in order to raise money to free Louisa's mother who was still enslaved at the time the narrative was published:

> "Should any of our readers be willing to contribute to this object, as we hope many will, let them inclose, if it be but a single dollar, either to Evans & Co., bankers, Cincinnati, Ohio, or to Rev. H. Mattison . . ." (49).

The second purpose, to provide evidence that slavery should be abolished, becomes apparent in chapters twenty-six ("Conclusion and Moral of the Whole Story") and twenty-seven ("Slave-Burning, or the 'Barbarism of Slavery' ") as well as in the questioning: "Did Mr. Cook always treat you well, as to any insults?" (10), "Well, how did he whip you?" (12), "Did he cut through your skin?" (15). Thus, we may predict that Louisa, the narrator, may have been more strongly interested in the first purpose, and the interviewer, H. Mattison, more concerned with the second purpose. Whereas these are not opposing intentions, each of the participants (interviewee and interviewer) disclosed information and asked questions accordingly. As a result, there was some overlap and a few areas of disparity. So the whole of the narrative was shaped by information which was selected to fulfill both purposes and not necessarily by a desire to tell the life story of an ex-slave. The final product is a text that irregularly focuses on particular events and does not provide a complete or rounded view of the narrator's life.

This discontinuity suggests that the voice of authority often shifts as the narrative is molded to suit its dual purposes. In the beginning the voice of the interviewer, Mattison, is clearly present as he describes the narrator and sets the stage for the full narrative. Even the question/answer format which begins in chapter III and continues through chapter XII illustrates the dominant role of the interviewer:

> Q: "Had she any one she called her husband while she was in Georgia?"
> A: "No."

Q: "Had she in Mobile?"
A: "No."

Q: "Had she any children while she lived in Mobile?"
A: "None but my brother, the baby when we were all sold."

Q: "Who was the father of your brother, the baby you speak of?"
A: "I don't know except Mr. Cook was. Mother had three children while Mr. Cook owned her." (7–8)

Chapters XIII through XXIII include letters exchanged between Louisa and her mother (since both women were illiterate, various third parties wrote their letters for them) with accompanying comments by Mattison. There are some first person accounts and direct quotes scattered throughout these chapters, but the interviewer's third person singular narration is dominant. Beginning in chapter XXIV the interviewer switches to third person plural narration (". . . we [ministers] took Mrs. P., and went to the Bishops' rooms . . .", ". . . we [Louisa and I] are obliged to close it [the narrative] after all that has been done . . .") because the chronology of events indicated that he had become involved in Louisa's life as one of her supporters at this point in time. Chapters XXVI[6] and XXVII appear to be Mattison's own dissertation on the evils of slavery and he included newspaper accounts of torture in Chapter XXVII. These chapters seem to have been added to the end of the narrative as a means of strengthening its abolitionist impact. Thus, it is obvious that Louisa's voice no longer can be heard after Chapter XVII. In earlier chapters, her voice was fairly free of editorial comments and marked only with quotation marks. However, in Chapter XVII, the editor subtly intervenes: " 'While in Ohio, going from Xenia to Springfield in the cars,' says Mrs. P., 'I was expecting a letter. . . .' " From this point on, Louisa's narration[7] becomes less frequent until it is completely absent in the last few chapters.

Interestingly, Mattison focuses on skin color and gender in his introduction entitled "LOUISA PIQUET, THE OCTOROON SLAVE.—CHAPTER I.—ILLUSTRIOUS BIRTH AND PARENTAGE." He goes to great length to emphasize her physical appearance, especially color:

. . . of fair complexion and rosy cheeks, with dark eyes, a flowing head of hair with no perceptible inclination to curl, and every appearance, at first view of an accomplished white lady. No one, not apprised of the fact, would suspect that she had a drop of African blood in her veins . . . (5)

Having isolated Louisa from her race by virtue of physical features, he also highlighted her good Christian standing and "lady-like bearing" even though the slavery experience could be observed in her "menial-like diffidence, her plantation expression and pronunciation, her inability to read or write . . ." (5). According to Mattison, these qualities assured readers that Louisa Piquet was upright, decent, and truthful. Notwithstanding, his focus on skin color which continued throughout the narrative exceeded basic issues of credibility. He posed several questions related to birth and color including:

Q: "Was your mother white?"
A: "Yes, she pretty white; not white enough for white people. She have long hair, but it was kind a wavy." (8)

Q: "Were there any others there white like you?"
A: "Oh yes, plenty of them. There was only Lucy of our lot, but others!" (16)

Q: "Were your children mulattoes?"
A: "No sir! They were all white. They look just like him [the master/owner]." (19)

Q: "Is he [Louisa's husband] a white man or colored?"
A: "He's a mulatto. His mother is brown skin, and his father white, and that makes a mulatto, you know." (26)

Q: "Is she as white as you are?"
A: "Oh yes; a great deal whiter." (25)

"While I was living in Mobile, a gentleman there owned a colored man that was more white than I am." (8) [Years later in New York] "Then he told her [Louisa] he had been in New York ever since he ran away; that no one ever thought he was colored. . . . Mrs. P. wanted to know who he married. He laughed, he said, 'You know I would never marry any but a white girl.' " (41)

The last example above Mattison titled "A WHITE SLAVE LOVE ADVENTURE," and in this chapter Louisa recounted the story of a fellow slave who proposed marriage to her, but had to run for his life before they could be married.[8]

The first part of the story is found in Louisa's words in Chapter IV and the last part of the story is paraphrased by Mattison in Chapter XIX.[9] Although these two episodes were effective in demonstrating the outcome of one person's life, the issue of "race mixing" certainly must have raised one of white America's worst fears: miscegenation. Therefore, it is doubtful that this "WHITE SLAVE LOVE ADVENTURE" chapter could have strengthened Mattison's antislavery argument. However, it might have fulfilled a kind of voyeurism that one may experience when writing about someone else's life, or it could have been a somewhat covert means of expressing sexism and racism that frequently tainted the motives of even some of the most dedicated abolitionists like Mattison:

> The darkest and most prominent feature of the whole narrative is the **deep moral corruption** which it reveals in the families concerned, resulting from the institution of slavery. (50)

> Thus it is that we have near 30,000 mulattoes in the Slave States; to a great extent the contributions of slaveholders and their sons to the common stock of southern chattels. (51)

> Alas for those tell-tale mulatto, and quadroon, and octoroon faces! They stand out unimpeached, and still augmenting as God's testimony to the deep moral pollution of the Slave States. (51)

It is ironic that he used the term "darkest" to describe one of the many problems of slavery. Even at this early date in the culture contact between whites and Africans, negative connotations were attached to words and phrases which described sinful and/or wicked deeds. Moreover, according to Mattison, one of the obvious manifestation of moral corruption in the slave states was the appearance offspring produced from master/slave relationships. Whereas this information may have indeed elicited sympathy from some, it is not clear whether he was arguing against the rape and forced concubinage of black female slaves or was he simply enumerating the evils of miscegenation?

Most important, however, is Louisa's view of her own life. Would she have focused on skin color in her narrative had it not been for the interviewer's questions? What other aspects of slave life would she have talked about instead? We can only speculate. It is apparent that Louisa did not choose to pass for white as she could have done, and she never seemed to be mistaken or confused about her status as a slave or as a freed slave. So the attention to color may have been imposed by the interviewer.

Furthermore, Mattison's emphasis on physical features and lady-like behavior hint of a male framing of a female subject as object. He constantly searched for details that suggested something less than the most virtuous gentlemanly and ladylike conduct between master and female slave:

Q: "Well, how did he whip you?"
A: "With a cowhide."

Q: "Around your shoulders, or how?"
A: "That day he did."

Q: "How were you dressed—with thin clothes or how?"
A: "Oh, very thin; with low-neck'd dress. In the summer time we never wore but two pieces—only the one under, and the blue homespun over. It is a striped cloth they make in Georgia just for the colored people. . . . (12)

Q: "Were others stripped and examined?"
A: "Well, not quite naked, but just same." (16)

Even though one could argue that this was Mattison's technique for gathering information for his antislavery argument, the redundancy of certain types of questions (i.e., physical features, moral behavior, sensuality) insinuate a belaboring of ideas to the point of fixation resembling eroticism. So it is likely that various trends in the narrative are due primarily to Mattison's influence and/or world view rather than any purpose or design by Louisa.

Similarly, the interviewer/interviewee relationship is an interwoven complex of variables that cannot be easily disentangled. On the surface, Louisa and Mattison complemented each other in their respective needs and purposes. She needed to earn money to free her mother, and he lacked primary sources [e.g., slave narratives] to further his argument against slavery. She could neither read nor write, but he was literate and a member of the power structure (i.e., white male, minister). These prerequisites for collaboration, however, did not necessarily create an equitable interaction between the two. As Couser has observed, "the submission of minority autobiographers to the authority of their collaborators is a function of their limited power, literacy, and access to media of communication" (118). Thus, the asymmetries in their relationship created a situation that almost guaranteed the muting of the narrator's voice and point of view.

Finally, the situation or condition of elicitation was another crucial factor in determining the dominant voice in Louisa's narrative. Although Mattison does not indicate where the interview took place, it is clear that time is an important element for both interviewee and interviewer. The immediate past (i.e., slavery, mother's continued captivity) is an issue for Louisa, and the present (i.e., the institution of slavery) is a main concern of Mattison. So there is some tension manifest in the narrative because both collaborators are working against time:

> . . . we [Mattison & Louisa] are obliged to close it [the narrative] under a cloud of disappointment and gloom. The mother and brother are yet toiling in bondage in Texas. . . . (48)

At this point, Louisa had not raised enough money to free her mother from slavery, so it looked as if the narrative had not served one of the purposes for which it was created. Slavery was still alive and well despite the most vehement protests by abolitionists. Therefore, the critical time factor heavily influenced the selection of details and events included in the narrative as well as the strong abolitionist stance reflected in Mattison's comments. In this atmosphere of crisis, the focal aspect of Louisa's life was slavery. There were very few particulars about other aspects of Louisa's experiences such as life after emancipation, her children, and her subsequent reunion with her mother. Yet, a great deal of space including two extra chapters (XXVI and XXVII) were devoted to expounding Mattison's views of slavery. So this was not a life story as much as it was a political document.

Returning to one of the initial questions: Who is the authority of Louisa Piquet's narrative, we find a complicated, but reasonable answer. According to Mattison in Chapter I:

> The story of her wrongs and sorrows will be recited, to a large extent, in her own language, as taken from her lips by the writer, in Buffalo, N.Y., in May, 1860. (6)

"In her own language" suggests that Mattison adheres closely to Louisa's oral narrative style ("to a large extent") which indeed lends more credibility to the narrative. This approach would not only secure Louisa's voice as the narrator of her own text, but also give the appearance of authenticity since we are told early on that she has "plantation expression and pronunciation" (5). However, when one reads the actual text, there are relatively few southern black English features than would have been predicted from the editor's previous testimony: "She have long hair, but it was kind of wavy" (8). Therefore, even if one argues that some linguistic variation is natural, and that transcription of the narrator's words into conventional English was necessary for the purpose of readability, Louisa's conspicuous use of "standard" English, "Shall I go and get it?" (30) is suspicious.

For the preceding reasons and others, it would be easy to suggest that H. Mattison, the editor of the text, is the primary authority of Louisa's narrative. However, such an extensive generalization ignores the strength of authority that Louisa brought to her own life story. Although she was illiterate, she did not completely relinquish all power to the editor/interviewer.

> Q: "Where was that? In the street, or in a yard?"
> A: "At the market, where the block is?"

Q: "What block?"
A: "My! don't you know? The stand, where we have to get up?"
(17)

Q: "It seems like a dream, don't it?"
A: "No; it seems fresh in my memory when I think of it—no longer than yesterday. . . ." (18)

The last excerpt ("It seems like a dream, don't it?") is especially significant in that Mattison suggests that the slave experience, and particularly Louisa's separation from her mother on the auction block, was no more than a bad dream. Louisa does not hesitate to set the record straight. She vividly remembers the agony of parting with her mother:

Mother was right on her knees, with her hands up, prayin' to the Lord for me. She didn't care who saw her: the people all lookin' at her. I often thought her prayers followed me, for I could never forget her. (18)

So the narrator's voice is clearly identifiable. Louisa Piquet takes an active role in shaping the narrative text of her life.

Moreover, Louisa's experience with "ghostwriting" did not begin with her introduction to H. Mattison. Previously she had managed to get letters to and from her mother who also was illiterate. These precious documents were written and read by others:

Q: "What became of the first letter you had from your mother, while you were in New Orleans?"
A: "I never saw that. Mr. Williams only told me he got it, and what was in it. I only knew she was in Texas. I thought it was all Texas." (30)

"The letter is, of course, written by some white person, and is printed exactly as it is written." (32)

It was no small accomplishment to communicate through someone else's writing their deepest feelings and concerns, yet Louisa and her mother managed to stay in touch with one another through a medium that neither could comprehend without assistance.

Silences were also present in the narrative, and functioned both as a mechanism for protection as well as a means of control. For

Louisa, like many other ex-slaves, emancipation was bittersweet. Although she had gained her personal freedom, she left behind close family and friends still in bondage. So the whole of her story could not be told for fear that it would jeopardize others still enslaved:

> [There is a kink about mailing a letter, so as to have it reach a slave, that we never before dreamed of; but Mrs. P. does not wish it published for fear it will hinder her from getting her letters.] (30)

> Just here might come in a chapter more romantic and thrilling than any thing as yet narrated in this pamphlet, but, for reasons that we must not name, it must remain unprinted for the present. The time may come, and we hope soon will come, when it may be published without prejudice to any party or interest. (35)

> "Then he ordered me, in a sort of commanding way (I don't want to tell what he said), and told me to shut the door. . . ." (11)

> [Here Mrs. P. declines explaining further how he whipped her, though she had told our hostess where this was written; but it is too horrible and indelicate to be read in a civilized country.] (15)

The first two examples hint of maintaining silence in order to protect self and others, but the last two examples are different. They suggest that public standards of morality should not be breached. In other words, no matter how horrible a deed of cruelty to a slave, obscene language and sexually explicit descriptions usually were disguised by euphemism or completely omitted in a printed text. This form of censorship not only protected social mores, but also reinforced the silence imposed from within the plantation system.

Second, the collaborators go to great lengths to establish Mrs. Piquet's upright "moral character," otherwise, any trace of indecency would have weakened Mattison's overall antislavery stance and marred Louisa's reputation. Yet, what is most important is that Louisa was the one who made the decision not to reveal certain details. So while silences served important functions, they also permitted the narrator some amount of control. Thus, the answer to the question of authority is neither clear-cut nor definite. It appears that even though Mattison may have made the final decision about the published form of the narrative, Louisa was not a silent partner.

Does collaboration contaminate both the process and product

of autobiography? Not necessarily. The relationship between the collaborators (interviewer/interviewee) is the determining factor. The more control a narrator exercises in the elicitation process, the more likely the text will reflect her intent, style, and point of view. Ultimately, the written form of a collaborated life text may closely resemble an autobiographical text composed by a single author. At the very least, the presence of an "other" in creating a life text may result in a different type of personal narration, but the autobiographical nature of that life story is still intact.

ORAL NARRATION PROCESS AND PRODUCT: A SAMPLE NARRATIVE

Based on a text from my study of African American women's oral narratives, the next segment of the discussion focuses on the issue of editing. Specifically, how do editorial/interviewer decisions impact the autobiographical content of a life text?[10]

The written drafts of the texts that follow represent three distinct stages of transcription and editing. The first text/stage contains raw data of the interview. As many linguistic features as possible are initially transcribed. This includes actual utterances as well as conversation fillers (e.g., ah, uh), false starts, repetitions, and interruptions (. . .). Here the written text is checked and double-checked against the tape. The audio tape is the source/authority that determines which corrections and clarifications are made.

Notice that the question/answer format reflects the flow of the interview process and the relationship between collaborators. In this case (side #1 of tape), the initial phase of this interview suggests that the interviewee is dominant or in a controlling position at this point. She uses metalanguage ("Is that all you wanted to know about that?"), clarifications ("What else did you say?"), refusals ("I don't tell my age to anybody") and interruptions to regulate and enforce her role as narrator. Even though this particular narrative style may seem to be imposing at times, it is important that an interviewee participate in elicitation as fully as possible. Collaboration requires that both the interviewee and interviewer are not passive, but are dynamic and interactive. Similarly, the end product is not a static document, but according to Ron Grele, a "conversational narrative,"[11] an *exchange* between interlocutors. It is dialogue rather than monologue.

Text #1
(unedited)

Q: O.K. let's begin . . .

A: (interrupts) Then you'd better play it back so I can hear it now . . . I grew up in Townson, Georgia. Townson is a suburb of Alatoona. Nine miles from Alatoona. Is that all you wanted to know about that?

Q: Uh . . .

A: (interrupts) What else did you say?

Q: Uh, do you have any brothers and sisters?

A: I have three brothers, one of which is still living. And I have two sisters living. None live in Alatoona but in, a, in, Washington, North Carolina. My younger sister joined a new religion in Santa Monica, California. And she moved back to Washington where my other sister was. And she is more or less not as active as she was in California. My family has many children. We believe that nine is a sacred number. My mother had nine children. My youngest sister's the ninth one and ah my two sisters were born in the ninth month of the year. Which is September. My brother, my two brothers which are, one died nine years after my mother died. And the other one died nineteen years to one day after my mother died. So nine seemed to have followed my family. And we are just beginning to realize it. And I have been losing my hearing for seven years. And the one and the other one [year] and the seven make nine, therefore nine also.

Q: On my goodness.

A: So nine seems to follow us,

Q: What are you in the birth order of children in your family?

A: I'm the third child. But the first one that's lived, the two older ones are dead. And my, my um, as I said my older, my two sisters, were born in the ninth month which was September and my, my birthday is in November, which is the third month, and ah, one of all multiples of nine.

Q: Um, were your parents professional . . .

A: (interrupts) Well my daddy um, taught school, and, and um, but he really earned his living as a postman. My mother was just a housewife and a mother.

Q: And um, did you a, finish high school early?

A: Yes. I did. I finished high school very early. But at the time I went to high school, there were no public high schools in Townson and so I had to attend high school at the University. I went there for six years. To Alatoona University, and finished a normal education. And after that, my daddy sent me to the University of Ohio from which I received two degrees.

Q: Ah, how old were you when you finished high school?

A: I don't tell my age to anybody.

Q: Alright um, I'm simply asking that because a lot of the women that I've interviewed finished high school at fifteen.

A: Well, I don't know, I guess I finished high school before then, at, um, about fourte, um, no, no, not high school, um a let's see, no I didn't finish high school at that time. But Alatoona University around fourteen.

Q: Um, um, and ah . . .

A: (interrupts) What High School?

Q: No, what field did you get your degrees in?

A: Ah, Sociology, and Education

Q: And after you finished college did you go on to a career?

A: Yes. I taught school for quite a number of years in Alatoona, and I also did post-graduate work too, at Alatoona University, New York University, and the University of California.

Q: Oh, how wonderful. Ah, in your career, did you at any point feel, that, that something happened to you because you were a woman?

A: No, I realize that ah, there is almost two strikes against a, black women. First, the fact that they are minority in most places. As, bein' black kinda ah, of, obstacle, in the way. And also bein' a woman is an obstacle.

Q: Is there, is there anything in specific, that would happen because of those factors, and, and how did you react?

A: Well, um, not necessarily. I suppose um, living in the South where there was um, um segregation, it had to be hard, and that fact has black, bla, black people, men and women would have done much more, they would have gone further if they had, not had that obstac, obstacle.

Q: Um, um, um, a, when you first started teaching, what, what kind of student did you often run into?

A: Well, I, ah, ah, now, I started teaching first as an ele, elementary teacher. I did not like it at all. I really tried, to get out of the teaching profession. But then after I went back to school and, because I had finished a normal course, as I said at Alatoona University before my daddy sent me to the north. Because see, the, the, the students that I in whose classes I was in, at that time had gone on, and I wanted to go too, I mean he wanted to send me to ah, another university. Then when I came back from there I was given a high school. Put into high school. And I loved teaching. Then, because the students, were on a higher level, and we could, I mean, we could discuss, we could discuss things that would ah, man to man, you might say. And ah, it was very enjoyable, and there's two things that I a want to be remembered as, as I say from time to time and that is as a teacher and a writer. I like to write. I have written two books as I might have told you, when you were here before. I've written the mini-biography of my daddy. And then I've written my reflections on literature, and ah, I have um, a hard back copy of those two books. And I have ready for publication another one, and there are other books.

Q: Oh my. What inspired you to write?

A: Well I don't know, um they say that I kinda have a talent for writing. I have always, no, no, I was chairman of the English Department, when I retired, retired from teaching, and um, the, the, the um, I wanted to go into journalism. And so the editor of the paper said that if you've been teaching English you don't necessarily need to do that. And I know my um, dear friend Jean says you [me] are a writer. Now, ah she's finally convinced me, that I am a writer.

The second stage of the process moves away from the tape to focus on the written text. The conversational/interactive nature of the interview is extracted so that narrative features can be organized to resemble a written text.[12] Questions are removed, repetitions deleted, and uncertain or confusing utterances are clarified. At this point the interviewer's role becomes backgrounded and the interviewee's words become foregrounded. Eliminating the interviewer's words/questions changes the shape and the focus of the text. The relationship between questions and answers then becomes critical and ultimately determines how a text will be read. Can the interviewee's words stand alone and unsupported by the interview questions?

As text #2 indicates, the narrator's answers form a subtext separate from the interviewer's questions. This does not diminish the importance of questions, but suggests that their primary purpose is to create scaffolding for the main text. In other words, questions provide a bridge between the text and the narrator, and ultimately may become inconspicuous in an edited version of the transcript.

Also, as text #2 demonstrates, recounting one's life is not necessarily chronological. The narrator alternates between the past (e.g., childhood) and present (e.g., personal philosophy about African American women) mingling her insight (i.e., hindsight) with the facts and events of the past. This may be some small indication that although some narrators may tend to begin at the beginning of their lives (e.g., birth, childhood), this may be only an orientation or focusing strategy that does not necessarily lead to a linear unfolding of one's past. Many salient events, not in any particular order, may come in between the beginning of the autobiographical narrative and the end.

Most information in text #2 is understandable without the accompanying question, but at least three paragraphs appear to be out of context. The paragraphs which describe her personal philosophy ("There is almost two strikes against a black woman," and "Living in the south there was segregation") seem not connected to the main body of the text. Also, the last paragraph ("I don't know what inspired me to write.") seems to be an obvious response to a question. This means that these paragraphs require special attention when editing the text for the third and final draft, otherwise the likelihood of readers' misunderstanding is increased.

Text #2
(first edited draft)

I grew up in Townson, Georgia. Townson is a suburb of Alatoona. Nine miles from Alatoona.

I have three brothers, one of whom is still living. And I have two sisters living. None live in Alatoona, but in Washington, North Carolina. My younger sister joined a new religion in Santa Monica, California. And she moved back to Washington where my other sister was. And she is more or less not as active as she was in California. My family has many children. We believe that nine is a sacred number. My mother had nine children. My youngest sister's the ninth one and my two sisters were born in the ninth month of the year. Which is September. Of my two brothers, one died nine years after my mother died. And the other one died nineteen years to one day after mother died. So nine seemed to have followed my family. And we are just beginning to realize it. And I have been losing my hearing for seven years. And the one year and the other one and the seven make nine.

I'm the third child, but the first one that's lived. The two older ones are dead.

My daddy taught school, but he really earned his living as a postman. My mother was just a housewife and a mother.

I finished school very early. But at the time I went to high school, there were no public high schools in Townson and so I had to attend high school at the University. I went there for six years. To Alatoona University, and finished a normal education. And after that, my daddy sent me to the University of Ohio from which I received two degrees.

I finished Alatoona University around age fourteen.

I have degrees in Sociology and Education.

After I finished college I taught at school for quite a number of years in Alatoona, and I also did post-graduate work too, at Alatoona University, New York University, and the University of California.

There is almost two strikes against a black woman. First, the fact that they are minority in most places. Being black is a kind of obstacle. And also being a woman is an obstacle.

Living in the south there was segregation. It had to be hard for black people. Black men and women could have done much more, they would have gone further if they had not that obstacle [racism].

I started teaching first as an elementary teacher. I did not like it at all. I really tried to get out of the teaching profession. But then after that I went back to school, and because I had finished a normal course, as I said at Alatoona University before my daddy sent me to the north. Because the students in whose classes I was in, at that time, had gone on, and I wanted to go too. I mean he [daddy] wanted to send me to another university. Then when I came back from there I was given a high school. And then I loved teaching because the students were on a higher level, and we could discuss things man-to-man, you might say. And it was very enjoyable. And there's always two things that I want to be remembered as, as I say from time to time, and that is as a teacher and a writer. I like to write. I have written two books as I might have told you. I've written the mini-biography of my daddy. And then I've written my reflections on literature, and I have a hard back copy of those two books. And I have ready for publication another one, and there are other books.

I don't know what inspired me to write. They say that I kind of have a talent for writing. I was chairman of the English Department. When I retired from teaching, I wanted to go into journalism. And so the editor of the paper said that if you've been teaching English you don't necessarily need to do that. And I know my dear friend Ruth tells me that I am a writer. Now she's finally convinced me that I am a writer.

The third and final draft of the transcript is reorganized to form a more coherent, story like whole. Some chronological placement is observed, but not rigidly so. The main concern is to arrange information to effectively describe various episodes in the narrator's life as clearly as possible.

Notice that paragraph #1 combines information from some of the briefer paragraphs. More details from the main text are added to paragraph #2. This gives a more vivid picture of the narrator's description of her childhood home. Her philosophical statements were placed in paragraphs #9 and #11. In paragraph #9, the statement ("See as a black woman you have two obstacles to overcome . . .") provides an effective philosophical conclusion for a real-life event/problem. In paragraph #11, the statement ("I realize that there are almost two strikes against black women") functions as a transition for the next paragraph. So placement of philosophical statements that may not have specific contexts once the questions are removed can be strategically useful in maintaining the narrator's intent and meaning.

Again, the final draft of the transcript reflects reorganization of the data into a smoothly flowing narrative with some chronological sequencing. Except for substituting fictional names for real ones, the narrator's language is not modified. Her speech style is closely maintained and features of dialect are preserved as much as possible.

Text #3
(fully edited)

1   I grew up in a small suburb nine miles from a large southern city. I have three brothers, one of which is still living. And I have two sisters living. None in my hometown but in a neighboring southern state. My mother had nine children. I'm the third child, but the first one that lived. The two born before me died. My youngest sister's the ninth one and my two sisters were born in the ninth month of the year which is September. Of my two brothers, one died nine years after my mother died. And the other one died nineteen years to one day after my mother died. So nine seemed to have followed my family. And we are just beginning to realize it.

2   My daddy taught school, but he really earned his living as a postman. My mother was just a housewife and a mother. My daddy built the house we had. You see when we first moved to town there was a man here who complained so much about the water falling off of our house over on his house. So then my daddy decided to go around to the other street and get two lots together. And he put the house on the end of one side near the street you know. And then on the other side of the lot we had garages. And at one time it was just like an undertaker's shop almost, 'cause so many cars were there. I had a car, my sister had a car, my brother had a car, numbers of cars had been there. At the end of that lot he built a house, a little house for his mother and father.

3   I remember my grandmother, my mother's mother, died at our own house. I am named after my grandmother, you see. Now I know my mother's mother too. I went to see her once. But she was so old and I was so young that I wanted to leave immediately. I thought she was gonna die before I left. So that's the little thing I remember about her from childhood. I remember my grandaddy. We used to go every summer down to his house. He was a tenant farmer. He would give us some of everything, you know: figs, peaches, watermelons and all those kinds of things. My grandmother used to take me there, you know. She used to like colors. She liked red shoes. Now I'm doing the same thing that my grandmother did. So I think things go round in a circle and repeat themselves and all.

We would sit on our big porch. We had a big porch, round porch, you know, and daddy would sit out there sometimes. He was a wonderful man. And so he would say, "Now, I want one of my boys

135

. . . ," He's always talking about the boys. "I want one of my boys to be a lawyer. I want one to be a doctor, one a business man," you see there's just three of them. And I would say, "Well, what do you want me to be?" And he said, "Oh you'll just grow-up and

4 be a good wife, and mother," as my mother had been. "And you have children, and do that sort of thing." But he would never say what he wanted us girls to be. But at the same time he educated all of his daughters. He had a very, very deep respect for woman-hood. When I left home he went with me to present me to the community, you know. When my sister left to teach school he went with her there. When my younger sister went to a college out of state, he went up there with her, too.

I finished high school very early. But at the time I went to high school, there were no public high schools in town and so I had to attend a local university for high school. I went there for six years. To

5 the university, and finished a normal course of study at Alatoona University and after that, my daddy sent me to a university in the north from which I received two degrees, one in Sociology and one in Education.

College was enjoyable. Because when I was registering at the university there was a girl registering who was from here. And we had

6 become good friends throughout the whole five years that I was there. This college town was almost like my second home. And whenever I would go there if I was anywhere else, they would come and get me and take me to their house. So we were very, very good friends.

After college I taught at a high school for quite a number of years

7 in my hometown, and I also did post-graduate work too, at the local university, and at a northern university, and a university out west.

I just kinda gradually went into teaching. Because when I started teaching I said, "Oh I'll teach two years and then I'll get married." But you see my daddy had several children, and so I wanted to get out of school. So that's why I took a normal course which is two years above high school. See, and then later on, I went back to the university. So I just kinda slipped into teaching. Because daddy just thought I'd just become a wife and mother, just like my mother, you know. But I was

8 always independent and aggressive. I was never like my mother, I was never a homebody. You could eat off of her floor because she kept an immaculate house. But see, I'm not a housekeeper. As you see this table all torn up and all now. I'm an outdoor person you see. Generally, I'm not like my mother. But my daddy, always taught me to be independent. He always said, "Now listen, I want you to be indepen-

dent whether you marry or not." I think there is a point at which you have to become not too independent and all. But I think there is a point at which all of us might stop.

See there were so many graduates every year. And the only thing they could do was to teach. So consequently when women got married, the black ministers here went to the Board of Education in order to open up jobs for the male graduates. And they kept saying that when a black teacher married she would have to give up her job because there were so many others [males] and there was nothing else for others to do. Because I know when I married they didn't even allow the pension to be received by the widow, see. You see it was really discrimination even in the salaries and all. Here's one example of that. I know a man that was teaching and who was not the chairman of the department. I was chairman of the department. And it so happened, that I saw his check. And I know that advance in salary should have been mine instead of his. And so what I did, I called the Board of Education. "Mr. Black," I say, "Now I'm the chairman of the department." But he let that man keep that same salary he had. And just put me on the same salary he was. So that shows discrimination between men and women. See as a black woman you have two obstacles to overcome: being black and then being a woman too. Because I don't think that's fully disappeared yet. I think that that's still in existence now.

9

I started teaching first as an elementary teacher. I did not like it at all. I really wanted to get out of the teaching profession. But then after I went back to school and because I had finished a normal course, as I said at the local university before my daddy sent me up north. Because see the students in whose classes I was in, at that time, had gone on, and I wanted to go too. I mean he [daddy] wanted to send me to another university. Then when I came back from there I was given a high school. Put into high school. And I loved teaching then because the students, were on a higher level, and we could we could discuss things man to man, you might say. And it was very enjoyable, and there's two things that I want to be remembered as, as I say from time to time, and that is as a teacher and a writer. I like to write. I have written two books as I might have told you. I've written a mini-biography of my daddy. And then I've written my reflections on the humanities and I have a hard copy of these two books. And I have ready for publication, three other books.

10

I realize that there is almost two strikes against black women. First, the fact that they are a minority in all places. And being black is a

11   kind of obstacle, in a way. And also being a woman is an obstacle. I suppose living in the south where there was segregation highlighted, the fact that people, men and women, would have had much more if race had not been an obstacle.

Ideally the editing process should be a joint endeavor like the interview process. It is common practice, for example, to have a narrator review and correct transcripts of the actual interview (and even this changes the shape of the original text). However, when that is not possible, the editor/interviewer must make decisions that best reflect the overall purpose of the interview as well as the narrator's point of view. Undoubtedly, it will be neither easy nor without some flaws.

On a structural level, the text as a whole consists of at least three subtexts: (1) the interviewer's questions, (2) the interviewee's answers, and (3) the complete text (questions and answers). Each subtext may exhibit slightly different aspects of the whole. Division of a narrative into separate components may not be always desirable, but it can facilitate editing and analysis by reducing the amount and type of information present in a single subtext. On the other hand, editorial decisions, particularly if made without input from the narrator/ interviewer, can be more reliable if based on the whole text. So the extent to which editing influences the autobiographical content of a narrative depends on a variety of factors including harmony of purpose between interviewer and interviewee, and selection of textual features (e.g., $-/+$ questions, answers containing personal philosophy). At this point, the most important question for the editor to ask and answer is—Does this text reflect the narrator's view of herself? The question may be different if the purpose of the interview is something other than oral autobiography.

INTERVIEWER/INTERVIEWEE RELATIONSHIP

The interviewer/interviewee relationship is usually described according to an antagonistic model of narrative interaction. The adversarial perspective inherent in this model defines interviewer and interviewee as binary opposites and/or as a dichotomy of potentially conflicting intentions and viewpoints. The person/interviewee who lived the life and the person/interviewer who elicits the life are expected to naturally assume contending (win/lose) roles, and vie for speaking turns as well as control of the interaction. Okihiro observes that "the interview involves at least two different world views . . . Are they parallel, or do they clash and what are the implications if they do not correspond?" (202).

Bicultural collaborations are illustrations of the "clash" of world views. As Couser has remarked, these kind of collaborations are seldom ones of "true equality or reciprocity" (26). He explains that "minority narrators may lack the clout to discredit the results" (12), and submission to a collaborator/editor/interviewer by a minority narrator may be the result of her/his "limited power, literacy, and access to media communication" (118). So bicultural collaboration, while it is very valuable, naturally poses problems in the interview situation. If the interviewer is from a dominate group (e.g., white Americans, males) and the interviewee is a member of a minority or oppressed group (e.g. African Americans, women), then the asymmetrical relationship that obtains is likely to create an advantage (i.e., position of power and control) for the interviewer no matter how sympathetic or sensitive she/he may be.

On the other hand, what happens if the interviewee and interviewer share the same cultural background, social status, and world view? Will the implied lack of "objectivity" contaminate a narrative beyond recognition? In reality there are interviewer/interviewee relationships which bear no resemblance to the antagonistic model (e.g., cooperative model).[13] When the interlocutors are from the same group, then the process and the product of oral narration assume a very different appearance. I had many of the same social characteristics as my interviewees. I was an educated, African American female as were the women in my study. Therefore, the most salient variable was age. So I approached the interview situation as a participant/observer. In other words, I was an insider, someone who shared many commonalities with the interviewees, but nonetheless, someone who did not have the experience of long life. I neither pretended nor felt that I was the so-called expert. I arrived at the interview situation to be informed by women who were simultaneously my superiors *and* colleagues.

COOPERATION/COLLABORATION

Both the narrator and I assumed a cooperative stance. Even though we followed a question/answer format, narrators were free to shape the interaction as they saw fit. As is illustrated in the following example, narrators could introduce additional and sometimes seemingly extraneous topics into their stories as they felt was necessary:

Q: And the grandparents on your fathers side?
A: My grandfather was a coachman for a very wealthy family in the north. My grandmother did not work. And there is a very interesting story about them too. You want me to relate that?

Q: Yes.
A: Well, the story as my paternal aunt told me . . .

Q: That was a wonderful story.
A: I thought I would like to write about it someday.

Q: Yes, please do. What was her maiden name? (36:1, p. 1)

In this instance, the narrator's request for permission to tell an additional anecdote about her grandfather indicates her awareness of the task at hand and her willingness to cooperate. She also is careful to document the source of the story ("my maternal aunt told me") which allows the listener to understand the narrator's role in the telling process (i.e., this was not a first-hand account witnessed by the narrator herself). Furthermore, this is only one of many instances where narrators have demonstrated that family history was kept alive by an oral history cycle—stories were handed down from generation to generation by elders in the family.

Narrators also requested permission or prepared to tell additional anecdotes by hinting that there was more to talk about.

A: So we [my sister and I] said that's [teaching in the south] going to be our basic concern and . . . at some point if you'll ask me what one of the joys I have been able to achieve in going to the south to teach, I'll be glad to tell you about it.

Q: Yes, I will want to hear that. Would you talk about Ms. Brown? When did you first meet her?
A: Well, you might as well have asked me what was the greatest joy of my teaching experience in the south. First, I have to start telling you how I went south. . . . (3:2, p. 2)

Here the narrator demonstrates a keen sense of the narrative process by suggesting that she had more to tell, but that this may not be the appropriate time to tell it ("at some point if you'll ask me"). Also, she appears to have a chronology in mind ("First, I have to start telling you . . .") that may indeed make the story more understandable or relevant. From another perspective, it may appear that the narrator wanted to tell this particular story all along, and in a very subtle, but persistent manner, managed to insert the story without disrupting the interview.

Repairs or requests for clarification would also reinforce the cooperative efforts of the interviewer and narrator. In example #3, the narrator explains her father's personality in terms of his relationship with other family members, but she does not initially make clear the identity of those family members:

Q: Tell me about his personality.
A: My father?

Q: Yeah.
A: Oh, he was, well, I guess I would say now as I think about him, he was a soft and easy going gentleman because he never verbally voiced any disapproval of my grandmother, but I'm sure that he didn't quite think that, he didn't think that his little granddaughter need to be spanked all the time.

Q: You mean his daughter?
A: Yeah. That's what I mean. Course, I know I should've been spanked, probably more. But the other thing I learned very early, no matter what you did or what you didn't do, you better tell the truth about it. Because I never could figure out how grandma would know when you didn't tell the truth. She always knew, so you got a spankin' for what you did and then you got a spankin' because you had told a fib. (62:1, p. 7)

The narrator prefaces her description of her father by marking her view as retrospective ("now as I think about him"). This may be some indication that her present opinion may differ, in some degree, from a previous opinion of her father. My request for clarification ("You mean his daughter?") not only elicits an explanation, but also prompts the narrator to elaborate on the issue of punishment and learning.

Cooperation can also be established or reinforced by utilizing nonverbal cues. During this particular interview, the narrator at times became very pensive (e.g., facial expression and long pauses between words), and once I recognized this, I asked that she verbalize her thoughts:

> A: But I remember my aunt saying to me when I got ready to go to college. She persuaded me to go into teaching . . . and so I believed her and I did it and she was right you know, cause that was the size of what you [a black woman] could do in those days.
>
> Q: You're thinking of something.
> A: Yes, yes.
>
> Q: Go ahead, go ahead.
> A: I got tickled as I thought about Mary McCleod Bethune, you may know this story. . . . (1:1, p. 5)

The narrator tells a delightful story about Mary McCloud Bethune, but, more importantly, this digression motivated her to entertain connections between the various elements of her past. As is seen in this next example from the same narrator, she naturally makes associations between many strands of her life that may appear to be unrelated:

> Q: Were your parents college graduates?
> A: Yes, now my mother was, but my aunt, oh that's another story, but I won't tell, it has nothing to do with your job . . . my aunt did not graduate [from Howard University]. That's why I was laughing because there was another story, because she was very bright, very brilliant, but she didn't graduate.
>
> Q: You can tell me the other one [story] too.
> A: Well, alright. . . . (1:1, p. 6)

The narrator is trying to resist her tendency to associate dissimilar elements of her life story ("but I won't tell). However, as her previous performance has indicated, these asides are many times the heart/core of her narration. In this instance, the story of her aunt's missed opportunity to graduate from college was a prime example of failure to adhere to the family's beliefs about education and personal integrity. These beliefs could not have been fully uncovered without this particular story.

Exchanges between narrator and interviewer can guide the narrative in directions unexpected by either party. Rigid adherence to a script or list of predetermined questions frequently proves to be unproductive:

A: The first organizational plan for the administration of the office . . . was done by a black woman—yours truly!

Q: What year?
A: 1976 or '78. I can get the dates. I've got a lot of old [past] things I've done.

Q: Will you tell me about some of those things?
A: O.K.

Q: Give me . . . tell me one gem when you think of your trip to Africa.
A: You want a humorous one or you want . . . [a serious one]?

Q: Give me a humorous story.
A: We were at Nairobi and we went on our way to Kampala and. . . . (34:3, p. 4)

The interviewer's request for specifics ("What year?" "Will you tell me . . .?") together with the narrator's willingness to explore topics previously overlooked ("I've got a lot of old things. . . ." "You want a humorous one . . .") reveals another dimension of the narrator's life (e.g., foreign travel) equally important, but heretofore understated. The narrator's travels in Africa were extraordinary and revealed an aspect of her personality that was not apparent beforehand.

Another important variable in establishing cooperation was that of group membership. Many of the women acknowledged that they were interacting with a member of their own social group by marking their language overtly:

> ". . . as a black woman, I think that you might have . . .".
>
> ". . . was done by a black woman—yours truly!"
>
> "cause that was the size of what you [a black woman] . . .".

Although there is no way to account for covert cues of such rapport, most of the women felt very comfortable talking to someone who shared their same background and experiences. On many occasions, it was important to establish rapport and isolate the "other" ("I think white folks always ask me that question").

In the interviews, cooperation was facilitated by a variety of factors. The interviewee's sense of the narrative task allowed for a collaborative shaping of the text and effective dissemination of details. Narrators' comments such as:

> "You want me to relate that?"
>
> "You want a humorous one . . .?"
>
> "If you'll ask me . . .".
>
> "But I won't tell. It has nothing to do with your job."

demonstrated their awareness of the constraints of the interview situation as well as their desire to share information not requested by the interviewer, but central to understanding the many facets of their lives. Second, the feedback that I offered from the interviewer's position was intended to encourage a narrator to follow her own instincts:

> "That was a wonderful story."
>
> "Yes, please do.
>
> "Yes, I will want to hear that."
>
> "You're thinking of something."
>
> "You can tell me the other one too."

The reciprocity of the interaction not only built a strong narrative, but also provided many women with a unique opportunity to speak candidly about their lives. Gluck and Patai have concluded that "It is also true that the telling of the story can be empowering, validating the importance of the speaker's life experience" (2).

REPAIR AND WHEN THE ANSWER IS NO (OR NO≠NO)

In spite of our efforts to cooperate, there were some instances of a breakdown in communication and the need for repair. When my questions lacked clarity, for example, then the momentum of the interview slowed until an understanding could be reached by both parties:

> Q: Is that book available anywhere or is it out of print?
> A: No. It's been registered, oh it's been long out of print. A couple of relatives have copies of it. I have a copy of it. And um, so it's got a lot in it that would be very boring such as the program that was at the Baptist church and who sang what songs. A lot of things in it that are rather mundane, you know, tedious in that sense.
>
> Q: And so there are no copies in the public domain as far as you know?
> A: Well, in the public domain. You mean in the library?
>
> Q: Yes.
> A: Oh, I think in the Library of Congress. . . .
>
> Q: Yes, other than that.
> A: Not that I know of. Good if there were. (57:1, p. 8)

Notice that I seem to be unaware that the question has been answered and ask three times about the availability of the book: "Is that book available . . .?," "And so there are no copies . . .?," "Yes, other than that." The first time the narrator answers and elaborates on some particulars of the book. The second time the narrator asks a question ("You mean in the library?") and gives a different answer ("Oh, I think in the Library of Congress. . . ."). The third time the narrator answers no ("Not that I know of.") With each subsequent response, the narrator's answers become shorter and shorter. Her question to me clarifies the confusion only partially and finally we drop the topic unsure of the initial question and whether or not it had been answered.

At other times the question was clear, but the narrator did not have the knowledge and/or experience required to answer the question. As sometimes happens, I repeated the question twice in the hope that the narrator would elaborate:

Q: What did some black women of your generation do if they did not get an education?
A: They did domestic work . . . I think that's about all. What else is there to do for people if they don't have an education?

Q: I mean, what about your contemporaries?
A: Well, I think my contemporaries did whatever they could do. What anybody is doing now . . . So um, I can't think of what they might have been doing. What might they have been doing?

Q: I don't know. I was just asking. If you had. . . .
A: Well, I don't know, and I can't think right off. I can't remember because, you see maybe I was associating mostly with people who were in the same category that I was. And I didn't observe too much of what others were doing. (26:1, p. 13)

The narrator not only does not expand her answer, but perhaps senses that I am searching for something specific, so she asks me the question ("What might they have been doing?). My response is defensive and does not explain my question, so the narrator interrupts me and finally reveals the reason that she does not know more than she has said.

In another instance, the narrator did not understand the relevance of my question:

Q: How did you know that you were going to college? And at what point did you know that?
A: It was just understood. My father went to college. My mother graduated from high school. You know, and that sort of thing. It wasn't a discussion or debate. It was a natural evolution, let's put it that way. Everybody always asks me that. I don't know why that's so strange.

Q: Well I have a theory that I'll tell you about after we finish. That's why I asked.

A: Yeah. I think white folks always ask me that question. (57:2, p. 8)

She associates my question with those asked by outsiders ("white folks") which would imply *my* lack of knowledge about my own people. However, rather than an issue of race, I think that the misunderstanding evoked by the question was a function of age and point of view. From her position, the narrator perceived her situation (going on to college after graduation from high school) as "normal," but I was trying to establish that it was unusual for most women, especially African Americans, to attend college during that time period. Nevertheless, I felt that it was important for her point of view to prevail. There was at least one other instance where age explicitly was an issue:

A: There was this wealthy man . . . I can't think of the name . . . You wouldn't know the name. See that's before your time. See how quickly history passes.

Q: Yeah.
A: And things pass into history so if you don't take . . . the opportunity when it comes, you miss it . . . (4:3, p. 6)

In this example, the narrator is trying to supplement her memory, but when she finds me no help, attributes it to age. This sparks a digression which turns out to be a brief, but insightful account of the narrator's view of the past.

These repairs indicate that power and control in an interview is dynamic. It shifts back and forth between the interviewer and interviewee depending on several variables including the topic, specificity of questions, and relevance of the topic to the interviewee's experiences.

From a different perspective, when a narrator answers no, a different kind of communication breakdown occurs. No may have a variety of meanings from "I don't want to talk about that" to "I don't remember" to "I really do not know that information." In many instances, no is an initial response while the narrator continues to think and talk. Ultimately, the she may provide affirmative information to a question she initially responded to with *no*. One narrator claimed that she did not know much about her grandfather:

Q: What caused him [grandfather] to pursue that [pharmacy] as a career?
A: Cause he had an inner motivation, I'm sure.

Q: Did he have a pharmacy as far as you knew?
A: No. He was, he did have a drug store at some point. He had a little store down south. . . . [brief story about whites burning down his store]. So anyway, when I graduated from college down south my father said he [grandfather] was not coming to the graduation because he was not going to go to the deep south. And I, upon asking why, then he explained the story about um, the ah, issue of, of uh, the drug store. (57:1, p. 10)

She speculates about her grandfather's intention and reveals that she did learn something about her grandfather from her father. It may be that the narrator only counts first-hand knowledge as valid here rather than knowledge passed down by someone else. In a continuation of that same topic she reveals more:

Q: Did your grandfather continue to practice pharmacy a after he left the south?
A: I don't know any of the details of what he did at that point there [up north]. But by the time I remember seeing him in the 1930s, see I was born in '24 so that was many years before that he was practicing. I don't know what he did at that point. But I remember when I came to visit the farm when I was six, seven, maybe nine years old he was quite old and he was, I think, remember, had a job as a night watchman, or something. Some very sedentary, low-key job that was not related to his profession. But at that time he was quite old. (57:1, p. 11)

Again, even though the narrator explains why she did not know her grandfather very well, she does provide some important information: (a) her grandfather lived to old age and (2) he worked when he was very old at an job that had nothing to do with his training as a pharmacist. This menial job for a college-educated man may be a function of age and/or race, but, nonetheless, it was an important detail to be uncovered.

Another narrator also speculates about the details of her grandparent's lives, and the few facts that she does have about them are extremely important:

Q: Did she [grandmother] work outside of the home?
A: No. Her customers would come to her.

Q: And do you know how far she went in school?
A: I have no idea how far she went in school, but I'm sure it wasn't very far.

Q: And you don't remember her husband, your grandfather?
A: I don't remember him. I can remember what my dad talked about. He [grandfather] had been a cobbler and a carpenter. I mean, he was a skilled tradesman. And then he was a turn-key of the jail in a southern city. (58:1, p. 14)

The knowledge is second hand, but her ability to recall her father's stories about her grandfather fills in the missing information. This is another instance of the cycle of oral history being maintained in an African American family.

Thus, *no* sometimes is not negative. It may be a filler or place holder while the narrator searches her memory. This is not to suggest that we dismiss or always doubt narrators' negative responses, but that we understand the importance of reading between the lines.

UNASKED QUESTIONS

Sometimes I would ask narrators to switch places with me and ask themselves questions that I did not ask. The results were always enlightening:

Q: Is there a question that I didn't ask, but should have?
A: Oh, that's a good one. Uh, did you ever try to become a president someplace else, or another position? And I have two bad experiences which are pure sexism and racism. (57:3, pp. 16–17)

In this instance, the narrator had never spoken overtly about sexism or racism. Even though she was a professional in a field rarely populated by African Americans or women, she did not relate any of her experiences to discrimination due to race and/or sex. Yet, when asked about the question I did not ask, she gave a very lengthy and emotional description of her confrontation with racism and sexism in higher education.

In the next example, the narrator almost misunderstands my question. However, after a request for clarification, she provides a very thoughtful answer:

Q: If you were doing this interview, what question would you ask that I didn't?
A: What would you have asked me?

Q: Yeah. What would you ask you that I didn't ask you?
A: Oh, I don't know. Um, because you were very interested to find out how I grew into the groove where I am. And I think that was, that's a critical question. And I think that um, as a black woman, I think that you might've asked me um, how I could possibly steer other women, you know, that's other young black women. What does the future truly hold, you know, how can we help them. That wouldn't change my life at all, or then again it might. But, I do think that these are some of the things that we [African American women] really have to consider. What do we now have to do. . . . (58:3, pp. 11–12)

The role reversal here leads the narrator to express her concern for future generations of African American women. She doubts the impact of the question on her own life, but feels that it represents an issue that must be considered by all African American women.

METACOMMUNICATION

Metacommunication refers to self-monitoring processes that most of us engage in during social/linguistic interactions. According to Stubbs, metacommunication is the "verbal monitoring of the speech situation" (48) and includes such activities as checks on whether a speaker is being understood by the listener (e.g., "Can you hear me?"), messages about channels of communication and if they are operative ("Do you want me to phone him?" "Do you want me to repeat that to her?" "Do you want me to speak louder?"), cues for taking turns speaking, checks on whether or not a message has been received and understood ("Do I make myself clear?"), and management of who speaks and how much (48). As can be predicted, in an interview situation, metacommunication is the support for information exchanged between the interviewer and interviewee. In my study, there are many examples of metacommunicative strategies (see discussion of cooperation): "You want me to relate that?" "Is there a question that I didn't ask, but should have?" These strategies are natural, automatic. However, when examined in the context of an interview situation, metacommunication takes on additional meanings.

In the following excerpt, as the narrator unfolds remote memories, she also describes her thought processes:

Q: Now you said earlier that your grandmother had raised you with this finger.
A: Uh-huh.

Q: What does that mean?
A: When she said this that and the other, then that finger came down and I guess to her it meant, "You heard me, I said it." I don't know why she did it that way. And I hadn't always remembered that. It's only fairly recently when I think back about things that happened when I was growing up at home that I realize she would say whatever she was saying and that [finger gesture]. And I guess that finger went up and down when you [a child] were talking when you shouldn't be. Because you see, you weren't to interrupt adults . . . Now I never thought of that until I was talking to you here today. Isn't that a riot? (58:1, p. 10)

The language of her description ("And I hadn't always remembered that. It's only fairly recently when I think back . . ."), indicates that the narrator is thinking about the way she thinks or remembers. This process which is a part of metacommunication may be referred to as metacognition. That is, monitoring one's own thoughts. Later, she specifically points out that these memories represent a new line of thinking: "Now I never thought of that until I was talking to you here today." Thus, we find in the interview situation oral narration as discovery ("Isn't that a riot?). Interviewees/narrators pay attention to their thought processes and by so doing identify new thoughts/

ideas, a different way of perceiving an old idea/memory, or uncover a distant memory not usually accessed.

Language can function in the same manner. Speakers often use language to talk about language or metalinguistic strategies. ("How could you talk to me like that?" Stubbs refers to this as "language which refers to itself" (49). The following speaker frequently refers to her inability to use words to describe the events of her dream:

> A: One other thing I want to tell you . . . I don't know how to put this in words um . . . I was asleep and I saw something happen . . . I saw lights, diamonds of lights, tears and tears . . . I never liked diamonds, you know, because my mother told me that they [whites] would kill Africans when they were mining them [diamonds] and so I never wanted anything to do with diamonds. But now [after the dream] I love diamonds. And that's the closest I can put it in words . . . I saw these diamonds and then I was somewhere where it was void of light and I saw this dazzle . . . I don't know but it was a glorious dream . . . I don't know what that means. I can't interpret it for anyone, but it's something, that's all I know . . . It [the dream] was real, but don't ask me. I can't explain it . . . I don't think I've ever told anyone . . . I don't know why I'm telling it even now, because . . . but for some reason I feel like talking about it today.
>
> Q: That makes me happy.
> A: Yes. I don't know, maybe there's something you have, that you're supposed to do with your life. . . . (29:1, p. 14)

Caught up in the recollection of a mystical experience, the narrator repeats several times her inability to verbalize the events of her dream, "And that's the closest I can put it in words. . . ." Here the discovery is the significance of her dream and the narrator's admission of her silence ("I don't think I've ever told anyone. . ."). In fact, she questions her own motivation (" . . . but for some reason I feel like talking about it today.") for discussing her dream and extends the mystical import to the interviewer (" . . . maybe there's something you have, that you're supposed to do with your life."). Although this kind of insight may not be common, metacommunication often is the vehicle through which such experiences are explained.

Whereas the interviewer/interviewee relationship is complex, it is the key to understanding authority in an oral text. As previous discussion has shown, authority is not static, but rather a malleable feature that shifts and changes according to the requirements of the interview situation. The narrator/interviewee is the authority and expert of her own life, and together with the interviewer, she creates a narrative text. Furthermore, similarities in social status and culture may be an asset rather than a liability because both collaborators share overlapping concerns, experiences, and purposes. Ignoring the pretense of objectivity, we then may find that subjectivity expressed through common experiences and world view actually enhances the richness of an oral narrative text. Released from the obligation to explain to an outsider, a narrator is free to describe events in detail and without the risk of uninformed judgment or inquiry.

Is the question of authority and control generalizable to all collaborative texts? Many scholars support the idea that autobiographical texts must be created by a single individual acting alone and in isolation of her/his environment. However, women and most people of color tend to view themselves connected to the whole/group, so the power of authority/control abides in the community and not the individual. According to Clifford and Marcus, "the principle of dialogical textual production . . . locates cultural interpretations in many sorts of reciprocal contexts, and it obliges writers to find diverse ways of rendering negotiated realities as multisubjective, power-laden, and incongruent" (15). Thus, there may be several voices and realities embedded in the narrative of a community-identified author/narrator. So the Eurocentric model that has dominated American autobiography cannot be applied cross-culturally. It is neither appropriate nor useful.

Returning to the original and related question, oral narrative as autobiography presents an interesting dilemma. There are no simple or easy answers, but the autobiographical nature of collaborated life texts cannot be dismissed. Whether or not they should be counted as "official" autobiographies and accepted into the canon may be irrelevant because their autobiographical content stands, regardless of whether it is "acknowledged" by scholars and/or critics. Also, the quest for authority may shed some light on the issue, but it eventually may lead to a dead end if we are always seeking a single author and an equally singular reality. Therefore, for these and other reasons previously discussed, it is fair and logical to argue for an expanded vision of autobiography that includes *variations*, especially oral forms, and recognizes cultural differences. Smith and Watson argue that:

> There are other modes of life story telling, both oral and written, to be recognized, other genealogies of life story telling to be chronicled, other explorations of traditions, current and past, to be factored into the making and unmaking of autobiographical subjects in a global environment (xviii).

Expanding the parameters of autobiography does not weaken the genre, but strengthens it by creating a larger and more representative pool of features. Autobiography is not an inert literary or historical mode, but a fluid pattern of discourse that assumes a specific configuration of features according to the culture and world view which shapes it.

NAPPY AT THE ROOT: SPEAKING/WRITING A WOMAN'S LIFE

Adrienne Rich's 1982 essay, "Split at the Root"[1] was an exploration and questioning of personal identity as well as a vivid description of the duality or "split" one feels when attempting to belong to two different and sometimes opposing cultures. In the essay, Rich also identified a process of telling that was simultaneously enlightening and intimidating. She admitted that this piece of writing was a necessary, but "dangerous act" (100) because in order to define her Jewishness she had to claim her father and by so doing "break his silence" (100) about their Jewish lineage. The telling that Rich described was not a neutral process of simply putting her thoughts on paper, but an emotionally charged exercise of writing her life within the paradox of exposé and restrained disclosure. Adrienne Rich was discovering what African American women had known since they began writing autobiography during slavery—making one's private life public is not without cost. Speaking/writing their own lives was a risky undertaking embedded in the malevolence of an historically prejudiced society that penalized them at least twice for being both African Americans *and* women. So for these women the act of telling is not only "split," but also "nappy." Like permed or color-treated hair, the texture of their narratives is often different above and below the surface. Above the surface, there is acceptable public appearance (e.g., straight hair/"standard language"), but close to the root/core is a more natural and appealing form (e.g., nappy hair/the language of resistance that sometimes is disguised or hidden).[2] Consequently, African American women's personal narratives are woven into a whole by threads of discourse strategies that conform to and defy conventional notions of both spoken and written autobiography.

AFRICAN AMERICAN WOMEN'S AUTOBIOGRAPHIES: ACTS OF DISCLOSURE AND CONCEALMENT

African American women writing autobiography or any other form of literature would appear to be a contradiction in terms according to colonial standards. That an enslaved African could write anything, but especially literature, was considered a violation of nature and an offense to white society. Yet, in spite of severe punishment and laws prohibiting the education of slaves, early writers like Phillis Wheatley forged extraordinary paths to American literature. Henry Louis Gates commented that each African American writer after Phillis Wheatley expanded a canon "whose foundation was the poetry of a black woman" (x). Unfortunately, this inauguration of African American literature by a woman was not necessarily an historical headline, but an enigmatic footnote immersed in skepticism regarding the intellectual capacity of slaves:

> Since the beginning of the sixteenth century, Europeans had wondered aloud whether or not the African "species of men," . . . **could** ever create formal literature, could ever master "the arts and sciences." If they could, the argument ran, then the African variety of humanity was fundamentally related to the European variety. (Gates, ix)

For Africans it was a losing proposition. If they could produce literature, it was explained in terms of their possible relation to Europeans and not due to some aspect of their own intelligence or culture. If they could not write creatively, then this was considered proof that they were destined to be slaves. So the literary/artistic works of Africans in the "New World" were subjected to harsh scrutiny tempered by disbelief and prejudice.

Historically, African American women arrived at autobiography through an indirect route. William Andrews reminds readers that for African American women: "the power to write their own stories as they saw fit did not come to female slaves as early as it did to male slaves" (xxxiv). So not only did women have to confront the skepticism that generally accompanied slave narratives, they also had to break free from the "assistance" of sympathizers. Harriet Jacobs, for example, took the risk of publishing *Incidents* on her own rather than having it submerged in *Uncle Tom's Cabin* as was proposed by Harriet Beecher Stowe (Yellin, xix).

Ghostwritten or "as told to" accounts were problematic for several reasons. Although these narratives gave women a voice and a vehicle for initiating change, a suspicious white readership usually raised questions of authenticity. Is it possible that a slave could write a personal narrative without considerable help from a white tutor/ sponsor? In addition, William Andrews concludes that "from 1760 to 1865, we find that only rarely did escaped female slaves ask for or receive the kind of attention that encouraged them to dictate or write their life stories" (xxxii). This difference in attention due to the gender of the narrator skewed both the production and promotion of slave narratives and ultimately the history of the period. As Nellie McKay observes, "in all categories of writing, considerably fewer nineteenth-century texts by black women than men survive" (142). She further explains that women tended to write spiritual narratives, whereas men wrote more "heroic" and political narratives (139). Of course heroic/political narratives conformed to male concepts of personal life writing popular during that time period.

Other constraints which influenced the way African American women lived and subsequently wrote about their lives included ideals of womanhood that largely excluded slave women, while at the same time holding them responsible for defiling the standards. Frequently referred to as the "cult of true womanhood," Hazel Carby explains this social convention as "mythical . . . requisites of womanhood" (20). Its basic tenets of four central virtues: "piety, purity, submissiveness and domesticity" (23), if practiced faithfully, promised white women happiness and influence. Carby argues that this creed, originating in the plantation south, was an insidious method of subordinating all women and simultaneously fortifying male dominance.

Slave women especially were exploited by a secondary code of "opposing definitions of motherhood and womanhood" (20) that forced them into habitual roles of breeders and concubines against their wills. The concept of strength extrapolated from the secondary code, for example, was thought to be a particularly appropriate description for enslaved African women:

> While fragility was valorized as the ideal state of woman, heavy labor required other physical attributes. Strength and ability to bear fatigue, argued to be so distasteful a presence in a white woman, were positive features to be emphasized in the promotion and selling of a black female hand at a slave auction (25).

Thus, slave women were judged to be very different from their white counterparts and, therefore, were mis/treated accordingly. As to be expected, this discrepancy in life-styles, images, and worthiness fostered erroneous assumptions between the two groups of women and eventually alienated African American women and white women.

The secondary code designed for slave women generated at least two stereotypes. According to Deborah Gray White, Jezebel and Mammy were images of African women popularized by slavery and still strongly present in modern American culture. The Jezebel image characterized an African American woman as a creature "governed almost entirely by her libido . . . sensual . . . promiscuous . . . lewd and lascivious" (29–30). In contrast, Mammy was "special," a "premier house servant" (47). She was an expert in domestic/household matters, could do anything and do it better than anyone else, "was completely dedicated to the white family" (49), especially the children, and "served also as friend and advisor" (49). Deborah Gray White argues that the image of Jezebel and Mammy were more myth than reality and were fully misleading then and now. For early African American women autobiographers, this circumstance made their writing task particularly burdensome because they had to refute both racist and sexist myths in order to establish their own identity and credibility.

Thus, the tradition of African American women writing autobiography, especially in the early years, must be understood in the context of historical racial and sexual oppression. This crippling double bind made it difficult, if not impossible for these women to freely speak or write about their lives in any form, but especially in autobiography. As a result, when African American women finally gained control of writing their own life stories, they articulated their experiences from within a paradox of disclosure and concealment.

African American women autobiographers wrote candidly about some aspects of their lives. Childhood usually contained more pleasant memories than adulthood, but the condition of slavery reduced even the children to a subhuman existence as can be seen in Annie L. Burton's[3] description of children's meals: "This bowl served for about fifteen children, and often dogs and the ducks and the peafowl had a dip in it" (4). Punishment was another topic reported frequently. The amount and degree of details about beatings and torture varied from narrator to narrator. Some women[4] seemed to speak of their own punishment in an almost objective manner while others were very explicit about the maltreatment they received. Mattie Jackson recalled very difficult periods in her enslavement: "I was not allowed enough to eat, exposed to the cold, and not allowed through the cold winter to thoroughly warm myself . . . I was kept constantly at work of the heaviest kind—compelled to move heavy trunks and boxes—many times to wash till ten and twelve o'clock at night" (26). She also witnessed her own mother's humiliation and abuse:

> Mr. Lewis was a very severe master, and inflicted such punishment upon us as he thought proper. However, I only remember one severe contest Mr. Lewis had with my mother. For some slight offense Mrs. Lewis became offended and was tartly and loudly reprimanding her, when Mr. L. came in and rashly felled her to the floor with his fist. But his wife was constantly pulling our ears, snapping us with her thimble, rapping us on the head and sides of it . . . the [the Lewis'] had a cowhide which she [Mrs. Lewis] used to inflict on a little slave girl . . . nearly every night. This was done to learn the little girl to wake early to wait on her [Mrs. Lewis'] children (10).

The reluctance of some women to speak out about incidents of personal injuries may be attributed to a variety of emotional and social factors including denial, embarrassment, self-protection, and narrative purpose/intent. Survivors of severe oppression such as slavery may employ metaphors and other kinds of indirect language to disguise/buffer the remembered pain. As a case in point, Annie Burton entitles the first section of her narrative, "Recollections of a Happy Life" (3) and proceeds to tell the audience that "the memory of my happy, care-free childhood days on the plantation, with my little white and black companions, is often with me" (3). Whereas this may seem a little strange, Ms. Burton could have been constructing this image for the benefit of a white audience, or she may have been creating an idealized portrait of childhood in order to block out or replace unpleasant memories of slavery. It is, therefore, important to identify the extratextual meaning of narrative strategies which frequently divulge more than the words on the page.

Concealment was a strong counterpart to disclosure. Sometimes found in the same narrative, these seemingly contradictory strategies actually released the voice of African American women autobiographers. They could expose as much information as they were comfortable with and at another time resort to discreet language or even camouflage to convey sensitive issues to astute readers. Harriet Jacobs' *Incidents in the Life of a Slave Girl* is an important example of subterfuge which almost lost the narrative to obscurity.

Jean Fagan Yellin, editor of the 1987 reprint of Jacobs' narrative explained that the first edition in 1861 contained a title page listing the editor, L. Maria Child, but no author, and the narrator called herself Linda Brent (xiii). So until Yellin and other researchers confirmed Harriet Jacobs as the author of the narrative, it was largely dismissed. Jacobs, however, appeared to be convinced that anonymity was the best way to protect family and friends still enslaved at the time of her writing:

> I had determined to let others think as they pleased but my lips should be sealed and no one had a right to question me (232).

She was determined to speak out, but felt equally responsible to safeguard others. Therefore, in the preface of her narrative, she admits that names, places, and dates were fabricated for a good reason:

> Reader, be assured this narrative is no fiction. I am aware that some of my adventures may seem incredible; but they are, nevertheless, strictly true . . . I have concealed the names of places, and given persons fictitious names. I have no motive for secrecy on my own account, but I deemed it kind and considerate toward others to pursue this course (1).

Readers could admire the courage of a narrator not concerned about her own personal safety, but dedicated to the well-being of others. This also may have helped them to accept the "truth" of Jacobs' account. However, Harriet had another reason to seek anonymity as was evident in the text of her narrative. Yellin explained that Jacobs was deeply troubled by failing to adhere to "moral" standards and even in middle age felt her "youthful distress" and "terrible guilt" (xiv). As was told in *Incidents*, unmarried Harriet became pregnant by a white owner in order to prevent her own master from raping her. At the tender age of fifteen, she was tormented by Dr. Flint's constant sexual harassment:

> My master met me at every turn, reminding me that I belonged to him, and swearing by heaven and earth that he would compel me to submit to him . . . I longed for someone to confide in. I would have given the world to have laid my head on my grand-mother's faithful bosom, and told her all my troubles. But Dr. Flint swore he would kill me, if I was not as silent as the grave . . . I was very young, and felt shamefaced about telling her [grandmother] such impure things, especially as I knew her to be very strict on such subjects (28–29).

This young victim of sexual abuse kept silent and tried to control her own fate as best she could. Her grandmother did indeed condemn her, but, nonetheless, supported Harriet in trying to protect her children. Thus, in her narrative Jacobs suggests that (a) due to rampant sexual abuse, slave women should not be judged by the same moral standards ["Cult of True Womanhood"] as white women and (2) the sexual abuse of slave women must be discussed if it is ever to be eliminated. During this era, speaking publicly about sex or any tangentially related topic invited societal sanctions, so Jacobs' proposal was quite revolutionary in its vision and intent. Hence, concealment was a narrative strategy influenced by both external (societal, political) and internal (personal morals, beliefs) constraints which made it clear that African American women could not speak their minds freely nor without penalty.

Incidents was not the first African American woman's narrative to make special use of concealment. *Our Nig*, resurrected by Henry Louis Gates in 1983, was first published in 1859 under the unusual pseudonym of "Our Nig" (xi). He believes it to be the first novel published by an African American author in the United States. Gates refers to the novel as a "fictional third person autobiography" (xi) and reports that it was the death certificate of her son that established Harriet E. Wilson as the author of the novel (xiii). In explaining Wilson's sentimental novel, Gates observed that for "one hundred and twenty-three years" (xiii) since its publication, the novel was "ignored or overlooked . . . by even the most scrupulous scholars" (xiii). He is not certain about why such an oversight occurred, but perhaps the title or subject matter (racism in the North, a successful interracial marriage) contributed to the oversight.

Most interesting is the language of Wilson's novel. Meaning was submerged in euphemisms, metaphors, and oblique allusions to sexual transgressions:

> As she merged into womanhood, unprotected, uncherished, un-cared for, there fell on her ear the music of love, awakening an intensity of emotion long dormant . . . She knew the voice of her charmer, so ravishing, sounded far above her . . . She surrendered to him a priceless gem, which he proudly garnered as a trophy, with those of other victims, and left her to her fate . . . Conscious that the great bond of union to her former companions was severed . . . she determined to leave the few friends she possessed and seek asylum among strangers. Her offspring came unwelcomed, and before its nativity numbered weeks, it passed from earth, ascending to a purer and better life (5–6).

The concealment found in *Our Nig* is steeped in the language of the sentimental or "woman's novel" (xxxii) of that era. According to Gates this kind of novel focuses on the trials and sometimes happy ending of a long-suffering heroine. What may be most striking for modern-day readers is the rhetoric of the novel which appears to echo the ideas of the "Cult of True Womanhood" and the archaic formal speech of the period. In the preceding excerpt, which is the beginning of Chapter One of *Our Nig*, Mag Smith's story, a now familiar prototype of dysfunctional female/male relationships, is told in a very indirect and "polite" matter. She believes the lies of a gigolo and loses her virginity ("surrendered to him a priceless gem"). He, of course, does not marry her and moves on to his next victim leaving Mag pregnant ("her offspring came unwelcomed"). The baby dies early and by his death both mother and child are spared further disgrace and ostracism. So concealment in this instance appears to be a function of the type of novel and the social mores of the time.

There is, however, another form of concealment in the autobiographical features of the novel. There are significant correlations between the lives of Frado, the main character of the novel, and Harriet Wilson. Both women suffered many of the same tragedies (poverty, desertion, sexual oppression) and both desperately wanted to improve their lives. This intermingling of the author's life with that of the heroine is more than a coincidence. It is a safe means of telling one's own life story through several layers of camouflage. Whether or not Harriet Wilson was aware of this strategy may not be as important as her proficiency in embedding her voice within the narrator's voice.

Before leaving the discussion of disclosure and concealment in African American women's autobiographies, we must consider Zora Neale Hurston's controversial autobiography, *Dust Tracks on a Road*. Many scholars, including her biographer Robert Hemenway, regard Hurston's autobiography as an assortment contradictions at best, or a complete fabrication at worst. In his introduction to the 1984 edition of *Dust Tracks*, Hemenway immediately alerts readers to the problems of the text:

> *Dust Tracks on a Road*, one of the most peculiar autobiographies in Afro-American literary history, presents an image of its author that fails to conform with either her public career or her private experience. (ix)

There could be several alternative explanations if there is such a discrepancy in *Dust Tracks* including the notion that Zora suffered from a psychological condition commonly known as multiple personalities. Because this is not a reasonable hypothesis, one must ask if it is insane to write an autobiography and not reveal one's "true" self? Who is the authority of a person's life story—the autobiographer, the biographer or neither?

Reminiscent of "popular" reactions to slave narratives, Hemenway questions Hurston's truthfulness by mentioning what he considers troubling details of her personal life:

> As a guide to Hurston's private life, *Dust Tracks* proves equally confusing. It ignores the public record, omitting mention of her second marriage and refusing to name her first husband. It avoids placing personal events within a historical framework (x).

Is an autobiographer *obligated* to recognize *all* facts of public record? Does a reader have the right to know *all* of the details of an autobiographer's life? How important to *history* is Hurston's first husband's name as well as her second marriage? Surely, placing personal events in a historical context is more than a matter of naming names.

Hemenway theorizes that "autobiography is not history" (xii), and exonerates Ernest Hemingway from telling the whole truth in *A Moveable Feast*: "He recasts events as he remembers them from the advantage of age, reporting only the emotional reality of a man settling scores for posterity" (xii). Is "emotional reality" different from any other kind of reality? Hemenway allows Ernest Hemingway to recast "events as he remembers them," but expresses a less tolerant view of the same feature in Hurston's autobiography:

> she tests that reader's good faith, challenges credibility, and asks for a considerable suspension of scrutiny. Hurston redramatizes her life for the autobiographical text, manipulating character and event. . . . (xii–xiii)

Why can Hemingway be excused from telling the truth and not Zora Neale Hurston? Is it really an issue of truth-telling or a larger problem rooted in the differential perceptions of female and male writers? Elizabeth Fox-Genovese also refers to *Dust Tracks* as troubling and raises interesting questions about Hurston's relationship to her own text:

> Like the fool of Shakespearean drama, she fawns and flatters, reserving to herself the right to speak difficult truths that her demeanor and role appear to belie. Like the trickster of Afro-American folk culture, she speaks with a double tongue. Like the exile, she re-creates her own previous life as a function of her nostalgia. How, in the midst of this deliberate evasiveness that borders on willful duplicity, are we to locate the core of her self-representation? And how are we to locate it in relation to black women's tradition in autobiography (178).

Again, Hurston's concept of self cannot be pinpointed and, therefore, must be suspect. She is likened to a fool and trickster because a "core" self cannot be found or appears to be two things at once. Yet, for women, especially African American women, living out multiple roles is the rule rather than the exception of life. Hurston is candid in her portrayal of this dilemma and dares to suggest by her own example that these multiple roles are not linearly organized within one's life, but are interactive, overlapping, and sometimes in conflict with one another. This may be a distasteful admission of the condition of African American women's lives, but it does not make Hurston a liar.

Much of the criticism leveled at *Dust Tracks* seems rigorously unforgiving. In many instances, Hurston is penalized for being bold enough to exercise the same options as a male writer. Like her male counterparts, she does not explain *everything* including significant relationships in her life. Zora has the courage to tell the truth at times and at other times is mysteriously silent. Furthermore, Hurston refuses to be categorized and brazenly chooses to be several things at once. By so doing, she defies conventions in both the African American and white communities. She simply cannot be put in her place, if she has one. So the degree to which Hurston's autobiography has been harshly criticized, and in some respects dismissed, may reflect the author's standing or lack thereof, in a male-dominant arena, rather than the quality of her text. Notwithstanding, Zora Neale Hurston maintained her duality without apology:

> I have had the corroding insight at times, of recognizing that I am
> a bundle of sham and tinsel, honest metal and sincerity that cannot
> be untangled. My dross has given my other parts great sorrow . . .
> But on the other hand, I have given myself the pleasure of sunrises
> blooming out of oceans, and sunsets drenching heaped-up clouds.
> (347)

The purpose of Hurston's concealment and duplicity is a matter that probably will be debated for some time. However, the possibility that she may have wilfully and cunningly created an autobiographical self difficult to locate or explain, violates canonical expectations and yet opens up greater alternatives for narrative strategies in women's autobiographies.

Thus, as history has informed us, African American women writing autobiography is distinctive. It is simultaneously an expression of identity and an act of resistance. DuBois once described African Americans' lives as a "double-aimed struggle" (46) to exist. That is, they experienced an ongoing, internal conflict between distorted/negative images of self and positive images of self, self as African vs. self as American. Adhering to one often meant automatically rejecting the other. For African American women there is the added dimension of gender. As Barbara Christian so eloquently explained:

> For what Afro-American women have been permitted to express,
> in fact to contemplate as part of the self, is gravely affected by
> other complex issues . . . To be able to use the range of one's
> voice, to attempt to express the totality of self, is a recurring
> struggle. . . . (234)

For African American women the act of writing autobiography is essentially a redefinition of self in the diaspora and simultaneously a means of resisting false expectations based on a racist and sexist mythology of women. Even though African American women compose their life stories for a variety of reasons, establishing identity and exerting resistance are inherent, if not unconscious, parts of the telling process. They must define themselves in their own terms in order to exercise authority over their own life stories. Joanne Braxton maintains that a fuller understanding of an African American woman's autobiographical text occurs when one views this woman at the "center of her own (written) experience" (6).

Furthermore, the African American autobiographical self, male or female, is intricately linked to the community. So the definition of self necessarily includes community. Joycelyn Moody, in comparing selected nineteenth- and twentieth-century African American women's autobiographies suggests that "for the contemporary authors, community precedes autonomy, and only collective authority permits personal ability" (646). It is only by knowing the African American community that can one accurately know and define one's self. Nellie McKay, after surveying works of other feminist scholars, also proposes that identity for women and minorities is formed through connections with others (182) and that "community identity permits the rejection of historically diminishing images of self imposed by the dominant culture; it allows marginalized individuals to enhance alternative selves constructed from positive (and more authentic) images of their own creation" (175).

Modern-day writer Itabari Njeri, for example, in her very intriguing autobiography, *Every Good-bye Ain't Gone*, explicitly defines herself in the first chapter of her text:

> I was born in Brooklyn, the daughter of a Marxist historian and a nurse. I had studied most of my life to be a musician, an opera singer. In the 1970's I embraced what was considered to be radical black politics. I rejected my slave name for an African one. I began to wear traditional African clothes. (19)

Like African American women writers before her, Itabari explains herself within the context of her vision of family and community. Unlike many of her foremothers, she also describes herself in terms of her career aspirations. Identification with the African motherland is of prime importance at this point in her life and becomes a constant thread throughout her story:

> I used to be reluctant to tell people my slave name unless I surmised that they wouldn't impose their cultural values on me and refuse to use my African name. I don't care anymore. When I changed my name, I changed my life, and I've been Itabari for more years now than I was Jill. (225)

Thus, this definition of self according African values becomes a form of resistance and self-assertion. Rejecting a Western name in favor of an African one empowers the author to redefine herself in her own terms. Sometimes, however, her own terms are not without cost. Njeri describes attending her cousin's winter wedding in "African regalia" covered with a wool coat, but with sandals on in the snow:

> "No," I tell my mother, my big toe a brighter red than my nose as we meet in the church vestibule." "I'm not cold." Hell no. I'm an African. (216)

This comical recollection allows the author to make fun of herself and at the same time emphasize her commitment to an African identity. Her physical resistance to Western customs such as naming and dress represented a deeper rebellion against cultural practices which have continued to enslave African Americans on some level.

Njeri's nonlinear autobiography winds in and out of the past and present, sometimes skipping several consecutive years of her life. Yet there is continuity and wholeness to her story. Moreover, the author demonstrates that perceptions and definitions of self are dynamic rather than static. These ideas of self shift and change shape according to many internal and external variables:

> I abandoned classical music because it was incompatible with my newly aroused sense of cultural identity. In time I would come to see that black nationalism almost inevitably leads to a kind of cultural chauvinism indistinguishable from racism, the very thing I thought I was fighting. (19)

Itabari's discovery of the flaws in her world view created a modification in her identity. She could not remain the same person once she realized the limitations of "cultural chauvinism." Such revelations inspired her to change her life on other levels:

> I spent my college years as a political organizer for CAP, probably the most sophisticated Pan-African organization of the era . . . But like most nationalist organizations, it was a bastion of sexism— women bowing and scraping before men . . . after three years in the organization, I decided to leave. It was stifling. (220–221)

She admitted that her stay in the organization was influenced by the fatherly guidance of Amiri Baraka, but she could not continue to suppress her independent nature for a cause that neither recognized nor appreciated her value as a woman and as an intellectual. With this departure from the organization came a predictable change in life-style as well as some sense of loss:

> I spent the rest of the year singing part-time, doing secretarial work part-time and deprogramming myself from the CAP experience. The latter meant that I could show my legs and cleavage again. But I couldn't expect everybody to speak to me in Swahili when we met. Nor could I expect everybody to share the same code of conduct, as we did in CAP. . . . (222)

Itabari Njeri creates a dynamic image of self that moves through time and space to weave a fascinating life chronicle of a modern African American woman. Acts of identity and resistance form common strands which braid her story into a patterned whole and at the same time connect her experiences to those of earlier African American women autobiographers.

Finally, Joanne Braxton submits that the "study of black women's participation in the literary genre of autobiography reveals much about the ways in which the experience of racial and sexual difference influences the development of identity and the selection of language within a given narrative" (8–9). Braxton, in her ground-breaking work on African American women's autobiography, argues that their autobiographies are a "corrective to both black and feminist literary criticism" (9). From that starting point, she analyzes selected African American women's nineteenth- and twentieth-century autobiographical writings including slave narratives and diaries.

Braxton observes that social and historical changes such as the Civil Rights Movement had a direct and significant impact on African American women's autobiographies, especially those published during the 1960s (142). Although she does not discuss them in detail, the political autobiographies of this period such as Septima Clark's *Echo in My Soul*, Anne Moody's *Coming of Age in Mississippi*, and, in 1970, Ida B. Wells' *Crusade for Justice* are extremely important. They not only reflect the social climate of the period, but also describe African American women's contributions to major political movements. So even though the history of the Civil Rights Movement initially was written as if women were on the fringes, these autobiographies correct this false impression.

Joanne Braxton's observations are keen and insightful, but sometimes fall short of exposing larger issues. The majority of autobiographies that she lists, for example, even some published during the 1980s, are either out of print and/or not on library shelves. Although she does not discuss the problem of availability of African American women's autobiographies this, in itself, is essential to maintaining the "tradition within a tradition." Publishing an autobiography is important, but keeping it in print and accessible is equally important. Otherwise, many fine works will forever remain on the periphery of autobiography—unknown, unread, and unanalyzed.

WRITING/SPEAKING

As can be seen from the preceding discussion, writing and speaking a woman's life is a reflexive process that is autobiographical in nature and sociohistorical in scope. A woman's linguistic reconstruction of her self, on tape and in writing, is a complex undertaking shaped by external and internal forces. How is the spoken form different from the written form? Two narratives, one written and one spoken, of women matched for age, occupation, education, and social class are compared in response to the question.

The narrators are Pauli Murray[5] and Elmira Bowen[6] born in 1910 and 1908, respectively. Both women were born into college-educated, middle-class families in the southeast. Elmira Bowen was the first African American woman to graduate from law school at a university in the midwest in 1930, and Pauli Murray graduated from the Howard University Law School in 1946.[7] Although there is no record that the two women ever met, both had successful law careers, were civil rights activists, and deeply religious.

Murray's autobiography originally entitled *Song in a Weary Throat* was published by Harper and Row in 1987. It was later retitled *Pauli Murray: The Autobiography of a Black Activist, Feminist,*

Lawyer, and Poet, and reprinted in 1989 by the University of Tennessee Press. Pauli Murray died in 1985 while working on a revision of her autobiography. I elicited Elmira Bowen's oral narrative at her home in the southeast in 1988 and 1989 for a total of 5 hours of audio tape. The discussion that follows examines excerpts from both narratives in order to establish differences in speaking and writing one's own life story. A true comparison would contrast Bowen's actual *oral* performance with Murray's written text, but because that is not practical, the edited *transcript* of Bowen's narrative will be used instead.

To begin, a word-for-word comparison would be unwieldly and unrevealing. Murray's 435-page written text appears formidable when contrasted with the 150-page transcript of Bowen's oral interview. Therefore, instead of an item-by-item analysis selected structures and themes will be examined for their respective spoken and written features.

Both narrators experienced discrimination first hand. Bowen's recollection of an undergraduate experience was poignant but concise:

> It so happened that I was with the first class of young Blacks to enter the university and I had some rather interesting experiences there. All the girls were called into the dean's office and we were all told that we should be as unobtrusive as possible on the campus, that we were members of the subject race; the university did not really want us, but as it was a city university it had to take us. And we left that interview just about in a state of shock because we hadn't been prepared for that and we immediately met with the young [black] men on the campus and told them about it. And we all decided that we're going out for everything. That everybody [all of the black students] in that freshman class is gonna come away with some distinction. We didn't burn any buildings down or anything like that, we just decided, we were gonna show them. And we all did . . . And the success of it was that the next year, the same official . . . called us back and apologized. He said, "I made an error and I want you to know that you are a credit to your race." (36:1, p. 8)

The story starter, "It so happened . . ." introduces the situation that the narrator euphemistically refers to as "interesting." She divulges some of the details of what could have been a very ugly racial incident on campus. The episode is related by the narrator's voice outside of the action, as indicated by past tense. However, in the middle of the segment, the voice switches to present tense, "we're going out for everything," which then allows the narrator to speak from inside of the action. When Elmira switches back to past tense, the resulting philosophical retrospective, probably inspired by the sixties, hints of a kind of nonviolent activism with a positive outcome. Finally, at the end of the segment Bowen uses reported speech to emphasize the resolution of the problem, "I made an error. . . ." Even though these are not unbiased remarks ("you are a credit to your race"), there was a slight change in attitude and, therefore, in her estimation some small progress.

Pauli Murray devotes an entire chapter to her law school rejection by the University of North Carolina and refers to the incident throughout many subsequent chapters. She painstakingly cites laws that applied to her situation as well as correspondence from white officials:

> My application pending before the University of North Carolina was suddenly transformed into a public controversy by the surprising and far-reaching decision of the United States Supreme Court in **Missouri ex rel Gaines v. Canada** . . . Two days after the Gaines decision was announced, the University of North Carolina rejected my application solely on racial grounds . . . The rejection was not unexpected, but seeing the reason in black and white was infuriating. I wrote immediately to Dr. Frank Graham, then president of the university. . . . (114–115)

In the midst of her almost objective description of the incident, she mentions her feelings about being a victim of racism, "the reason in black and white was infuriating." This seemingly unintended pun ("black and white") further illustrated the separation of the races that characterized American society and precipitated in Murray's rejected application.

Both women discussed their experiences as practicing attorneys. Bowen did not dwell on her adventures in the courtroom, but did take the time to highlight some important aspects of that experience:

It wasn't as difficult in law school as it was when I came out, took
the Bar, and started to practice. Because I had to overcome the
tradition of a male, this being a male field. And I would go down
to the courts and take my seat in the section which is reserved for
lawyers and the bailiff would come over and say, "Young lady this
is reserved for lawyers. You have to sit back there." And I was
continually having to prove myself, but I took all that in stride
because you know you're in a pioneer field and you have to go
with the flow of it, you know. (36:1, p. 8)

Here Bowen is sensitive to her position as one of the few women in
the field and is philosophical about what that meant to her. Again,
she uses reported speech sparingly, but certainly for emphasis. On
the other hand, Murray is almost totally philosophical:

The awkwardness of my position gradually disappeared as my work
as a lawyer improved and was accepted. Later I looked back on
the job at Paul, Weiss, Rifkind, Wharton & Garrison as decisive
for my future growth. When I left the firm after three years, I
carried with me the assurance of having been tested by the most
exacting standards of the legal profession, an experience that enabled me to face new challenges with greater self-confidence . . .
For months I had to struggle with phantoms lurking in the background, secret fears that gaps in my knowledge or inadequacies in
performance would be attributed to my race or sex. Only as I
learned through dogged effort to handle day-to-day assignments
with reasonable competence were those nagging fears laid to rest.
(314)

She, too, is sensitive to issues of race and gender. However, Pauli
takes full advantage of the opportunity for retrospection and provides
an analysis than spans both the past and future of her life at that
time.

Another similarity was that of religion. Bowen and Murray were
deeply committed to their religious beliefs and lived their lives
accordingly. At the peak of her career, Bowen took the very bold
step of leaving the country to carry out her Faith's call for pioneers
(missionaries):

I was at the point materially where I was getting satisfied and
ambitious so that I really had to decide what priority my religion
had in my life. And on this basis I went to Morocco. It was a
tremendous experience for me as it is for any pioneer [missionary].

> Particularly if you've never been out of the country before. And if you're going to a place where you have no contacts, no people that you know, and your sole reliance must be upon God because you have nothing else. And for me it was even more so I think because I was black, I was a woman. I was alone in a far eastern culture . . . but I must say, God's protection was with me because never during those four years that I was in Morocco, did I ever have an unpleasant experience, as a woman. (36:2, p. 15)

Alone and unassisted, Elmira embarked on what would become many years of service to her Faith in several African countries. Again, she expresses awareness of her status as a single woman in a foreign culture, and by so doing recognized the depth of her beliefs. For Pauli Murray, the death of a close friend guided her to the ministry:

> Renee's death changed my life . . . I felt an urgency to complete my mission on earth in the days left to me . . . As I reflected upon these experiences, the thought of ordination became unavoidable. Yet the notion of a "call" was so astounding when it burst into my consciousness that I went about in a daze, unable to eat or sleep as I struggled against it . . . Once I had admitted the call of total commitment to service in the church, it seemed that I had been pointed in this direction all my life . . . I took the fateful step of applying . . . for admission to holy orders. (426–427)

As was her pattern, Murray devoted an entire chapter to describing her call to the ministry. One of the first women to officially be ordained as an Episcopal priest in 1977, she assumed the position after years of challenging the provision that had reserved the priest-hood for men only.

Finally, both Bowen and Murray traveled and lived abroad, especially in Africa and small "third world" countries. Elmira Bowen's first trip was an adventure as well as a religious experience:

> From the very moment that I entered the country it seemed as if unseen hands and unseen power arranged contacts that were helpful, educational, and very wonderful to me. A typical example of this was when I got off, I sailed to Morocco on a steamship, and on this cruiser, I did not know it, but at the same time there were four other pioneers [missionaries] and after we had gotten settled we met each other . . . When I got to Tangier and got off the

boat, I was surrounded with all the luggage that I had brought to stay a year and the Arab porters who spoke no English were rushing at me from all directions, screaming for my luggage, and I was standing there daring anyone to touch it. And in the midst of this great confusion, I heard someone saying my name. (36:2, pp. 15–16)

Uncharacteristic of most women's autobiographies, Bowen portrays herself as fearless: "I was standing there daring anyone to touch it." This does not appear to be a boast, but rather an honest appraisal of her behavior under the circumstances. She has already told the listeners that she was alone, and that she had no one to depend on but God. Murray's experience was similar, and she was very detailed in her account of this first voyage:

Early in 1959, Maida Springer, who had just returned from a conference in Ghana, gave me a clipping from the *London Times* advertising faculty openings in the newly established Ghana Law School in Accra. I answered it immediately . . . For the next twenty-six days I live in the tiny, self-contained world of a seagoing freighter, learning to endure its ceaseless groaning and creaking, heaving up and down and sideways on an awesome ocean which seemed to stretch to infinity. Commanded by Captain J. B. Bye . . . the boat carried a foreign crew of forty, eight American passengers, and a cargo of six thousand tons of rice, potatoes, tractors, and other heavy machinery consigned to West African ports. From New York we sailed north two days to take on four hundred tons of Canadian flour at Halifax, Nova Scotia . . . As a neophyte, who had never traveled outside the United States, I could hardly have found more experienced and reassuring companionship to prepare me for my new venture. Six of the other seven passengers . . . were veteran travelers to Africa, and they took delight in briefing me on what to expect. . . . (318–319)

The author is very specific about names and dates. She pays attention to even the smallest details such as the contents of the cargo. It is interesting that she refers to her trip as a "venture" rather than an *adventure*.[8] This subtle use of language may be some indication of her uneasiness with this new undertaking or it may well be a figurative expression marking her exploration of new territory.

Pauli Murray's autobiography was written from a political point of view. Even before she attended law school she was politically active and interested in making a difference. This overall theme generated coherence across the various chapters of her lengthy text. As the writer of her own life story, she could easily exercise this option and frame her entire life according to a central theme applied retrospectively. Bowen, on the other hand, related her life in segments with each one sometimes having a different theme, and some having no theme. Her strong religious beliefs formed the main theme of her life. These beliefs were the undercurrent of many segments, and were boldly expressed in others. So in a way, Elmira also chose to reveal her life through a central theme—religion. If Bowen were to write her autobiography as she plans to do, we may expect to find the same kind of thematic organization as that found in Murray's autobiography. Chronological ordering characteristic of many written life stories also may impose organization around a central idea or theme.

Writing one's own life versus speaking one's own life may be differences in degree rather than kind. As previously discussed, some of the major differences in the narrator's stories were due to time and space limitations.[9] In the case of an oral narrative, the interview situation naturally imposes time restrictions that writing does not. Even if an interviewer and an interviewee had an unlimited amount of time to record a life story on tape, there still would be some aspects of that life that oral elicitation could not capture. On the other hand, writing lacks the spontaneity of oral language. It is missing the discovery that speaking unprocessed experiences sometimes brings to the surface. Because writing is consciously edited, it is manipulated and controlled in a manner that often camouflages authentic features of a narrator's speech. Also, writing cannot convey the various shades of meaning that can be expressed verbally through prosodic features such as pitch, loudness, and length. Neither mode is *better* than the other. Both are invaluable tools of research and interpretation. In fact, we must utilize *both* written and oral narratives in order to preserve women's lives and contributions.

6

TELLING A LITTLE STORY: ORGANIZATION AND STRUCTURE IN AFRICAN AMERICAN WOMEN'S ORAL NARRATIVES

The structure of a narrative text is influenced by a variety of factors including the interviewee's personal qualities (e.g., narrative style) as well as external features (e.g., interview format). From the word level to the level of the whole text, elements of structure take shape according to a configuration of variables which are activated by the interview process. These structural features not only are interesting in themselves, but they also reveal meaningful information about the speaker and the process.

SPEAKING THE UNSPEAKABLE

On a macro level or the level of the whole text, several variables must be considered such as story structure, narrative style, and suppressed discourse. Each of these variables influences the whole text in distinctly different ways. The issue of linearity, for example, affects the manner in which an oral text is elicited and later reorganized in a written form.

According to "Western" tradition, a story or narrative is conceptualized as primarily sequential and/or chronological. Stories are expected to unfold in a straight line from beginning to end without significant deviation from the main topic. This expectation, however, derives from an idealization of narrative texts and cannot be validated in all circumstances. Some scholars including Shirley Brice Heath (1983) offer overwhelming evidence that oral stories vary from culture to culture in their structure, conceptualization, and functions. Some Americans recognize "Once upon a time" as a story starter, but others are more familiar with "Did I tell you about the time that . . ." as a story starter or beginning. Similarly, recollections of personal life stories are not neat and orderly beginning from childhood and progressing through adulthood. Instead, as the narratives in my study indicate, narrators begin at various points in their lives, not always at childhood. The final text contains a complexity of life events and crises woven into a multifaceted whole, shifting between the past and present. This discourse variation or intertextuality within a single narrative creates several levels of micro-structure which parallel and intersect one another, but do not necessarily form any type of immediately detectable sequence or chronology. It is according to Wolf and Hicks a "network of texts within texts" (331).

Narrative style, the overall pattern of discourse characteristic of a particular narrator and dominant in a text, further illustrates the nonlinear features of some oral narratives. In my study, there were at least three narrative styles: unified, segmented, and conversational. Few narrators used one style exclusively and some segments of discourse could not be classified in any of the categories. However, most large units of discourse such as a question/answer segment or "frame" (Tannen, 1989) assumed a specific pattern according to a narrator's unique style of speaking.

A unified style contains words and phrases that are all related to a central topic or idea. Contiguous parts of the narrative fit together as a whole.

> Q: How did you become interested in foreign languages?
> A: In the early days it became fashionable . . . I guess in all cities and in all social circles for adults to study a foreign language. There were French clubs and Spanish clubs and German clubs. And my parents were members of that kind of a society and they studied French and enjoyed it very much. And they also studied Spanish. And then in their schooling they had taken German. Chicago was kind of a center of German activities. And so all of us grew up in the family speaking a little bit of French, a little bit of Spanish, a little bit of German. And

so forth. And we would be told to sit down in German or get up and go to the piano in French. Or study something in Spanish. And we even made up our own language . . . And I think that sparked my interest in foreign languages. Also, my mother was studying Spanish, she tells me, at the time I was conceived. So who knows? (3:2, p. 20)

Each utterance is related to the central topic—interest in foreign languages. The narrator supports her answer as completely as possible by providing several examples and details. She does not deviate, but focuses exclusively on the question at hand.

On the surface, a segmented style appears to be the opposite of unified. Contiguous parts of a narrative are composed of a diverse assortment of seemingly unrelated utterances.

Q: What made you decide to go back to school?
A: Look at me, I quit school to go find knowledge. Well, you need knowledge to find knowledge. You gotta know where to search for knowledge. That's why I guess it took me so long . . . I was forty years old when I had that vision, but I said, I wrote my folks and I said, "You know they tell me that life begins at forty and I have not yet begun to live. I'm just now beginning." So I went back to school and finished high school. Well, I didn't finish there but I got back to school right then in Tennessee. And then I came home. In 1954 I went out west. So I enrolled in high school there and got my degree in the adult night school. Then I went on to college. (4:1, p. 6)

The narrator at first responds indirectly by discussing her search for knowledge. This brief preface sets the stage for her answer and at the same time signals the importance of her quest for knowledge, her motivation for leaving and then returning to school. Even after she answers the question ("So I went back to school . . ."), the narrator goes on to supply a specific time and location for her return to school. This sequential ordering of the last few utterances does not match the preceding utterances whose connectedness is not entirely revealed until the question is answered. Such ordering at the end of her answer may be an overt attempt to be factual and/or another means of signifying the importance of the event. Thus, a segmented style is created in part by shifts in focus on topics of varying importance. As previously illustrated, this style contains utterances that may not be immediately or directly related to the topic. Instead, utterances are loosely affiliated with the topic and their meaning/connection may not be clear unless the whole segment is taken into account.

Conversational style occurs when a narrator reconstructs past conversations verbatim. A narrator modifies voice, tone, and/or pitch in order to represent different speakers and different emotions. She uses conversation as means of illustrating an idea or event:

> Q: Did anything in your life ever happen or not happen solely because you were a woman?
>
> A: When I went to City College I remember, I'm not going to call any names, a young man, friend of mine said, "I don't have any time. Will you, will you do this paper for me?" And I said, "No!" I didn't mind doing anything for anybody, but I, I, isn't it funny how you are? I said, "No, I'm sorry, I can't do that. You have to do it yourself." **He looked at me.** You know, he gives me this dirty look. He did his paper because **nobody** [none of the girls] would do it for him. And he got an A. If I had done it for him, he would have gotten a B. Isn't it funny how people are? It's an interesting thing. (5:1, p. 1)

The narrator's indirect, but poignant example suggests that the answer to the question is yes, but instead of saying so, she reconstructs the conversation. Her explanations between quotes provide additional information about her beliefs and motivation. In the last section of her answer where she discusses grades, the narrator perhaps unknowingly implies that the work done by a girl would be imperfect, "B" compared to the perfect score "A," that the young man received.

Narrative style is an unconscious macro-level organizational framework that shapes a narrative into a coherent whole. Patterns or styles vary from narrator to narrator and one text may contain more than one style. Whereas these patterns are not necessarily always discrete, they expose the overall design of an oral text and simultaneously uncover meaning that may be submerged in the arrangement of its parts.

Finally, the issue of suppressed discourse is central to analyzing and interpreting African American women's oral narratives. As sociolinguistic theory indicates, social inequities are reflected in language. So the racism and sexism that has characterized African American women's lives is manifest in language used by and about them. Specifically, their oral narratives contain many instances of suppressed discourse, an internal censorship of one's own speech. Often spontaneous and sometimes unconscious, it most obviously appears as the modification of natural speech in order to disguise meaning or diminish the impact of a particular situation or event.

Suppressed discourse can take many subtle forms. As one narrator demonstrates, the impact of her experiences is modified/explained by prefacing each episode with a statement of her own personal philosophy. Such statements also occurred at the end of an episode or at *both* the beginning *and* end. As a result, a kind of embedding occurs in which an episode is immersed in or buffered by statements of personal philosophy:

> Q: Have you ever felt that some things happened to you just because you were black?
> A: Yeah (pause) now ah (pause) racism, oh it's one of those things you know is going to be there. For instance, during the time that I was working at the college and traveling back and forth to the Farm Security Administration (pause) because Mrs. Roosevelt always saw to it that I was tied to that which helped (pause) to ah (pause) rehabilitate families and to provide education for children who otherwise would not have had an education (pause). Ah (pause) I hear people say things like, "I'd love to do something with that little Ms. Brown but you know she's Mrs. Roosevelt's little chocolate drop." So on undercurrent, I heard all this racism, but they were afraid of her [Mrs. Roosevelt]. (27:3, p. 56)

The narrator's preface, "racism . . . is going to be there," acknowledges racism as a factor inherent in her life as an African American woman. So the reported speech of what others [whites] said about her, ". . . Mrs. Roosevelt's little chocolate drop," fits into the framework she initially established. This racial slur, however, is reported without any reference to her feelings about being called a "little chocolate drop." Omission, as we will later discuss, is another feature of suppressed discourse. When this same narrator describes being denied a national award because she was black, she concludes her description with a philosophical statement about the impact of the event on her life:

> And then ah (pause) one other experience I had that was very (pause) very ah (pause) poignant was the fact that something I had done [musical composition] had been selected for a national award and they didn't know, when I had written this, that I was black, and when they [contest officials] found out, the award was no longer available. I try to forget things like that because I (pause) I (pause) I (pause) I don't (pause) I just don't think bitterness is going to help us get anywhere (pause) and ah (pause) so (pause) whenever possible I try to (pause) forget those sort of things. (27:3, p. 56)

Whereas an audience could accept the narrator's philosophy at face value, her remarks that this childhood memory is very "poignant," and later, "whenever possible I try to forget things like that . . ." seem contradictory. This may have been an incident that was *not* possible to forget. Whatever the reason for the contradiction, enveloping a traumatic event in her personal philosophy may well serve as a buffer for a painful remembrance. It may be forgiven, but not forgotten. Even though the narrator's attitude is noble, it is one of the few reactions permissible according to societal constraints. To have responded otherwise (e.g., display/voice anger), the narrator would have been "uncharitable" or bitter. There is no safe or acceptable public forum for exposing and candidly discussing one's adversities, especially if they are a direct result of racism and/or sexism.

Denial by negation is another trait of suppressed discourse. Often when asked a direct question about sexism or racism many narrators would initially give a negative answer, but then proceed with a positive response or example. No did not always mean that an event did not occur or that a situation did not exist:

> Q: Were you one of the few women at that time, who was in that particular department?
> A: No, there were a lot of women, but I don't think that they went on [to doctoral studies] you know. We had lots of women. I (pause) they (pause) I don't know of any of them going on, out of my class. (30:2, p. 24)

Here the narrator hedges (marked by pauses) in her answer which must be qualified. Yes, there were women in her class, but few like her who were enrolled in the doctoral program.

> Q: Did you experience any kind of discrimination as the only black woman in the department doctoral program at that time?
>
> A: No, I didn't, there were seven of us who were, six white, seven of us who were working to come out that year, and we had no discrimination among us. It was a question of studying together . . . so it was a great comraderie there. . . . (30:2, p. 30)

When the question becomes even more specific, the narrator continues her general but, again, qualified response. She views herself as part of the group, "there were seven of us," rather than an outsider. The qualification of her reply, "we had no discrimination among us," only partially answers the question. There may have been no discrimination among the students, but did the professors and other university staff discriminate against African American females?

In this same stretch of discourse, the denial becomes stronger when the questions become more challenging. As can be seen in the following example, when pressed about the number of African American students on campus, the narrator continues to maintain a fiercely positive stance:

> Q: There couldn't have been many blacks at State at that time?
>
> A: Oh, don't say that, no don't (pause) don't say that (pause) there were plenty of them there, plenty of them there. I suppose the only school that had more was Sagimon State, but there were many there, but they weren't at that level, on the doctoral, but they had plenty of them there. (30:2, p. 26)
>
> Q: So there were lots of black graduate students?
>
> A: . . . well they had plenty of them. But not at the level I was studying.
>
> Q: So on the doctoral level . . .
>
> A: Oh no, I never did see anybody [black students] on the doctoral level, but some on the Master's level with me. (30:2, pp. 26–27)

At this stage in the questioning the narrator inadvertently exposes her concern for a positive viewpoint when she requests of the interviewer "don't say that." Again, as her response develops, a restriction applies. Yes, there were African American students on campus, but she was the only one in a particular department's doctoral program. Thus, at this time, progress in integrating African American students into predominantly white universities was limited because most were concentrated on the undergraduate level. Breaking through this artificial ceiling into a doctoral program, as the narrator had done, could not have been without some difficulty. The subtle denial that is present in this segment of the narrative is an excellent illustration of suppressed discourse. This narrator does not freely discuss issues of race and gender.

Another important aspect of suppressed discourse is omission and use of indirect speech. That is, specific information is omitted or substituted at key points in an interviewee's narration. This seemingly unconscious strategy creates a euphemistic effect that is noticeable if you listen closely. One narrator, in a very moving description of her encounter with racial violence, tended to omit certain adjectives and only indirectly referred to race:

> A: I was on my way to Mississippi again and um (pause) I had to change buses (pause) I never liked Alabama and I had to change buses in Alabama . . . At that time they [government officials] said that if people [African Americans] were traveling interstate they could (pause) sit anywhere . . . [i.e., in the white waiting room]. Whenever there was a [civil rights] law, even though I was scared to death, I believed if the law is here we must begin to use it or it will fade into oblivion. So when I got off the bus, I asked one of the red caps carrying the bags. I said, "Where is the interstate [white] waiting room?" because I wanted to be sure where I was going (pause). . . . And then here comes this old sort of (pause) he was almost a redneck, not quite (pause) who's pretending to be drunk (pause). He said, we [white people] made this waiting room [**colored**] over there for you" . . . So he eventually went over further into the [white] waiting room and got a real redneck . . . and he came over with this man and he said, "Alright, come on, we don't want you in here". . . . And so, I took my things and the redneck and his friend followed me to the door then they pitched me out the door. Yes, they did. (5:2, 6)

The brackets [ ] indicate places where adjectives could have been used. The "interstate" waiting room, for example, was the white waiting room, yet the narrator did not initially signal that distinction. Instead, one must infer from the context that there were two different waiting rooms reserved for white and *colored* passengers, respectively.

Overall, the narrator rarely marked her speech for race except for use of the term "redneck." She applied this term with caution ("almost a redneck" versus "real redneck") in describing her attackers. Meaning is conveyed largely by context and role of the character. The narrator's use of omission and indirect speech ("old, sort of [redneck]," "almost a redneck") may have been an attempt to politely describe an ugly racial incident and/or a kind of shock absorber that protected her as well as the audience from the pain of the experience.

Although not all instances of omission, negation, indirect speech, and embedding qualify as suppressed discourse, it is likely that information left unsaid is signaled by one or more of these features. The ultimate effect is a kind of ominous silence that occupies the space between the words of a narrator and the life that she is reconstructing. Context provides some additional meaning, but the whole may never be uncovered.

SOME LITTLE WORDS ABOUT STRUCTURE

Separating an oral narrative into various components can be problematic in that the totality of a text is rarely the sum of its parts. As indicated in the preceding discussion, not only are there inconspicuous variables (e.g., suppressed discourse) that must be taken into consideration, but equally important is the relationship between structure, meaning, and the social context in which narration occurs. As a consequence, analytic approaches that focus exclusively on sentences and words may not be particularly revealing or informative. However, variation on the level of discourse, especially that found in a single speaker's narrative, can uncover numerous and different shades of meaning submerged in the social fabric of a text. Thus, the following discussion will examine intertextuality, embedding, passive voice, and the adjective *little* as key elements of discourse structure within an individual narrative.

INTERTEXTUALITY

According to Wolf and Hicks (330), intertextuality may be defined as discourse variation within the performance of a single speaker. It is characterized by multiple voices or stances, each with its own distinct linguistic features. The researchers found at least three different voices in their study of intertextuality in the speech of young children:

1. narrative—"past tense, third person and predicates denoting observed actions" (330)
   example—Once upon a time three bears lived in the woods.
2. dialogue—present tense, first person singular, second person singular, and predicates which make the character's inner life and visions public (e.g., 'know,' 'glad') (330)
   example—I said, "I am disappointed by that decision."
3. stage-managing—"second person pronoun (we're)," external, departs from the narrative to make comments on characters, events, and actions (e.g., asides) (339)
   example—We're not going to use this room; its too small.

These three voices run parallel and interact within the same narrative. The result is a rich mixture of voices that create a "network of texts within texts" (331).

Unlike the Wolf and Hicks study, I found tenses not to be so discretely centered around voice. In many instances, a single narrator would shift back and forth from past to present in a single sentence: "And then here comes this old, he was almost a redneck, who's pretending to be drunk." This shifting may be due to a variety of factors, including the idea that defining characteristics of voice/intertextuality may be fluid rather than static. Also, use of multiple voices may be an age-graded phenomenon with children using tenses in fixed voice positions and gradually expanding to the adult model of flexible and innovative applications of verb tense within the narrative mode.

Also, I found the same three voices, but with more elaborate and complex functions. The manager voice, for example, was not as frequent as the other two voices. It served not only as an external commentary on some aspect of the narrative (e.g., "Thompkins Hall is the dining hall . . .") but also was a technique for organizing and developing the text itself (e.g., "I will come back to that later." "You want me to talk about that?"). The manager voice provided narrators with an unobtrusive means of stepping outside of the narrative to modify, adjust, explain, and/or organize the text.

The narrator voice in my sample assumed a participant/observer stance depending on the emotional import of the event or situation. Recollections of racial violence or emotional trauma, for example, usually evoked a more distant stance or that of the detached observer. On the other hand, narrators were frequently participant/observers of their high school and college experiences. With this combined stance, they could switch from being a part of the action to being outside of the action according to their own narrative style and the unique demands of a particular episode. However, unlike children's narrative voices in the Wolf and Hicks study, these narrators sometimes enveloped value judgments in their narrative commentaries: "But I was only angry. It wasn't because I was brave." Conceivably this kind of retrospective evaluation may be a result of aging. That is, the wisdom gained from experience and reflection may lead older adult narrators to not only comment but also evaluate themselves, others, and past situations.

In a very moving account of racial confrontation, a narrator develops the action through her narrative voice and simultaneously offers profound insights about fear, violence, and the will to live what she believed. This excerpt unfolds a moving story that illustrates multiple functions and versatility of the narrative voice.

Text #1
Gathering Silence

Well, at any rate, from Gulfport I had another experience which was not happy. I was on my way to Mississippi. I had to change buses. I never liked Alabama and I had to change buses in Alabama and it meant I had to wait about an hour and so at that time they had said that if people [black] were travelling interstate they could sit anywhere. And whenever there was a law even though I was scarred to death, I believed if the law is here and we must begin to use it or it will fade into oblivion. So . . . when I got off the bus I asked the one of the red caps carrying the bags. I said, "Where is the interstate waiting room?" Because I wanted to be sure where I was going . . . So he said, "Oh, you can sit anywhere in there," in this main waiting room.

So I went in and somehow I didn't feel altogether certain about this so I sat in the last row that was the easiest one to get out the door if I needed to get out. And I had a book with me and of course I read the same page over and over again. First it was the bus driver. Came to me and said, "Oh, I think you have the wrong waiting room." I said, "Oh, I'm an interstate passenger." You know as though I didn't know from anything. And he said, "Let me see your ticket." And so I did and he said, "Oh, you're alright." So I thought well, I'll set here comfortably, but I still didn't feel right about it 'cause it was Alabama.

And then here comes this old, he was almost a redneck, who's pretending to be drunk. He said, "We made this waiting room over there for you." And I said, "Oh, I'm an interstate passenger." But he was too ignorant to understand any of that, but I just pretended he wasn't there. And so he stood around trying to talk to me and I was trying to talk to him in some intelligent way, but I was getting nowhere fast. So I stopped it. So he eventually went over further into the waiting room and got a real redneck. He [the drunk] came over with this man and he said, "Alright, come on. We don't want you in here." I said, "But I'm an interstate passenger," knowing full well he wasn't listening. And he said, "We don't care what you are. We don't want you in here." And he started to pick up my things and at that point I got mad. I said, "Don't you touch my things!" I said it with a sharp voice, you know. He stepped back. But I was only angry. It wasn't because I was brave.

I said, "Now don't you touch my things," and I said, "I'm leaving here because I don't want to cause trouble for the rest of these people [black]," because all the porters had gathered together. And I thought, you know the thoughts that go through your mind are like turning on electricity. They're kind of immediate and fast and I said, "Now these men have families and there's no sense in their families being disrupted for my pride over anything like that because it will be better if I just go on and do what I have to do. Go on out the door and let these men keep their jobs and don't have any problems." And so I did just that. I took my things . . . and the man and his friend followed me to the door then they pitched me out the door. Yes, they did . . . Yes, they did. And of course you're so embarrassed. So I went and I said to the porter, I said, "Now I'm gonna call the FBI. Of course they're probably not gonna do anything, but if anything happens to me I'll let them know who they should contact." But it was more embarrassing than it was injurious. So at any rate, I got my stuff together and I first went into the black waiting room and you know there's a silence that gathers, that let's you know that in the split second of time that things have been happening that everybody in there knows what has been happening, and I felt that. I sat there for a while then pretty soon it was time for my bus and I went on to where I was going. (5:2, pp. 5–7)

The narrative voice in the preceding passage performs at least two functions. One function is to advance the action of the narrative. It primarily is marked by past tense and employs predicates denoting past actions either observed or carried out by the narrator:

"I was on my way to Mississippi."

"And so he stood there trying to talk to me. . . ."

The second and more striking function is that of evaluation. The narrator carefully assesses the situation and places value or judgment on the behavior of those involved including herself. By so doing, she makes the audience privy to her own beliefs and fears:

"Well, at any rate, from Gulfport I had another experience which was not happy."

"I never liked Alabama. . . ."

"I believed if the law is here and we must begin to use it or it will fade into oblivion."

". . . and somehow I didn't feel altogether certain about this so I sat in the last row that was the easiest one to get out the door if I needed to get out."

". . . I read the same page over and over again."

"You know as though I didn't know anything from anything."

". . . but still I didn't feel right about it 'cause it was Alabama."

"But he was too ignorant to understand any of that, but I just pretended he wasn't there."

". . . knowing full well he wasn't listening."

"But I was only angry. It wasn't because I was brave."

". . . you know the thoughts that go through your mind are like turning on electricity. They're kind of immediate and fast. . . ."

"But it was more embarrassing than it was injurious."

". . . you know there's a silence that gathers . . . and I felt that."

The narrator's omniscient stance establishes motives and foreshadows results. She lets the audience "in" on the action (". . . knowing full well he wasn't listening") without revealing the outcome of the episode. Thus, the narrator speaks to the audience from a privileged position—from inside of the inside. The voice is not only speaking from inside of the action, but also from inside of the narrator's thoughts and feelings: like, believe, feel, know, pretend, be. This manner of telling creates an intimate bond between the narrator and the audience. Though not all narrators construct such an intimate relationship with listeners, this aspect of the narrative voice adds another complex dimension to the text. Furthermore, the authenticity of the narrator's experience is validated, in part, by the intense emotions that she recalls in conjunction with the event.

The actor voice or what has been referred to as reported speech or dialogue is distinguished by present tense and a participant stance. It also provides a view from within, but from within conversations and direct quotes reproduced by the narrator: She said to me, "I just don't understand." Frequently, a narrator marks the speech of others by the words say, said, tell, told. Reported speech serves several functions including emphasis, examples, and plot/story development. In my study, not all of the women used reported speech, but of those who did, the amount and frequency varied. (See "Language in Context: Telling it Like a Lady" in Chap. 2).

Out of the many instances of reported speech, there are several segments worth examining. These examples differ in frequency, style, and structure. Also, as mentioned previously, in some narratives there was not a single instance of reported speech, in others it was used sparingly, and in yet others it was used profusely.

Text #2
When I Grow Up

We would sit on our big porch. We had a big porch, round porch, you know and daddy would sit out there sometimes. He was a wonderful man. And so he would say, "Now, I want one of my boys . . ." He's always talking about the boys. "I want one of my boys to be a lawyer. I want one to be a doctor, one a business man," you see there's just three of them. And I would say, "Well, what do you want me to be?" And he said, "Oh you'll just grow-up and be a good wife, and mother," as my mother had been. "And you have children, and do that sort of thing." But he would never say that he wanted us girls to be. But at the same time he educated all of his daughters. He had a very, very deep respect for womanhood. When I left home he went with me to present me to the community, you know. When my sister left to teach school he went with her there. When my younger sister went to a college out of state, he went up there with her, too. (26:2, p. 5)

In this example of reported speech, the voice of the narrator and the voice of the actor intermingle in an interesting development of the episode. The voices switch between clauses each time the narrator reports her father's speech or her own words. The actor's voice produces the actual words, "I want one of my boys . . ." while the narrator's voice explains, "He's always talking about the boys." Ultimately, the narrator's voice resumes and maintains control near the end of the episode. It is as if the narrator is compelled to step outside of the action in order to explain her father's behavior to a modern-day audience that might not understand. However, this may not be necessarily the case. She may have been trying to convince herself that her father's differing expectations of his male and female children was not a serious breech of their relationship, but rather a traditional attitude that was harmless: "He had a **very, very,** deep respect for womanhood." It is not uncommon for narrators to gain new insight on a important past event as they are telling their lives. If this is true for the above narrator, then the audience changes near the end of the episode when the narrator's voice takes over. Initially, the narrator is speaking to a "general" audience, but, at the end, she may be speaking to herself as well.

The next segment is very different from the preceding one in that the narrator's conversational style dominates this stretch of text. There is little explanation, but a great deal of attention is given to developing a sequence of events:

Text #3
A Perfect Union

I had a strike in another place. A truck hit me and pushed me into a ditch. And the constable kept me in jail and he told he didn't care, he twisted my arm and twisted it out of place and then came to the hospital, he told me he didn't care, I asked to use the telephone . . . so I called and told them [union]. And they [police] wouldn't let the president of the local post my bond, . . . he called my husband and he told my husband what the bond was, and he said, "I want her out on bond," he said, and "Mr., Mr. Barnard . . . will be there. . . ." And just as I walked up to the . . . step on the county jail, they came to the county jail, I walked up on the step, Barnard walked behind me and says, "Mrs. Green," and he [jailor] turned around . . . "Come on here so and so and so," he said, "Come on here," and uh Barnard said, "Mrs. Green," I said "Yes," he said, "We're here." They kept me upstairs and locked me up, kept me up there. Bernard said, "I wanna post bond," I said, "You can't," so Barnard said, "Can I use the telephone?" "No!", so Barnard . . . he went to call and he left a man there, to see if anything that could happen . . . I said, "Well, my arm is out of place you gotta take me to the hospital." So they got me out . . . But he [police officer] was getting ready to work on me [beat me up] or begin to work on me because, see, he stood up at this truck and told me I was lying that the truck did not push me over . . . I said, "Why should I lie about it?" "Because you want some *money*. . . ." (56:2, pp. 18–19)

Notice that the reported speech does not begin where one would predict (third line—and he told me he didn't care). Up to this point, the narrator is outside of the action. Therefore, she can relay any event or detail without concern for sequence. So the compact version of the story is given first, almost as a preface. The long version begins with the first occurrence of reported speech when the narrator quotes her husband ("I want her out on bail"). Then the entire episode is continued in reproduced conversations between the narrator and others. In this instance, delaying reported speech establishes a focus for the important details that follow. This abundance of reported speech creates a dramatic effect and allows the narrator to enter and remain inside of the action.

Reported speech does not always occur as reconstructed conversation. It also can be presented in the form of thoughts or of written communication. An editor, for example, described how the males in her life tried to persuade her to become a teacher or a secretary:

> And I thought, "I don't, I **know** I don't want to go into secretarial work. I mean, I like people," you know, but . . . (53:3)

The narrator signals the beginning of the reported speech segment with, "And I thought," switches to present tense, then marks the end of the segment with, "you know." She not only reveals her thought at that time, but also provides a glimpse of how she probably "talks to herself," so to speak, when in the process of decision making. So presenting thoughts in the form of reported speech may not be irregular if we consider that some thinking is a kind of dialogue with oneself.

Another narrator presented her written language as reported speech. In discussing the process of how she decided to go back to school, the narrator describes a letter that she wrote to her folks back home:

> I was forty years old when I had that vision, but I said, I wrote home to my folks and I said, "You know they tell me that life begins at forty and I have yet begun to live. I'm just now beginning." So I went back to school and finished high school. (4:1, p. 6)

In this instance, the beginning of reported speech is marked by said, as if it were actual dialogue. The narrator easily could have used wrote—and I wrote . . . ," but did not. Therefore, many forms of language filtered through recall may be suitable material for reported speech, especially because there is no practical way of representing thoughts or written language in oral narration.

Even though reported speech seems to be a vital feature of oral narratives, its purpose and validity has been questioned. Deborah Tannen, in a discussion of reported criticism in conversation, suggests that dialogue or reported speech is not accurate in its reporting and is instead "creatively constructed" (1989: p. 105) by a speaker in the present time. In other words, reported speech is different out of context. It is not an accurate representation of either what was said or what was meant. Tannen further comments that communication is not simply a matter of exchanging information through a neutral medium—language—but rather a complex transformation of words and ideas shaped by a speaker's relationship with the audience. It is she says, "constructed dialogue."

Although Tannan's data is largely anecdotal, her observations change the way we think about reported speech. Certainly, one could argue, for example, that a single utterance is not the same when repeated by the same speaker several times. It is humanly impossible to duplicate the exact pitch, tone, and sometimes wording even when an utterance is repeated immediately and a number of times by the same speaker. In this sense, reported speech is not an *identical* reproduction of a past conversation. The extent of its deviation from the past is almost impossible to measure. Aside from audio or video recording (or time travel), we will not be able to accurately reconstruct most past speech events verbatim. However, exact words may not be as important as meaning which can be recalled in a variety of forms. So to further the argument about truthfulness in reported speech may not be as useful as examining the multiple functions of this versatile narrative strategy.

EMBEDDING

Embedding or inserting a story within a story occurred in many of the narratives. Once the manager's voice announced embedding ("Well, let me go back . . ."), the narrator's voice immediately resumed telling:

> My mother was one of these mothers that um (pause) she missed her education. (pause) **Well, let me go back and tell you how she learned to read.** Ah she would lay in bed in the cabin and the cabin was papered [wall papered] with newspapers and she would spell out the words on the cabin wall and taught herself how to read. So she was always so proud that she could read. (16:1, pp. 13–14)

There also is some marking of the end of an embedded story, but usually in the narrator's voice ("So she was always . . .") rather than the manager's voice. In this instance, embedding occurs on the discourse level and is complete in two sentences. However, it echoes throughout the remainder of the narrative in that the additional information provided by the embedded story is the framework for understanding the motivation for educational achievements of the children of the family.

Announcements of embedding, sometimes called story starters, can be performed by any of the narrative voices. In the following example, the speaker accomplishes embedding by providing "background" information in the narrator's voice:

> Interestingly enough, in 1931 when I received my A.B. degree, I became the first black member of Phi Beta Kappa at State. **And ah** (pause) **the background story about it** is that I read in the paper that ah, four or five parents were going to be invited to attend the initiation of the Phi Beta Kappa recipients in that year and I went over to the secretary of the chapter there, Mr. Black, and asked if my father could be invited. And ah, this man looked at me and said, "Well, we'd like to do that Miss Smith, but you see the only reason we can invite those particular parents is because they are also members of Phi Beta Kappa." I said, "Well, so is my father a member of Phi Beta Kappa." Whereupon he was sent an invitation and my dad came. (3:2, p. 25)

In this example, embedding is signaled by a clause ("And the background story about it . . .") rather than a complete sentence. Reported speech is used sparingly and only near the end of the embedded segment to highlight the resolution of the problem. Even though becoming the first African American member of Phi Beta Kappa at that university was a remarkable achievement, the embedded information diverts attention away from the speaker to her father. This may have been an effort to share the spotlight with her father or to point out his equally important accomplishment.

In some narratives, the embedding was more complex. The following example illustrates a structural pattern that resembles a set of concentric circles. That is, once a digression occurs, related ideas are enfolded one within another. The whole appears to be a disjointed group of sentences only marginally connected to a main idea:

> Well, I was born in Philadelphia in 1911. And my mother and father divorced during the first year and we went on living in Philadelphia. My mother was a pharmacist, **she had planned** to be a surgeon but ah, because of the cutting, you know women are much more sensitive to that, now they're not. We've become more scientifically involved (pause) and she spent her time working at one job and doing pharmaceutical work in the hospital in another job. And, in fact, the fact that she could do it at all, a black woman, in those days, was remarkable. She played the piano and so I take it that that's where my interest in music may have begun. And my aunt was smart enough to see that it was a real interest so she always took me to, I had season tickets to all the concerts, even as a little person. And when she could get, she would get off from work regardless of what her day had been like, come an get me and take me to the concerts. (5:2, p. 10)

In this dense segment, the embedding is unmarked ("she had planned . . ."). From this point on, many other ideas are presented, but as implanted parts of other ideas: "she had planned to be a surgeon" → "women are much more sensitive to that" → "she spent her time . . ." → "the fact that she could do it at all" → and so on. This rippling or wave effect provides much more information than is normally possible. Although it is difficult to sort out all of the individual parts, this type of embedding permits a narrator the opportunity to offer several different kinds of information (i.e., history, commentary, facts, etc.) in one segment.

In the preceding examples, the embedded information contained details about the lives of significant others. For the narrators, this strategy, whether conscious or unconscious, may have been a means of expressing their "community identity" (McKay, p. 175). As Nellie McKay and other scholars have suggested, African American autobiographers portray a sense of self intimately connected with the group or community, and not rigidly individualistic and self-sufficient as is found in white male autobiographies. If so, then we can argue that this type of embedding is yet further evidence that language reflects the reality of its users.

PASSIVE VOICE

Many scholars hypothesize that gender differences in the English language are best understood in terms of powerful language versus powerless language. Within this context, women tend to use powerless language, whereas men tend to use powerful language (O'Barr and Atkins, 1980; Frank & Ashen, 1983; Coates, 1986). Passive voice is one of the many grammatical structures that can be used to express aspects of power. In active voice, the agent of an action is the subject of the verb—**Mary** hit the ball. However, to transform an active sentence into a passive sentence, the subject and the object must switch places. The original subject now becomes the object of a preposition—the ball was hit by **Mary**—the recipient of the action. On the surface, this syntactic structure may appear to be no more unusual than any other structure. However, when examined in the framework of women's oral narration, special features emerge.

Many of the narrators described certain actions in full passive voice. Discussions of fathers and their influence on the family frequently took the form of passive as can be seen in examples a and e. Other topics that evoked the passive voice was various forms of oppression such as sexism (example c) and racism (examples b, d, and f). In general, the position of recipient is usually less powerful than that of agent or doer. Ultimately, we must ask: Is this use of passive voice related to chronic oppression and does it reveal specific information about perceptions self and the world?

> (a) I mean he [dad] wanted to send me to another university. **Then when I came back from there I was given a high school.** Put into high school. And I loved teaching then because the students were on a higher level . . . we could discuss, we could discuss things . . . man to man, you might say. . . . (26:1, p. 3)
>
> (b) And my maternal grandmother's father . . . **belonged to a family who had been given manumission by their owner at his death.** In his will and he had left them a certain amount of money so that they could leave the slave state and go to a free area. . . . (36:1, p. 2)
>
> (c) Oh, I think it is a worldwide focus because China for example . . . they took great pains to show us women in industry, women in education . . . **I asked pointedly if this was ac-**

    cepted by men. I said, "You know it is accepted in the West but we are still fighting through legislation. . . ." (36:3, p. 1)

(d) . . . the Republican party uh believes that people should help themselves and that kind of thing, **and uh help lift themselves by their own boot straps** and I think uh Martin Luther King asked a very proper question. **How can you lift yourself by your boot straps when you have no boots on.** . . ." (30:3, p. 2)

(e) . . . when we were going to high school, **all of us were told by my dad who really was the ah . . . a . . .** well both of my parents were scholars, but my dad seemed to advise us just what subjects to take. He wanted all of us to take Latin. . . . (3:2, p. 1)

(f) As we discovered later, [the law] was to protect the slaves from being transplanted in the 19th century before 1863, 1865. **Ah, just being transplanted by their masters into Central American countries.** And I understand there were many masters who managed to do that and get around that. . . . (3:3, p. 3)

Equally notable is that most discussions of the slave past of a narrator's grandparents or great-grandparents involved at least one occurrence of passive voice.

From a different perspective, Bolinger (1980, p. 29) argued that the agentless passive is most dangerous because it enables "the speaker to keep silent about who performs the action" (e.g., "the documents were submitted." vs. "The documents were submitted by the escapees.") Although omitting the agent is not necessarily fraudulent, he proposes that important information is missing when the passive is used in a way that conceals the agent.

(a) "And you read the part you were assigned. . . ." (27:1, p. 7)

(b) "I was told you are an outsider." (27:1, p. 9)

(c) "He was named Calvin." (27:1, p. 9)

(d) "I had been offered an opportunity to write case review articles for the university Law Review." (36:1, p. 7)

(e) "And we [African American females] were all told that we should be as unobtrusive as possible on campus, that we were members of the subject race. (36:1, p. 9)

(f) "We were not given any residential privileges. . . ." (36:1, p. 9)

(g) "I don't know, my father was very jealous I've been told." (56:1, p. 8)

Incidents of racial and/or sexual discrimination were more likely to be framed as agentless passives than any other topics. Some narrators may assume that the agent of such actions is understood and known to the audience or she may simply choose to omit that piece of information as a means of distancing. Sensitive or intensely emotional situations such as a family secret or hurt feelings may also elicit agentless passive.

In the context of the entire segment, examples a, d, and g are the most neutral of the agentless passives. In these examples, it was the school teacher, a college professor, and a relative, respectively, who were the undeclared agents of the actions. However, in other examples, silent "doers" imply a more complex meaning than is apparent initially:

(b) —by the African American community.
(c) —by a missionary.
(e) —by a white, male dean.
(f) —by the university administration.

In each of these cases, the agents represent a significant influence/force in the narrator's life and consequently major repercussions take place. In example c, the narrator's family loses track of their African roots because a missionary gives their African grandfather an English name; and in example e, the female students organize *all* of the African American students in their own honor society in order to combat campus racism. Unlike the full passive and depending on the context, the unnamed agent in this kind of passive construction can be the most powerful position.

ONE LITTLE WORD

Use of "little" as a comparative adjective assumed an unusual meaning in several contexts. Instead of the expected meaning—small or brief—the word "little," when coupled with particular nouns, establishes an oppositional relationship between the adjective itself and the noun it modifies. In excerpt a, for example, the "**little** dedication service" was not little, but enormous. The narrator describes in detail how numerous parents, students, city administrators, and out-of-town officials gathered at the dedication ceremony to honor her mother. Thus, little used in this manner is a form of understatement. The same is true of excerpt f. Newspaper coverage of the case was quite sensational and propelled this young female attorney into the spotlight early in her career.

(a) But ah, the city schools . . . paid such great homage to her [mother] . . . that a school was built in her name . . . and I think there's some introductory remarks in a **little** dedication service in which we attended that indicate what the public thought about her. (3:1, p. 2)

(b) My father was among the five or six parents who came up and first bestowed the key before the other graduating seniors were to receive their **little** diploma, and their **little** certificate, and their key. (3:3, p. 1)

(c) But uh, when I got that **little** job . . . that paid, I think twenty dollars a month or eighteen, which was the cost of tuition at the university. . . . (30:2, p. 2)

(d) My high school classmates, they were keen. That was a keen class. . . . You know, we were handling heavy debates and subjects and writing our **little** essays, like college people. (30:3, p. 5)

(e) That first year we published a **little** magazine . . . and we got contributions from any student on the campus who would give us a contribution. . . . (36:1, p. 9)

(f) And that **little** case was written up in the newspapers and I got a **little** publicity and I was really very happy over that one. . . . It may have been the early part of '34. Yes, I liked that case. I've kept a **little** scrapbook and that's one of my favorites. (36:2, p. 3)

All of the narrators produced at least one instance of little plus a noun as understatement. In general, it was the most frequently occurring adjective in all of the narratives. Furthermore, as the following excerpt indicates, it was not unusual for little to be used repeatedly in the same segment, but with different meanings:

Text #4
A Little Man

Oh, Dr. Carver scared the daylights out of me. When I went to Tuskegee I ah, was going up to Thompkins Hall, Thompkins Hall is a Lib, it's the dining hall and it has some very impressive looking stairs going up to the to the ah dining hall are ah, and on either side there is nice greenery. It's beautiful and it's all, I don't know what it is Wisteria and something else there, but it's beautiful and I started up the stairs going to ah, to dinner and this **little** voice said, "**Little** girl better go get your coat. And I stopped, and looked I didn't see anyone so I started upstairs and got two or three steps higher. "Yes, I think it's gonna rain, you better go get your coat." Well, that frightened me and I was always a person who had to see what was scaring me if I got scared of something I had to see what it was. So I tore down the stairs going in the direction where I heard this **little** voice, and when I got down there, there was this **little** man with some tiny **little** glasses on and a cap with the bib broken and a butterfly net. And ah, he was catching some kind of **little** bug. And, he told me, he says, "It's going to rain and you go get your coat now. Where are you from?" And I said that I was from Tennessee, so he said, "**Little** Miss Tennessee you go get your coat and he called me **little** Miss Tennessee from there on, and, when I described to Miss Cloptan who was the, the matron about this man who told me to come back and get my coat . . . And she says, "Well, that was Dr. Carver." And that's how I met Dr. Carver . . . So, I was assigned to, to Dorothy Hall and Dr. Carver's, I suppose you call it a laboratory was in the basement of Dorothy Hall, so I saw this **little** man again and I sneaked in there to see what he was doing. . . . (27:2, p. 26)

In the preceding excerpt, little is used nine times. In most instances, it appears that little does indeed mean small. However, "**little** voice" may mean high pitched or low rather than small. "**Little** man" used twice may mean small, but it also may well be another understatement. Even though Dr. Carver may have been small in stature, yet he was a world renowned scientist. So the double meaning conveyed by "**little** man" masks but does not completely conceal the understatement. Whether or not it is deliberate or unconscious, this particular pattern of diminishing the importance of individual achievements by juxtaposition may be a gender- or age-graded phenomenon or it may be a distinguishing feature of suppressed discourse.

Articulation of African American women's life stories in their own words involves a complex interaction of race, gender, and social status with language, history, and culture. All of these variables are important, and language especially can be most informative.

Commonly thought of as simply a means of communication, its power to reveal more than what appears on the printed page is often underestimated. Words, phrases, and even silences contain multiple layers of meaning beneath the literal surface, and particular combinations expose social realities otherwise concealed from view. What narrators say, **as well as** the way they say it, is extremely important. Therefore, oral narratives are valuable not only because they preserve life histories, but also because they capture an intimate use of language.

NOTES

INTRODUCTION

1. Several women requested anonymity, therefore fictional names are used for persons and places.

2. Maxine Hong Kingston, *The Woman Warrior* (New York: Alfred A. Knof, 1976), p. 43. Old Chinese sayings about the worth of girls: "Girls are maggots in the rice." "It is more profitable to raise geese than daughters." Also, Nancy Miller in *Getting Personal*, uses the "maggots in the rice" quote as an example of the need for feminist autobiographers to construct of self identity "at the intersection of cultural codes about women" (126).

3. George Gusdorf, "Conditions and Limits of Autobiography," in *Auto-biography*, James Olney, ed. (Princeton: Princeton Univ. Press, 1980), pg. 29.

4. G. Thomas Couser, *Altered Egos* (New York: Oxford University Press, 1989), pg. 126.

5. Clifford and Marcus point out the "complex and fertile recent debate . . . around the valorization, historical significance, and epistemological status of writing." They suggest that "writing is both empowering (a necessary, effective way of storing and manipulating knowledge) and corrupting (a loss of immediacy . . . of the presence and intimacy of speech)" (118).

6. Some studies of women's speech: Lakoff, 1975; Miller and Swift, 1976; McConnell-Ginet et. al., 1980; Kramarae, 1981; Thorne et. al., 1983; Coates, 1986, 1988. Selected studies of African American's speech: Labov, 1972; Wolfram, 1969; Stewart, 1971; Smitherman, 1977; Folb, 1980).

7. Mitchell-Kernan, 1971; Scott, 1974; Nichols, 1980; Goodwin, 1980; Marsha Houston, 1985).

2. THE EXCEPTION OF THE EXCEPTIONS

1. Linda Perkins, "The Education of Black Women in the Nineteenth Century," in John Faragher and Florence Howe, eds., *Women and Higher*

Education in American History (New York: W. W. Norton, 1988), p. 71. Patterson earned her degree from Oberlin College, the first institution of higher education in the United States to admit women and African Americans.

2. *Ibid*.

3. (30:2, p. 3) indicates transcript number, side of tape, and transcript page number.

4. Jeanne Noble reported that in the early twentieth century there was a total of five million African American students enrolled in college (89).

5. A two-year certification program at most colleges allowed students to quit school and teach after two years. It was routinely offered to African American women, many of whom did not return to complete their B.A. degree. According to Noble (89) although African American women outnumbered African American men in the first and second years of college, more men than women completed the baccalaureate degree at the end of four years.

3. CLIMBING THE LADDER OF SUCCESS

1. Cynthia Fuchs Epstein, "Positive Effects of the Double Negative: Explaining the Success of Black Professional Women," *The American Journal of Sociology*, 1972:919. Quoted in Giddings, *When and Where I Enter*, pp. 332–333.

4. ORAL NARRATIVES AS AUTOBIOGRAPHY

1. See *Six Women's Slave Narratives*, The Schomburg Library of Nineteenth-Century Black Women Writers, (New York: Oxford University Press, 1988). In the introduction to this volume, William Andrews identifies each text as a "dictated slave narrative." Prince sought out an editor in order that her story be told, and Jackson's ghost writer was a black woman herself.

2. In *Collected Black Women's Narratives*, The Schomburg Library of Nineteenth-Century Black Women Writers (New York: Oxford University Press, 1988).

3. "Written and rewritten over a period of forty-seven years, the three autobiographies present precisely drawn portraits that Douglass intended to will to history, so that he could be remembered exactly as he wanted to be" (103). Henry Louis Gates, Jr., *Figures in Black: Words, Signs & the "Racial Self"* (New York: Oxford University Press, 1987). Also see Andrews p. 314–72.

4. "Most critics . . . have had trouble with *Dust Tracks*. Much has been written about the 'lies' in the autobiography, its evasions and lack of honest self-disclosure . . . ." (179). Nellie Y. McKay in *Life/Lines: Theorizing Wom-*

en's Autobiography, Bella Brodzki and Celeste Schenck, eds. (Ithaca, New York: Cornell University Press, 1988).

5. Athens: University of Georgia Press, 1989.

6. This chapter also contained an addendum announcing that Louisa had at long last been able to raise enough money to purchase her mother and free her from slavery. It appears that the entire narrative had been completed *before* this event and was entitled "UNEXPECTED GOOD TIDINGS!" in this next to last chapter.

7. Except for Louisa's brief public notice in a local newspaper announcing her mother's freedom and offering thanks to supporters.

8. He asked Louisa to run away with him, but she refused.

9. Mattison does include a direct quote from Louisa regarding race mixing: "Now, it is astonishing, in the South, the white men run after the colored women, their own and others; but if a colored man speak to a white woman they want to shoot him." (41)

10. This approach assumes a worst case scenario—that the narrator/author cannot participate in the editing process due to relocation, illness or death.

11. Quoted in Gary Okihiro, "Oral History and the Writing of Ethnic History." In David K. Dunaway and Willa K. Baum, eds. *Oral History*. (Nashville, TN: American Association for State and Local History), 1984, p. 203.

12. There are many ways to edit and shape a transcript depending on the purpose of a specific project. If a life story or autobiography is the focus, then preparing the final text in story form increases readability for a general audience. Also, there are instances where questions can remain in the text and create no problem in understanding the content of a narrative.

13. The cooperative model is not suggested as an "opposing" model, but rather as an alternative model. There are many different models of narrative interaction. It is a *varied* mode of communication that should not be dichotomized into *only* two parts.

5. NAPPY AT THE ROOT

1. Adrienne Rich, "Split at the Root: An Essay on Jewish Identity," *Blood, Bread, and Poetry: Selected Prose, 1978–1985* (New York: W. W. Norton, 1986).

2. This is not to suggest that there is any relationship between "straight" hair and "standard" language or nappy hair and unconventional language. This analogy is intended to illustrate the difference in narrative language above and below the surface. That is, words are more than the sum of their parts, and the language of African American women's personal narratives often means more than what the actual words and phrases suggest. Denotative meaning is important, but connotative meaning may be much more

significant. Also see Marita Golden in *Bearing Witness*, edited by Henry Gates, Jr., p. 253.

3. Annie L. Burton, "Memories of Childhood's Slavery Days," *Six Women's Slave Narratives*, ed. Henry Louis Gates, Jr. (New York: The Schomburg Library and Oxford University Press, 1988).

4. "The Story of Mattie J. Jackson," written and arranged by Dr. L. S. Thompson in *Six Women's Slave Narratives*.

5. Pauli Murray, *Pauli Murray: The Autobiography of a Black Activist, Feminist, Lawyer, Priest and Poet* (Knoxville: The University of Tennessee Press, 1989).

6. Fictional name.

7. Her first application in 1938 to the law school at the University of North Carolina was rejected because of race (Murray, 115).

8. According to *Webster's New Collegiate Dictionary* the definition of venture is "to expose to hazard: risk, gamble." The second definition of adventure is "an exciting or remarkable experience.

9. Pauli Murray's autobiography is unusual in that "she recorded her life not at the end but as she went along, keeping records and notes of events small and great" (Murray, xi).

WORKS CITED

Andrews, William. *To Tell a Free Story: The First Century of Afro-American Autobiography, 1760–1865.* Urbana: University of Illinois Press, 1986.

Andersen, Margaret. *Thinking About Women: Sociological Perspectives on Sex and Gender.* 2nd ed. New York: Macmillan, 1988.

Bolinger, Dwight. *Language the Loaded Weapon: The Use and Abuse of Language Today.* New York: Longman, 1980.

Braxton, Joanne. *Black Women Writing Autobiography: A Tradition Within a Tradition.* Philadelphia: Temple University Press, 1989.

Carby, Hazel. *Reconstructing Womanhood: The Emergence of the Afro-American Woman Novelist.* New York: Oxford University Press, 1987.

Christian, Barbara. "Trajectories of Self-Definition: Placing Contemporary Afro-American Women's Fiction." In *Conjuring: Black Women, Fiction, and Literary Tradition.* eds., Marjorie Pryse and Hortense Spillers. Bloomington: Indiana University Press, 1985.

Clifford, James and George Marcus, eds. *Writing Culture: The Poetics and Politics of Ethnography.* Berkeley: University of California Press, 1986.

Coates, Jennifer. *Women, Men and Language.* New York: Longman, 1986.

Coates, Jennifer and Deborah Cameron, eds. *Women in Their Speech Communities.* New York: Longman, 1988.

Couser, Thomas. *Altered Egos.* New York: Oxford University Press, 1989.

Douglass, Frederick. *Narrative of the Life of Frederick Douglass, An American Slave: Written by Himself.* ed., Houston Baker, Jr. New York: Penguin Books, 1986.

Du Bois, W. E. B. *The Souls of Black Folk.* New York: The New American Library, Inc., 1969.

Folb, Edith. *Runnin' Down Some Lines: The Language and Culture of Black Teenagers.* Cambridge: Harvard University Press, 1980.

Fox-Genovese, Elizabeth. "My Statute, My Self: Autobiographical Writings of Afro-American Women." In *Reading Black, Reading Feminist:*

A Critical Anthology. ed., Henry Louis Gates, Jr. New York: Meridian, 1990.

Frank, Francine and Frank Anshen. *Language and the Sexes.* Albany: State University of New York Press, 1983.

Gates, Henry Louis Jr., ed. *Figures in Black.* New York: Oxford University Press, 1987.

Giddings, Paula. *When and Where I Enter: The Impact of Black Women on Race and Sex in America.* New York: Bantam Books, 1984.

Gluck, Sherna and Daphne Patai, eds. *Women's Words: The Feminist Practice of Oral History.* New York: Routledge, 1991.

Golden, Marita. "Migrations of the Heart." In *Bearing Witness: Selections from African-American Autobiography in the Twentieth Century.* ed., Henry Louis Gates, Jr. New York: Pantheon Books, 1991.

Goodwin, Marjorie Harness. "Directive-Response Speech Sequences in Girls' and Boys' Task Activities." In *Women and Language in Literature and Society.* eds., Sally McConnell-Ginet, Ruth Borker and Nelly Furman. New York: Praeger, 1980.

Gusdorf, Georges. "Conditions and Limits of Autobiography." In *Autobiography,* ed. James Olney. Princeton: Princeton University Press, 1980.

Heath, Shirley Brice. *Ways with Words: Language, Life and Work in Communities and Classrooms.* Cambridge: Cambridge University Press, 1983.

Hurston, Zora Neale. *Dust Tracks On a Road.* 2nd ed. Robert Hemenway, ed. Urbana: University of Illinois Press, 1984.

Jacobs, Harriet. *Incidents in the Life of a Slave Girl: Written By Herself.* Jean Fagan Yellin, ed. Cambridge: Harvard University Press, 1987.

Jones, Bessie. *For the Ancestors: Autobiographical Memories,* ed. John Stewart. Athens: University of Georgia Press, 1989.

Kingston, Mazine Hong. *The Woman Warrior.* New York: Alfred A. Knof, 1976.

Kramarae, Cheris. *Women and Men Speaking.* Rowley, MA: Newbury House, 1981.

Labov, William, ed. *Language in the Inner City.* Philadelphia: University of Philadelphia Press, 1972.

———. *Sociolinguistic Patterns.* Philadelphia: University of Pennsylvania Press, 1972.

Lakoff, Robin. *Language and Woman's Place.* New York: Harper & Row, 1975.

Lerner, Gerda. *The Majority Finds Its Past: Placing Women in History.* New York: Oxford University Press, 1979.

Mattison, H. *Louisa Piquet, the Octoroon: or Inside Views of Southern Domestic Life.* In *Collected Black Women's Narratives.* The Schomburg Library of Nineteenth-Century Black Women Writers. New York: Oxford University Press, 1988.

McConnell-Ginet, Sally, Ruth Borker, and Nancy Furman, eds. *Women and Language in Literature and Society*. New York: Praeger, 1983.

McKay, Nellie. "Race, Gender, and Cultural Context in Zora Neale Hurston's *Dust Tracks on a Road*." In *Life/Lines*, ed. Bella Brodzki and Celeste Schenck. Ithaca, New York: Cornell University Press, 1988.

Miller, Carol and Kate Swift. *Words and Women*. Garden City: New York, 1976.

Miller, Nancy. *Getting Personal: Feminist Occasions and Other Autobiographical Acts*. New York: Routledge, 1991.

Mitchell-Kernan, Claudia. *Language Behavior in a Black Urban Community*. Monograph of the Language Behavior Laboratory. No. 2. Berkeley: University of California, 1971.

Moody, Joycelyn. "Rippling Away the Veil of Slavery: Literary, Communal Love, and Self-Esteem in Three Slave Women's Narratives." *Black American Literature Forum*. Vol. 24, No. 4 (Winter 1990), pp. 633–648.

Murray, Pauli. *Pauli Murray: The Autobiography of a Black Activist, Feminist, Lawyer, Priest and Poet*. Knoxville: The University of Tennessee Press, 1989.

Nichols, Patricia. "Women in their Speech Communities." in *Women and Language in Literature and Society*. eds., Sally McConnell-Ginet, Ruth Borker, and Nelly Furman. New York: Praeger, 1980.

Njeri, Itabari. *Every Good-Bye Ain't Gone*. New York: Vintage Books, 1991.

Noble, Jeanne. "The Higher Education of Black Women in the Twentieth Century." In *Women and Higher Education in American History*, ed. John Mack Faragher and Florence Howe. New York: W. W. Norton, 1988.

O'Barr, William and Bowman Atkins. " 'Women's Language' or 'Powerless Language'?" In *Women and Language in Literature and Society*. eds. Salley McConnell-Ginet, Ruth Borker, and Nelly Furman. New York: Praeger, 1980.

Okihiro, Gary. "Oral History and the Writing of Ethnic History." In *Oral History*, eds. David Dunaway and Willa Baum. Nashville: American Association for State and Local History, 1984.

Perkins, Linda. "The Education of Black Women in the Nineteenth Century." In *Women and Higher Education in American History*, ed. John Mack Faragher and Florence Howe. New York: W. W. Norton, 1988.

Rich, Adrienne. *Blood, Bread, and Poetry*. New York: W. W. Norton, 1986.

Scott, Patricia Bell. "The English Language and Black Womanhood: A Blow to Self-esteem." *The Journal of Afro-American Issues*. 2 (1974): 218–225.

Smith, Sidonie and Julia Watson, eds. *De/Colonizing the Subject: The Politics of Gender in Women's Autobiography*. Minneapolis: University of Minnesota Press, 1992.

Solomon, Barbara Miller. *In the Company of Educated Women: A History of Women and Higher Education in America*. New Haven: Yale University Press, 1985.

Smitherman, Geneva. *Talkin' and Testifyin': The Language of Black America*. Boston: Houghton Mifflin Co., 1977.

Stanback, Marsha Houston. "Language and Black Women's Place: Evidence from the Black Middle Class." In Paula Treichler, Cheris Kramarae, and Beth Stafford, eds. *For Alma Mater: Theory and Practice in Feminist Scholarship*. Urbana: University of Illinois Press, 1985.

Stewart, William. "Continuity and Change in American Negro Dialects." In *Black-White Speech Relationships*, ed. Walt Wolfram and Nona Clarke. Washington, D.C.: Center for Applied Linguistics, 1971.

Stubbs, Michael. *Discourse Analysis: The Sociolinguistic Analysis of Natural Language*. Chicago: The University of Chicago Press, 1983.

Tannen, Deborah. *Talking Voices: Repetition, Dialogue, and Imagery in Conversational Discourse*. Cambridge: Cambridge University Press, 1989.

The Schomburg Library of Nineteenth-Century Black Women Writers. *Six Women's Slave Narratives*. Intro. by William Andrews. New York: Oxford University Press, 1988.

Thorne, Barrie, Cheris Kramarae, and Nancy Henley, eds. *Language, Gender and Society*. Rowley, MA: Newbury House, 1983.

Vansina, Jan. "Oral Tradition and Historical Methodology." In *Oral History*, eds. David Dunaway and Willa Baum. Nashville: American Association for State and Local History, 1984.

White, Deborah Gray. *Ar'n't I a Woman?: Female Slaves in the Plantation South*. New York: W. W. Norton, 1985.

Wilson, Harriet. *Our Nig; or, Sketches from the Life of a Free Black*. Intro. by Henry Louis Gates, Jr. New York: Vintage Books, 1983.

Wolf, Dennie and Deborah Hicks. "The Voices Within Narratives: The Development of Intertextuality in Young Children's Stories." *Discourse Processes*. 12, 329–351 (1989).

Wolfram, Walter. *A Sociolinguistic Description of Detroit Negro Speech*. Washington, D.C.: Center of Applied Linguistics, 1969.

INDEX

ABOUT THE AUTHOR

Gwendolyn Etter-Lewis is Associate Professor of English at Western Michigan University. She earned her Ph.D. in Linguistics at the University of Michigan. She specializes in sociolinguistics with a focus on gender differences in spoken and written language, and she has written about African American women's oral history for various scholarly publications. Dr. Etter-Lewis is the recipient of numerous honors and awards, including the Michigan Association of Governing Boards Distinguished Faculty Member of 1992, the 1991–1992 National Academy of Education Postdoctoral Spencer Fellowship, the 1992 Travel to Collections Grant and the 1991 Summer Seminar Fellowship from the National Endowment for the Humanities, and the 1989–1990 Ford Foundation Postdoctoral Research Fellowship.